The *SAVVY* Guide to Fantasy Football

The *SAVVY* Guide
to Fantasy Football

Michael Harmon

Indianapolis

International Standard Book Number: 0-7906-1328-X

Chief Executive Officer:	Alan Symons
President:	Scott Weaver
Chief Financial Officer:	Keith Siergiej
Chief Operating Officer:	Richard White
Acquisitions Editor:	Brad Schepp
Editorial Assistant:	Dana Eaton
Copy Editor:	Kim Heusel
Pagination Editor:	Kim Heusel
Cover Design:	Mike Walsh
Photos:	Provided by the author

Cover Photo is used with permission from AP Wideworld. Carolina Panthers receiver Steve Smith (89) fends off Atlanta Falcons defender Antuan Edwards (42) to score on a pass from quarterback Jake Delhomme during the second quarter of their NFL football game in Atlanta, Sunday, Jan. 1, 2006. (AP Photo/Bill Haber)

Manufactured in the USA.

Contents

ACKNOWLEDGMENTS

I would like to extend my thanks to the team at SAMS Technical Publishing, who worked tirelessly to help me turn pages of notes and granular ideas about fantasy football and the industry as a whole into this finished product:

To Richard White, for believing in this idea and offering me the opportunity to execute it.

To Dana Eaton, editorial assistant, who helped keep me on target and kept track of an endless stream of files and information

To Brad Schepp, acquisitions editor, who offered his assistance, support, and badgering when necessary to keep me headed to the goal line.

To Kim Heusel, copyeditor, who made sense of my late-night ramblings and polished the product.

I appreciate your comments, energy, support, and patience in this process.

Dr. Kim Beason of the University of Mississippi generously gave of his time and data to provide a snapshot of fantasy sports participants.

Craig Wiley originally pitched the idea and brought this opportunity to my desk, setting this all in motion.

Chapter 12 features several of the industry's leading analysts and game providers. They allowed me the opportunity to use screenshots to demonstrate the different aspects of fantasy football and graciously gave of their time and energy to offer historical nuggets and game advice:

- Roger Rotter of FOXSports.com
- Matthew Berry of Talentedmrroto.com and Rotopass.com
- Rick Wolf of Allstarstats.com and Sandbox.com
- Peter Schoenke of Rotowire.com
- Jeff Thomas of Sportsbuff.com
- William Del Pilar of KFFL.com

Thanks to my colleagues at FOX Sports who allowed me to pursue this endeavor. Larry Tobin, Andrew Hossum, Brian Grey, and obviously, Roger Rotter, offered their support and encouragement during the process.

The list goes on down the line, so I bid a sincere thank you to all of my family and friends who encouraged the process but made sure I stepped back from the computer on occasion.

DEDICATION

To my girls — For allowing me to explore
this fantasy world but keeping me grounded in reality

1 What Is Fantasy Football?

- ♦ Defining the Industry
- ♦ Are All Games the Same?
- ♦ Full Fantasy Games
- ♦ Simulation Games
- ♦ Salary Cap (Stock Market)
- ♦ Pick'Em
- ♦ How Do I Get Involved?
- ♦ What's the payoff?

The fact that you've picked up this text indicates that you've at least heard rumblings about or utterances of the term "fantasy football" in some context. That reference piqued your interest. Perhaps a family member or friend commandeered the television set during a Sunday brunch to catch up on the Arizona-Houston score. Maybe you witnessed a ceremony around the water cooler to award the dunce cap to that season's last-place finisher. Or maybe you caught a reference to fantasy football while casually watching your favorite team perform on an autumn Sunday. Whatever your entrée to this world, let's get the baseline definition of fantasy football out there and put everyone on equal footing. I can tell you this: You couldn't have picked a more interesting year to join the fray.

DEFINING THE INDUSTRY

Fantasy football refers to the set of skill-based games driven by the on-field statistical achievements of pro and collegiate athletes. Participants acquire players via a draft or auction process to create their fantasy team, and scores are derived based on the selected categories and point modifiers.

To give you a better sense of the magnitude of this industry in early 2006, when I entered the term "fantasy football" into Yahoo! Search, it returned nearly 59.1 million hits. The same search on Google yielded 38.5 million results. Get the picture?

The pregame shows and halftime segments of each network airing NFL action reference "fantasy numbers" or "fantasy stat lines." Analysts and reporters are called upon to make their fantasy selection for the game during the final whip-around segments ahead of kickoff. FOX, CBS, and ESPN all produced fantasy preview shows utilizing network talent in 2005. FOX Sports Net (FSN) has aired *The Ultimate Fantasy Football Show* for two seasons, a dedicated weekly show offering analysis, insights, and picks to aid participants' decisions each week. ESPN offers daily fantasy tips on ESPN News and provides a weekly radio show. Talk-show hosts spend countless hours taking calls regarding roster decisions, player injuries, and previewing the coming week's action. I personally appeared on over 50 stations during the 2005 NFL season to offer insights and aid in sit/start decisions. Suffice it to say, fantasy talk enters all sports discussions.

If you are accessing sports news through the Internet, the sites you traverse likely either house their own suite of games or are partnered with one or more providers to get their piece of this exploding industry. Figure 1.1 illustrates the typical format of a fantasy sports home page. The MyFantasyLeague.com home page displays the current standings, transaction history, and message board posts, and offers links to news and other tools to enhance the playing experience.

A comprehensive list of sites providing fantasy football games and information is included in Appendix I online at www.savvyfantasysports.com.

Figure 1.1. MyFantasyLeague.com home page

Are All Games the Same?

Fantasy football providers offer a myriad of games with varying structures and objectives. Naturally, the required time commitment also varies with the chosen competition.

 This is one of the first decision points in the fantasy gaming experience. As you contemplate an invitation to a league or consider starting a competition of your own, be sure to assess the amount of time available for your participation. The inability to regularly follow news, performance trends, and account for injuries usually leads to a subpar performance and frustrating experience.

The fantasy football gaming community can be broken into four distinct game styles. The following list ranks these game styles in order of the time commitment required.

1. **Full Fantasy:** In this style of game, participants draft a team from the player pool. Players can appear on only one team. During the season, participants make adjustments to their rosters via trades, free agency, and waivers en route to the playoffs and championship game. **Highest Time Commitment**

2. **Simulation Game:** Participants assume the role of general manager (GM) and attempt to assemble a team within a hard salary cap. There are no drafts. It's about creating the perfect squad and then assuming the role

of coach. Pick the offensive set, choose the defensive philosophy, and navigate your way through injuries to the title run. There is a college simulation game that forces you to go through the recruiting process and try to draw top talent to your school. It's a fun and challenging way to bridge the fantasy and reality realms. **High Time Commitment**

3. **Salary Cap:** Each player is tagged with a monetary value. Participants then choose players from the entire player pool and must field a full lineup while adhering to a hard salary cap. There is no draft in this style of games. Players can be added or dropped throughout the season. **Intermediate Time Commitment**

4. **Pick'Em:** Participants make selections for the winner of each game on the NFL schedule either straight up or using advanced scoring options such as confidence points or the point spread. **Lowest Time Commitment**

Full Fantasy Games

The overall concept of a full fantasy game is simple. Your job as owner/GM in this universe is to construct the greatest group of individual performers possible through the draft held prior to the season and then use the tools of waivers, free agency, and trades to improve your squad to challenge for the league title. Players can only appear on one team in each league, which is to say that only one team can draft Peyton Manning. One team can draft LaDainian Tomlinson, and so on.

Your fantasy team will rack up points based on the on-field prowess of individual players within NFL games in accordance with your league's scoring structure. In full fantasy games, the wins and losses earned by a player's particular team have no bearing on the player's fantasy value.

For instance, the 2005 Oakland Raiders finished with a record of 4-12 despite the threat of a potent offense with off-season acquisitions LaMont Jordan and Randy Moss leading the way. In fact, QB Kerry Collins threw three TD passes in a game on three separate occasions while guiding Oakland to a 1-2 record in those efforts. He was the leading fantasy scorer at the QB position in Weeks 1 and 17 despite losses to the New England Patriots and the New York Giants. Both opponents scored 30 points against Oakland, prompting Collins to exercise his right arm with regularity.

Conversely, the Chicago Bears won the NFC Central and secured home-field advantage with a record of 11-5. The Bears relied on RB Thomas Jones and a ball-hawking defense to achieve its huge record. Three Chicago quarterbacks combined to throw for 11 touchdowns for the entire season. Rookie Kyle Orton assumed the reins due to an injury to Rex Grossman and started 14 games for Chicago. He threw for nine touchdowns with a single multi-TD performance.

Therefore, selecting players on a team that is apt to give up large point totals on a fairly consistent basis doesn't necessarily doom your squad. Playing from behind may actually prove beneficial in the fantasy realm. With that said, while participants may draft as many players as they wish from a particular team, loading a team with one particular squad is uncommon. I've seen that draft strategy used to great success and miserable failure. In the end, it's about finding a balance between making the game fun with players you like and being competitive. Sometimes, the two ends of that statement don't necessarily meet. So, while the game concept appears quick and easy, piecing together the right team and managing to avoid the maladies of injury and bad play is not. One week's hero becomes next week's waiver-wire fodder in the turn of an ankle.

The league home page provides an overview of the happenings in the league. Figure 1.2 displays the appearance of a typical league home page. At a glance, participants can track the league's standings and the separation between their team and the team that they wish to overtake. They can view their spot in the waiver order before dipping into the free agency/waiver-wire pool, and, of course, the league home page houses the message board for witty banter and provocation of arguments.

Figure 1.2: Yahoo! Sports Fantasy Football PLUS league home page

Simulation

Simulation games forego the draft process of the full fantasy games, and instead force coaches to try and build toward a championship run within different constraints. The college version of this gaming style puts you through all the rigors that a college coach would face, from the heavy recruiting period to issues off the field, while navigating a

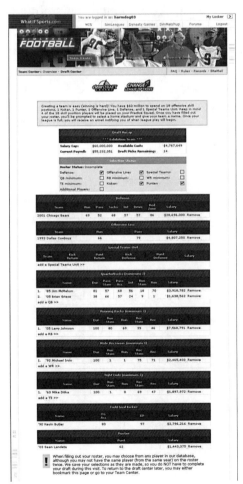

Figure 1.3.
WhatIFSports.com pro simulation roster page

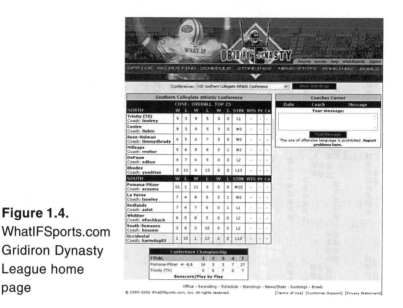

Figure 1.4.
WhatIFSports.com
Gridiron Dynasty
League home
page

full season schedule. Each coach begins in lower college football divisions and tries to build a winning program and ultimately get promoted to the elite Division I-A conferences. The professional game allows participants to assemble their ideal roster from the whole of NFL history under a hard salary cap. That means that participants can pair the 2004 Peyton Manning with the 1991 Jerry Rice and 1992 Emmitt Smith, provided they can still assemble a full squad under the cap. Figure 1.3 displays a sample of the type of roster that can be pieced together in such a competition.

In both the college and pro games, the coach then chooses the depth chart, offensive and defensive strategies, and level of aggressiveness in certain game scenarios. In these games, coaches need to account for offensive and defensive linemen, something that doesn't factor into the majority of straight fantasy competitions. Coaches need to push through injury issues and adjust their strategies for upcoming opponents, just as a real coaching staff does at the pro and college level. Figure 1.4 offers a glimpse of the league home page from the WhatIFSports.com Gridiron Dynasty game, where schools such as Trinity, Rose-Hulman, and Occidental make up initial job opportunities.

Salary Cap (Stock Market)

The salary cap gaming style offers participants the opportunity to build a squad without possessing a billion dollars of personal wealth. The game provider determines the fictional dollar amounts used to construct a team. Players are priced using a formula that takes into account past performance and expected future returns. Figure 1.5 illustrates the Sports Buff.com fantasy football roster page, complete

Figure 1.5. Sports Buff.com Salary Cap fantasy football roster page

with each player's cost against the salary cap. Participants must determine the best path toward assembling a full roster, whether to work for balance with moderately priced players or to devote a hefty chunk of their budget to one or two superstars and fill the remaining slots with bargain-priced players.

The game provider also establishes a scoring system by which players earn points for your team. The dollar values of players will rise and fall based on their performance in the current year, as past performance begins to account for a smaller portion of the player's value. As such, these games may alternatively be called "stock market" games based on the fluctuations in a player's value akin to that of a publicly traded stock. Participants can change out players for new ones on a weekly basis, so long as they adhere to the established salary cap. In this style of game, more than one team can possess a player (for example, several teams can spend the money to possess Peyton Manning or Larry Johnson). The difference is that the savvy player purchases a player at a lower base cost before his current season performance boosts his value. This, in turn, allows him or her to surround that player with other higher-priced performers and make a run to the league title.

Pick'Em

Pick'Em games offer a faster fantasy experience than the other gaming styles. The object in most games of this ilk is quite straightforward. Participants need select only the correct answer from the options listed. The standard format of a Pick'Em contest is displayed in Figure 1.6. The game site clearly marks which of the available options was selected by the participant and displays the results from that event

Figure 1.6. Yahoo! Sports Pro Pick'Em selection page

directly on the page. There are some specialty configurations that can be selected, most commonly choosing against the point spread or using confidence points. The confidence point option forces participants to rank how strongly they feel about their choice to win a particular game.

For most participants, the selection process will require a mere 10 to 15 minutes per week. Some participants may take a longer, more research-based approach, spending hours to review full histories and trends related to the games on the schedule. They analyze home and road trends, weather factors, and spend more time poring over injuries. On the whole, the Pick'Em style of game is the easiest by which to introduce a prospective fantasy gamer to the hobby.

HOW DO I GET INVOLVED?

Obviously, a base knowledge of the game and its intricacies makes one an instant league contender. Easy access to a computer terminal and an Internet connection certainly aids with finding last-minute injury substitutions and beating contenders to the new top option on the waiver wire. At the base of the game, however, commitment is the single greatest requirement. Participants must commit time and follow through to this endeavor even though there never seems to be a spare minute beyond work, sleep, and food. Those participants who check out for longer stretches of the season miss the blip in the schedule, perhaps the bye week for which they earn zero points at the position, or the latest injury catastrophe, and most likely return to teams that have slipped in the standings.

There are countless Web sites that offer updated injury reports and analysis to assist in setting that week's lineup. Fantasy columnists, myself included, work beyond the box scores and analyze trends, matchups, and target data to give readers the extra edge. These reports include information that most participants don't have the time to ferret out themselves, and help to provide reinforcement of decisions past and insight for the big move that will propel the squad toward the fantasy championship. A listing of gaming providers is available in Appendix I online at www.savvyfantasysports.com.

Beyond the stats, injury reports, and other analysis offered, most participants are driven by their innate fandom. As such, remember to have fun during your participation. After all, it's a game based on a game.

What's the Payoff?

The prizes available for capturing the league championship vary greatly. Participants in free fantasy contests may not receive prizes at all, save for bragging rights among their peers. For those participating in pay-for competitions, the trophy or other trinket received by the champion serves as the physical embodiment and reinforcement of those bragging rights.

Commemorative trophies, plaques, and items of clothing such as hats and T-shirts are the norm in the prizing realm. Jostens, a familiar name and longtime distributor of high school and college class rings, entered the market with a stylish line of rings designed for fantasy owners. Figure 1.7 illustrates two of the popular prize options available to commemorate a league title. A trophy with an engraved nameplate remains the industry standard of championship swag,

Figure 1.7. Fantasytrophy.com league championship trophy (left) and Jostens fantasy championship ring

while the ring equates the fantasy title to Super Bowl glory. Appendix II (online at www.savvyfantasysports.com) offers a listing of companies that offer a variety of prizing options.

There are, of course, leagues that forego the trinkets and niceties of trophies, shirts, and the like, and deal explicitly in cold, hard cash. In leagues among friends, family, and co-workers, it is not uncommon for participants to put forward a nominal amount of cash into a pool to pay for draft-day refreshments and registration fees to fantasy game operators, with the remainder divvied up among the league's top performers. In order to boost the payout, some leagues also charge transaction fees for each trade and waiver-wire move.

One of the new trends in the industry is the development of high-stakes games, where the cash prize to the victor is some multiple of the winner's normal annual salary. These contests appeal to the "know-it-all" effect of fantasy sports and are as much about ego as the large stakes. Krause Sports, which has published its *Fantasy Sports* magazine for 15 years, offers a high-stakes fantasy football contest with simultaneous drafts in Chicago, New York, and Las Vegas. Entry fees in these contests run from $1,300 to $5,000, and reward single league champions with prizes anywhere from $6,000 to $200,000 for the overall champion.

Armed with a basic concept of how the fantasy football industry operates, it's time to examine the evolution of the industry over the past 40 years. You can reread that. It says 40 years. Chapter 2 examines the ever-changing industry and how it has evolved from a small, underground activity into a mainstream force in 2006.

2 The Changing Face of the Fantasy Culture

- ♦ Origins of the Game
- ♦ Growth in the Online World
- ♦ Reviewing Demographics and Dollars

ORIGINS OF THE GAME

The general belief is that fantasy football games are a recent invention of the Internet explosion of the late 1990s. In reality, these contests can be traced back 45 years. Bob Harris and Emil Kadlec of Fantasy Sports Publications Inc., chronicled the genesis of fantasy football back to the early 1960s. Even more surprising to some might be the fact that fantasy football owes its creation to Wilford Winkenbach, a part owner and former public relations executive of the Oakland Raiders, and an *Oakland Tribune* reporter. The league was named the Greater Oakland Professional Pigskin Prognosticators League (GOPPPL) and included eight teams managed by individuals that met one of three overriding criteria. Team managers either had to be with an AFL team in an administrative capacity, a journalist covering an AFL team, or had purchased or sold at least 10 season-ticket packages for the Raiders' 1963 season. The last criteria for entry seemed to be a significant drop-off from the first two. Clearly, the founders had the idea that their game was suitable only for those at the league level and those in the know. My, how things have changed through the years!

Several components of the game have withstood the test of time. The league constitution addressed the weighty issues of draft processing, roster moves, lineup submissions and deadlines, and, of course, prizes for winners and losers. The trash-talking component of the game that captivates so many was most certainly in existence at the inception. There was a trophy presented at an annual banquet to the worst team in the league as a tribute to the coach's ineptitude. Winkenbach decreed that the trophy needed to be displayed prominently in that coach's home until the beginning of the next season.

The year of the game's inception speaks to the single most difficult part of operating and participating in a fantasy game during the pre-Internet world. All point totals and standings had to be calculated by hand. In the early days, the commissioner not only had the responsibility of settling disputes regarding trades and such, he also needed to be able to compile data quickly. Copiers and mimeographs at the workplace were commandeered after hours to distribute the all-important information to league members in a timely manner.

The only research and analysis available to owners were the few televised contests and stories in the local newspapers. In the original GOPPPL, information was freely exchanged within the offices of the Raiders and the *Oakland Tribune*. League members tracked their squads and obsessed about them at the office and local watering holes. The discussions in local bars piqued the interest of other patrons, and soon new versions of the game began to turn up all over the country.

The industry continued to grow slowly, but it wasn't until the advent of fantasy baseball in the 1980s that the participation increased exponentially. The popularity of both sports created a small cottage industry that ultimately witnessed a proliferation of magazines on the newsstands, fantasy games advertised in the backs of sports magazines, and the publication of injury reports in local newspapers.

GROWTH IN THE ONLINE WORLD

In the early '90s, the Internet became a force in the transmission of news and information. Fantasy participants used this new medium to vent their frustrations on message boards and began to create competitions online. Existing leagues that had long used the paper method migrated to this new source, where transactions and messages could be processed quickly and without a litany of telephone calls and paper mail.

It wasn't until 1990, when Prodigy created its *Baseball Manager* product that a company tapped into the Internet as a means for creating an online marketplace for the long-time pen-and-paper staple. The *Baseball Manager* release offered the first commissioner product to make the administration of a league easier, from roster submissions to scoring computations.

The explosion of the Internet in the latter part of the 1990s opened the industry to a variety of new players, from larger multipurpose destinations such as ESPN, CBS SportsLine, FOX Sports, and Yahoo!, to a number of specialized fantasy gaming and information hubs. The involvement of larger entities helped to bring the industry to the masses, with entertaining gaming options and information to feed the innate fandom. The barrier to entry in the niche market, particularly in the human costs associated with basic data compilation, fell to the wayside and everyone sought his or her own piece of an ever-expanding pie. As eyeballs and wallets began to gravitate to online games, these sites enjoyed advertising and sponsorship partnerships with traditional brick and mortar companies such as the auto manufacturers. Combine new interest from Madison Avenue with the continued growth of television ratings, and the fantasy industry is positioned as a major entertainment vehicle for some time.

REVIEWING DEMOGRAPHICS AND DOLLARS

To say that by joining a fantasy football league, that you're playing against the world might be hyperbole, but it's not altogether untrue. Participants from all over the world follow the exploits of their home teams. During this past NFL season, I received a number of letters from players in Europe, Asia, and seemingly every continent detailing their love of the game and how fantasy football helps to keep friends and family connected.

 Create a fantasy league to get your group of college or high school friends back together. Aside from the logistics of running a draft, the online gaming experience reduces all boundaries and helps you keep in touch.

I posed this simple question to friends and in my mailbag column: What is the appeal of fantasy football? Many of the answers spoke to the need to follow all games and how those contests involving two last-place teams still had a major fantasy impact.

One particular answer from Dan Lenz of upstate New York spoke to the joy of player evaluation and serving as a virtual general manager: "Fantasy football finally gives me the chance to be in charge of personnel. Most owners don't understand the real value of players, at least in terms of fantasy value, so this is a way to dominate."

Recent surveys on fantasy sports participation have placed the number of participants between 15 and 20 million. That number includes the entire span of fantasy competitions from the traditional sports offerings to single-event contests for award shows, less mainstream sports such as bass fishing, and filling out an NCAA Tournament bracket (that would push the number far north of the estimate, in my opinion).

A survey conducted by Ipsos in August 2005 produced a lower size estimate of the industry at 12.6 million individuals having participated in fantasy sports competitions, with 10 million participating since August 2004. Of that base of 10 million, 8.3 million individuals participated in fantasy football leagues. The survey indicates that 12% of the fantasy football population (1 million players) is comprised of women.

Dr. Kim Beason, of the University of Mississippi, conducted a similar study at the behest of the Fantasy Sports Trade Association (FSTA). His data presents quite a different picture of the typical fantasy sports participant. The notion of a "fantasy game" typically conjures an image of a middle-aged male living in his parents' basement. In fact, the average fantasy player is a 41-year-old male holding a bachelor's degree and earning a shade under $90,000 per year ($89,566).

To examine the economic impact of fantasy football on the various gaming providers and information hubs, Dr. Beason's survey examined the average amount of dollars spent on fantasy football. The results of the survey show that fantasy football participants spent an average of $161 per person for all league, tool, and information costs. The quick math says that over $1.3 billion (with a "b") were spent on fantasy football in the fall of 2003 (8.3 million participants multiplied by $161). That doesn't even include advertising or sponsorship deals for the participating companies.

The need to keep tabs on updated team and injury information while monitoring the waiver wire has led fantasy football owners to bring their fantasy football habit into the workplace. The executive search firm Challenger, Gray

& Christmas, Inc. estimated that U.S. businesses lose $36.7 million in productivity per day during the fantasy football season. The firm used a higher participant estimate of 14 million in line with Dr. Beason's past surveys to reach the dollar amount (14 million participants times $2.62, the average wage paid to American workers per 10 minutes). To combat this growing trend, some firms have limited employees' abilities to access fantasy sports as they would adult or gambling sites. Banking institutions have been a leader in squashing access to online sports access, putting keywords such as "fantasy," "sports," and "football" on the restricted list.

Most fantasy football participants (friends, family, and colleagues) that I polled admitted to checking in on game activity during the workday. They spoke of checking the previous night's results while booting up their machines and making sure that lineups were properly adjusted ahead of daytime baseball games. When asked if checking their teams was an appropriate function at the workplace, several wondered aloud about the difference in perception between coffee or cigarette breaks and their fantasy football hobby.

In the end, I would argue that the productivity loss as calculated by Challenger, Gray & Christmas offers a good shock value and makes us rethink the standard workday, but that the calculation is too simple. In an age when many workers exceed a standard eight-hour day without overtime pay so as to bring a project to completion, one has to wonder whether stepping away for a few minutes makes the worker a more productive and focused contributor for the rest of the day. Challenger, Gray & Christmas acknowledges in its findings that the boost in employee morale might just be worth the hit to the bottom line.

In Chapter 3, we'll move inside the white lines and address the necessary break in thought patterns that need to occur to separate brilliance on the gridiron with domination on the fantasy score sheet.

3 Making a Break Between Fantasy and Reality

- The Trap of Being a Homer
- Everyone is an Option
- Stars on the Field, but Viable Fantasy Options?
- Breaking the Plane: Scoreaphobic Players

Participation in a fantasy football league forces coaches to toe the precarious line between the fantasy world and real life. That is to say, during the extensive player evaluation period ahead of the draft, coaches must consider a player's role within the overall team concept and decide whether that role translates into fantasy points based on the chosen league configuration. The ranking process can best be described as part art and part science, where numbers are crunched to provided a basis and a visceral response places the players in order.

To successfully navigate the ranking process, the coach must be colorblind. All players are reduced to numbers and ordered, regardless of their team affiliation. Remember the *New Jack City* mantra: "Always business, never personal" and recite it endlessly as your draft time approaches.

There are three schools of thought related to the acquisition of players and roster management from the all-important draft to the conclusion of the season. Fantasy football participants weigh the importance of factors such as team affiliation, past performance, and strength of schedule differently. These styles of player acquisition and in-season roster management are identified and categorized in the following sections, using the rating system of "Good, Better, and Best."

Good: Some fantasy football participants wear their hearts on their sleeves, literally. They arrive to the draft in the colors of their favorite teams and often select more than one player on the home team. The thing that first attracts most participants to enter a fantasy football league is the passion for the game. For others, it's their only opportunity to get involved with a team in an "ownership" capacity. After all, most of us don't have an extra $800 million or $1 billion laying around for the next NFL expansion opportunity. Taken further, save a few teams such as New England and Pittsburgh, NFL ownership and management groups generally take a beating from local columnists and fan message boards. These participants are prone to gambling on the next "sure thing" on the hometown team instead of a proven performer on the dreaded rival.

Better: While the straight fan approach might be fitting for first-time participants, as they'll be sure to keep interested in their fantasy teams, it also generally leads to a mediocre finish at best. Unless they catch lightning in a bottle with high-scoring offenses such as the 2004 Indianapolis Colts or 2005 Seattle Seahawks, their fantasy team as a whole is in for a number of lackluster performances. Therefore, a combination of statistical analysis and that innate fandom is more beneficiary to participants. Draft lists in this context are based on numbers first, with decisions regarding rivalries and faith in the home teams as secondary concerns.

Best: In the ideal world, participants give total rule of their selections to the numbers. Emotions and team loyalty stay outside the draft room doors and any in-season visits to the waiver wire. It must be noted that all draft lists and rankings owe some of their composition to instincts and opinions about teams and players. At the base of the analysis, participants need to have informed opinions about the makeup of opponents and that individual player's roster to create their draft lists.

THE TRAP OF BEING A HOMER

One of the most alluring traps that ensnares fantasy football participants on draft day concerns the selection of the hometown players. Every off-season, longtime fan favorites are discarded in place of new blood via the draft or free agency, with some veterans being cut as part of a cost efficiency plan. The names in the box scores and rosters in the program change annually, but fans remain loyal to the logo on the helmet.

And that's where the draft-day dilemma occurs. If a player lines up at wideout or calls signals for your favorite team, then he surely is worthy of a fantasy selection. The inner fan and a "this is our year" attitude sometimes overwhelms logic.

It's not quite that simple. Each team has its players that fly off the board. In 2005 fantasy football drafts, four Indianapolis Colts offensive players came off the draft board by the end of the third round on average (Peyton Manning, Edgerrin James, and Marvin Harrison in the first round and Reggie Wayne in the third round). Nobody could argue with any of these early selections.

Name your team. I guarantee that at least one player warrants fantasy consideration regardless of how poorly you expect that player's actual team to perform. In fantasy football, every team's top running back and first wide receiver will be drafted no matter how suspect the team's offense is as a whole. For example, the hapless Houston Texans limped to a record of 2-14 in 2005. Despite low expectations for the team's performance in the AFC South, starting Houston RB Domanick Davis was drafted late in the first round or early second round on average. Many experts pegged third-year receiver Andre Johnson for a monster season and fantasy football participants agreed, making him a third-round selection on average. Even David Carr, who ultimately threw only 14 TD passes on the season, was targeted as a "sleeper" selection and drafted ahead of more established scorers. In hindsight, fantasy managers wished they'd moved one slot lower on their draft boards in selecting this trio, as each battled periods of injury or ineffectiveness in 2005.

I'll revisit this topic in Chapter 9, which examines the phenomenon and all-out celebration that is draft day.

EVERYONE IS AN OPTION

While some owners fall prey to the desire to own home-town favorites, others actively pass over players on their team's top rival. This stands as one of the chief arguments against fantasy football by its detractors. Naturally, football fans face a psychological block when confronted with the proposition of selecting a player whose performance may single-handedly propel your fantasy team to the ultimate heights while decimating your NFL favorite team's real-life hopes. As a result, managers adjust their rankings during the draft to push players in question a notch or two lower.

By way of example: If you're a fan of the Philadelphia Eagles, you may feel conflicted when faced with the prospect of drafting a power player from any other team in the NFC East. Clinton Portis and Tiki Barber were viable late first- and early second-round selections. An Eagles fan may have rationalized dropping Portis and Barber on their lists by citing their subpar 2004 showings (both with QB and offensive line issues at their base), while elevating players such as the aforementioned Davis from Houston or Buffalo Bills RB Willis McGahee, a second-half stud in 2004.

In my decade of playing fantasy football and my observance of literally hundreds upon hundreds of drafts, I've witnessed a number of managers pass over a player only to add a message of justification such as, "I just couldn't take a Giant, Cowboy, (insert team here)," when the player is finally drafted. The other participants in the league won't pass judgment on your team loyalty.

Remember, you're not cheering for that player's team to win a game. You still want your rival's team to finish 0-16. You just want that QB, WR, or RB to account for any of the scoring the team does accomplish. Shutouts are rare. It's undoubtedly better for you to earn points for that late scoring strike than your opponent.

I believe participants should stick to the rankings that accompanied them to the draft room. Naturally, managers should track the activity and be sure to shore up their rosters when players at a particular position are becoming scarce. But, simply diverting from the plan due to the color of a player's uniform is a recipe for disaster.

With all of that said, despite the explosion of the industry, fantasy football is still just a means to extend one's enjoyment of the NFL. If snubbing players from division rivals helps to make fantasy football a better experience, then so be it. Just don't look back to draft day when Terrell Owens signs a football or runs to the star in Big D in front of an adoring home crowd.

STARS ON THE FIELD, BUT VIABLE FANTASY OPTIONS?

The worlds of fantasy football and the NFL collide on the stat sheets and standing pages on another level, one where a player's ability to lead a team to victory (or at least be competitive) doesn't translate into fantasy superstardom. Quarterbacks stand out most in this area, as the ability to win a game isn't always dependent on a multi-TD performance a la Peyton Manning.

Among current NFL signal callers, Tom Brady and Ben Roethlisberger are cited as the two QBs who "just get it done." Play calling is predicated on a strong running game and short, efficient passes. It's easy to overlook that Brady led the NFL in TD passes in 2002 and passing yards in 2005. For Roethlisberger, images of the Steelers attack focus squarely on the running game of Willie Parker and Jerome Bettis. Few realize that Roethlisberger accounted for multiple TDs (rushing and passing) in seven of his 12 starts.

I offer a brief look at several quarterbacks to illustrate this point.

- **Troy Aikman, Dallas Cowboys:** The Hall of Fame QB and leader of the 1990s Cowboys stands among the greatest signal callers of all time. With a great offensive line, the legs of Emmitt Smith, and his accurate arm that found Michael Irvin so often, Aikman earned three Super Bowl wins. If you go inside the numbers, Aikman wasn't the classic fantasy quarterback, reaching 20 passing touchdowns just once. It should be noted, however, that a one-to-one comparison can be deceptive, as running games generally dominated the action in the '90s. Aikman placed in the top 10 in passing touchdowns with totals of 15 and 19 in two other seasons.

- **Michael Vick, Atlanta Falcons:** Vick ranks as one of the most exciting players in the NFL, blending a cannon for an arm with tremendous vision and elusiveness as a ball carrier. His wide receiver corps has not yet risen to his level, and his numbers continue to suffer. After five NFL seasons, there are still many questions regarding Vick's ability to run an NFL offense and achieve his potential as a passer. He tallied 15 passing touchdowns in 15 games last season with six touchdowns on the ground. Vick remains a top selection on draft day, often coming off the board as the fifth or sixth QB selected. Potential is a strong driving force, and Vick turns just 26 in June 2006.

- **Steve McNair, Tennessee Titans:** McNair is often described as a warrior, often playing through pain to lead his team to victory. The former co-MVP of the league turned in three successful fantasy seasons from 2001-03 with 25 or more total touchdowns in each of those seasons. He reached the 20-TD mark in two other campaigns on the strength of eight rushing touchdowns. However, the performances on either side of those seasons have been lackluster from a fantasy perspective. McNair has thrown for 16 or fewer touchdowns in each of his other five seasons as a starter.

BREAKING THE PLANE:
SCOREAPHOBIC PLAYERS

One of the more frustrating aspects of the fantasy season for owners involves running backs and wide receivers who are instrumental to a team's advancement down the field, but who disappear near the goal line. In some cases, a team's personnel will dictate the play calling inside the 5 where a role player overtakes the lead back or a seldom-used tight end makes up for the attention afforded the top receiver. In others, it's a function of ineptitude in short-yardage situations.

Zack Crockett of the Raiders has long filled this need for his team. He's averaged one TD per 13 carries in his career. And, even former Steelers tailback Jerome Bettis laughs about his peculiar stat line from Week 1 of the 2004 season: 5 carries, 1 yard, 3 TDs.

There are several top names currently afflicted with "scorephobia," my term for the "fear of the painted grass."

- **Duce Staley, Pittsburgh Steelers:** Staley was side-lined for virtually the entire 2005 season due to injury, but figures to be back in the mix at tailback for Pittsburgh in '06. He was the workhorse for the 2004 season, rolling up 830 yards and just a single TD due to the presence of Bettis. That TD came from 25 yards out.

- **Fred Taylor, Jacksonville Jaguars:** Taylor appeared to be headed to a career as a top scorer with double-digit TD totals in two of his first three years. However, a series of injuries kept him off the field and has slowed his TD pace. Taylor hasn't topped eight touchdowns in a season since 2000, and despite nearly 2,500 yards of total offense in the last two years, he tallied a total of only six TDs.

- **Reuben Droughns, Cleveland Browns:** Droughns took over as the featured back in the Cleveland set in 2004 after past success in the Denver system. He ran for 1,232 yards on 309 carries, but found the end zone on just two occasions. The Browns lacked playmakers to assist Droughns on offense save receiver Antonio Bryant (1,009 receiving yards, just four TDs), as evidenced by their league-low scoring total of 14.5 points per game.

- **David Givens, Tennessee Titans (formerly New England Patriots):** Givens was the No. 1 receiver in New England, accruing 59 receptions and 738 yards in the multi-target passing attack. It marked the second consecutive year in which Givens topped 50 catches and 700 receiving yards. He scored a total of five touchdowns during those seasons. Linebacker Mike Vrabel scored as many receiving touchdowns for the Patriots as Givens during this two-year period.

SUMMARY

Managers face a myriad of data points and trends to consider as they assemble their rosters. As much as I'd like to say that the numbers dictate all draft-day activity, it would be naïve to assume that team affiliations and gut instincts don't matter. The previous factors should guide you toward recognizing those players in adverse situations and to be more keenly aware of the distinction between those players who you love to watch for their gamesmanship and football prowess and those who you love to own for those raw numbers ... regardless of their uniform.

4 Commissioner Responsibilities

- ♦ Choosing a Site
- ♦ Establishing Waiver Rules
- ♦ Trading Rules
- ♦ Victory
- ♦ Preparing for Next Season

The selection or election of the league commissioner is one of the most important aspects of running a successful league, and it often gets little attention. The commissioner is often the person championing the idea of entering the fantasy football universe, and as such, he or she becomes the leader by default. Generally, the commissioner is the person bombarding your e-mail account with invitations or stalking you on your way to the break room.

The commissioner acts initially as a salesperson, extolling the virtues of involvement in fantasy football and selling the concept of owning your own team. The commissioner needs to be convincing in his or her delivery and messaging, appealing to building camaraderie or promoting the battle to be crowned "office know it all."

The commissioner also plays in the league, so it is imperative for the commissioner to have ample time to run his or her own team and address league issues. The choice of a commissioner or volunteering for the post shouldn't be taken lightly.

Choosing a Site

The commissioner needs to gauge the computer savvyness of members. A quick survey of the league membership should be done to assess their experiences and knowledge of different fantasy sports sites. Of chief import is whether they have user names and passwords for specific sites. The first step toward an active membership is the ease of use of the chosen site.

Commissioners, create a list of possible destinations for the league. Furnish the list to the league members and encourage them to rank sites on the list according to familiarity. Table 4.1 lists a number of the most trafficked sports and fantasy sports sites. A more extensive listing appears in Appendix II.

Table 4.1. A listing of popular fantasy sports web sites

Fantasy Football Game Sites	
Site	**URL**
All Star Stats	http://allstar.rotoworld.com
CBS SportsLine	http://cbs.sportsline.com
CDM Sports	http://cdmsports.com
ESPN.com	http://games.espn.go.com
FantasyFootball	http://fantasyfootball.com
FOX Sports	http://msn.foxsports.com/fantasy
MY Fantasy League	http://myfantasyleague.com
Rotowire	http://rotowire.com
Sandbox	http://sandbox.com
Sports Buff	http://sportsbuff.com
Sports Illustrated	http://sportsillustrated.cnn.com/fantasy
The Sporting News	http://fantasygames.sportingnews.com
Yahoo! Sports	http://fantasysports.yahoo.com

The commissioner should also evaluate the flexibility of the site. As the administrator of the league, he or she may be called upon to make decisions regarding fair play and balance during the season. Specifically, can the commissioner make roster and scoring adjustments as necessary? Figure 4.1 offers a sample of administrative tools available to league commissioners. The goal is to resolve disputes and maintain the integrity of the competition.

Figure 4.1. FOX Sports Fantasy Football Commissioner Tools Index

Be sure to review the site and examine any online tutorials (more commonly referred to as "tours") to view the available feature sets. The screenshots provide glimpses into the most traveled portions of the site so as to most effectively communicate the game experience. In reviewing the tour information, the gaming site will also promote its proprietary content and partnerships.

Review the Help and Rules information posted on each site. As the leader of the league, all questions will come to you. Therefore, it is in the commissioner's interest to choose a site that allows league participants to find in-depth answers quickly.

Another way to find out about the site's good and bad qualities is to inquire on the built-in message boards or to seek out blogs about fantasy football game sites. A query on the post is bound to elicit frank evaluations of the site and game play therein. Remember, those posting to message boards share the same passion about the sport and fantasy games as you do. Therefore, don't take offense if one or more members lash out at a seemingly innocuous question.

Post to your league's message board regularly. A weekly update or quick update about a team or player keeps participants interested and checking the league pages.

ESTABLISHING WAIVER RULES

Once the draft has been completed, all remaining players are available to the league through the available players list, also known as the waiver wire. The decision of how to handle these transactions is paramount to the success of the league. As owners contemplate the acquisition of a player from the waiver wire, they can view the current waiver priority order, as illustrated in Figure 4.2. In the best of worlds, the waiver wire helps lower-tier teams and slow starters to become competitive and thereby remain active.

Figure 4.2. Add/ Drop Functionality and Waiver Priority List

As the league's rules (commonly called a "constitution") are drafted, the administration of the waiver wire should be clearly outlined. Several popular options and the merits of each are outlined here:

- **No transactions:** It creates a great environment on draft day as everyone flexes his or her muscle to build the perfect team. However, it relies more heavily on luck and limits the need to actually follow the league.

- **Season-long rotation:** The initial waiver order is determined by some order (most commonly the inverse of draft order) and continuously rotates as players are acquired through waivers. All unowned players remain on waivers throughout the season, with one day of the week specified as the day on which all pending claims are run.

- **In place for a certain period post-draft:** All undrafted players go to waivers for a time period after the draft's completion. After this period ends, all claims are processed and the remaining players are available as free agents. Players released from rosters are subject to the waiver rules specified in the league's constitution (typically 2-7 days).

- **By standings, rotating:** The waiver wire in this context resets at a particular point in the week based on the standings. The last-place team receives highest priority.

- **Sun-Tues:** This system protects those members unable to watch games on Sunday by putting all players on waivers as soon as the deadline passes for the week's first game(s). All unowned players stay on waivers until Tuesday at 11:59 p.m. (generally Pacific Time).

- **Bidding:** Participants bid on unowned players using real or fictional dollars as set forth in the league constitution. This process forces participants to truly weigh a player's value, as they receive only a finite budget for the entire season. The player then goes to the highest bidder (with some tie-break system including standings or fantasy points).

TRADING RULES

Once the league approves a method by which to process trades, the managers need to adopt a voting policy (majority, commissioner rule, use of a third party) and, if applicable, the cost associated with the transaction. A stable and consistent voting policy between the commissioner and league members that is voted on and included in the constitution ensures that all personal biases are removed and that the trade is reviewed on its own merits. Some leagues create an acceptable statistical variance between the players or difference in the host site's player rankings. Whatever method is used, be sure to give each participant a voice.

VICTORY

Every manager plays for the glory of winning the league and demonstrating his or her brilliance among the group of friends, family, or associates. The pride and self-satisfaction of vanquishing all opponents stands as the best reward for a season of navigating through injuries, erratic plays, underperformers, and lineup decisions. But a trophy or knick-knack to celebrate the victory serves as a constant reminder to the also-rans and motivation to compete harder next season. Of course, private leagues among colleagues and friends also include a nominal cash outlay with payouts to the top finishers.

Most participants in office leagues, or those playing against family or friends, will continue to play for pride. A physical representation of the hard-fought win raises the level of competition.

A number of companies, new and old, specialize in providing goods to commemorate league championships. T-shirts, banners, plaques, and trophies are among the most

common prize offerings. Most gaming sites that require a registration fee will also furnish some type of prize to the league champion.

Figure 4.3. Traditional league prize: a T-shirt

The commissioner can also provide a "prize" to the last-place team. Trophy shops carry awards in the shape of toilet bowls or horse's rear ends to poke fun at last-place finishes. As fantasy football is all about creating a fun and spirited contest that routinely includes smack-talking, these awards serve as motivation to escape the league cellar.

PREPARING FOR NEXT SEASON

After prizes have been distributed, commissioners should immediately turn their attention to the next campaign and get feedback about the season just completed. The commissioner should ask questions about the overall performance of the gaming provider, with the ultimate goal of ascertaining whether the membership would like to explore new options.

Create a venue outside of the league, discuss the sport, and plan for next season. It helps to keep the group together and explore ways to improve the experience for the subsequent season. The creation of a Web site, online group, or blog such as those available through FOX Sports Blogs, Friendster, or Yahoo! 360 helps to keep the league alive through the long off-season.

The next chapter examines the basic principles of game play and introduces you to the fantasy football participant base.

5 Boot Camp: The Basics of Fantasy Football

- ◆ Who Am I Playing?
- ◆ What's the Cost?
- ◆ What Can I Win?
- ◆ Season Timeline
- ◆ Roster Configuration
- ◆ Scoring Configuration
- ◆ Playoffs

WHO AM I PLAYING?

The global popularity of the NFL, fueled by the season-ending spectacle that is the Super Bowl, has extended the fantasy football boundary far beyond the U.S. border. During the course of this past season, I received a large number of e-mails signed with country tags from all over the globe, with England, Italy, Sweden, Japan, and Iceland among them. I received a number of requests for assistance from military personnel stationed abroad who were using fantasy football as a means by which to hold on to a piece of home and to communicate with family and friends.

It is estimated that some 10 to 12 million Americans play fantasy football each year. Quick math says that roughly one in 20 participates in this world.

A survey conducted in 2004 by Dr. Kim Beason at the University of Mississippi yielded some results that may be surprising to casual observers of the industry and listeners of some sports talk radio hosts. Fantasy game participants are typically dismissed as geeks who spend all night in front of a computer after coming home from a low-paying job. Dr. Beason's survey suggests a much different picture: the average fantasy participant is a 41-year-old male professional with a yearly salary of $89,000.

But it's not just the men that are playing fantasy sports. A 2002 survey by marketing research firm Ipsos revealed that as much as 25 percent of the fantasy sports participant base is women. Regardless of which number you accept for the total fantasy football population, it means that approximately three to four million women are drawing up the virtual playbook. To put that number in perspective, four million people represents one half of the *Deal or No Deal* viewing audience.

Reasons for entering a league vary tremendously, ranging from those truly passionate about the sport to those being fed up with their "NFL widow" status. I received one message this fall from a mom in the Midwest who joined a league with her sons and husband and proudly declared that she had vaulted into first place during the playoff stretch. As the season wound down, tales of participation multiplied, with most citing their fantasy skills as a work in progress. Virtually everyone wanted to return for another season.

A large majority of the respondents to Dr. Beason's survey (in which 7 percent of the respondents were women) credited fantasy football as their gateway to the world of fantasy sports. An astounding 71 percent of survey participants first entered fantasy sports through fantasy football.

The easy access to computers for spot checks on available players and the latest news make fantasy sports a constant companion in the professional environment. In fact, the executive search firm Challenger, Gray & Christmas estimates that businesses lose roughly $36.7 million daily as a result of the fantasy football craze (high-end estimate of 14 million fantasy football players multiplied by $2.62, the average wage that an American worker is paid each 10 minutes). Dr. Beason's survey indicates that two-thirds of fantasy football participants checked their team online during work hours. Challenger, Gray & Christmas suggests that the amount of lost productivity may actually be beneficial to some companies, citing better morale and more focused efforts in the remainder of the workday.

Some firms have nixed access to fantasy sports in the workplace as they would access to adult sites. Financial institutions have been the leaders in taking this approach to online sports content, restricting keywords such as "fantasy," "sports," and "football" from office correspondence and flagging such queries behind the company firewall.

The majority of fantasy players (friends, family, and colleagues) I polled about their office dalliances argued that the 10 to 15 minutes spent on their fantasy teams each day were no more frivolous than the extended coffee and cigarette breaks that carried less of a stigma. They spoke of accessing their teams in the minutes while opening larger computer programs or of cutting lunches short to get a last-minute peek at their rosters before the beginning of daytime baseball. And there's that last check of items before shutting down the computer for the workday. Larger research projects concerning available players, trades, and upcoming schedule plays were left for home and their time off.

If anything, my years of experience in the industry would contend that the survey's result of 10 minutes per day is a very conservative estimate and that doubling — maybe even tripling — the amount would be more appropriate. The respondents to Dr. Beason's survey spent roughly 25 minutes per day managing their teams. Given the fact that longer workdays are becoming the norm in many sectors of the workforce, perhaps the short distraction that helps to refresh the mind and spirit isn't such a disruptive force.

WHAT'S THE COST?

There is only one cost associated with participation in fantasy sports that is incurred by all participants, and even then, that cost cannot be measured equally. The opportunity cost associated with the time spent at the keyboard clicking between available players and trade possibilities will differ greatly from player to player. Each participant must assess the amount of available time and take a quick check of his or her personality before entering this area. The amount of material available regarding stats splits, advice, and trend analysis can easily fill an entire day.

As for the monetary side of the equation, Dr. Beason's survey revealed that the average fantasy football participant spent $161 on research materials for the 2003 season. The highest cost relates to the cost of running the league. Among pay sites, commissioner and league services cover a wide price range, from $9.95 for a single team up to a staggering $1,250 for entry into the National Fantasy Football Championships. The typical league fee runs from $99 to $150 for up to 20 participants. Some sites, such as FOXSports.com and Yahoo! Sports offer a free game.

The typical magazine on the newsstand costs between $6.95 and $9.95. There are usually several magazines on the racks of your local Barnes & Noble or Borders in advance of the upcoming season. The remaining sports will be profiled in smaller sections of national titles, such as *Sports Illustrated* and *The Sporting News*.

The sliding cost of domain name registrations has spurred a proliferation of Web sites that offer free chat rooms, message boards, and quick-hit reactions to player movement and injuries. Like the premium fantasy games, a wide price range exists among content providers for player and team information. Figures 5.1 and 5.2 demonstrate two popular formats for the dissemination of player and team

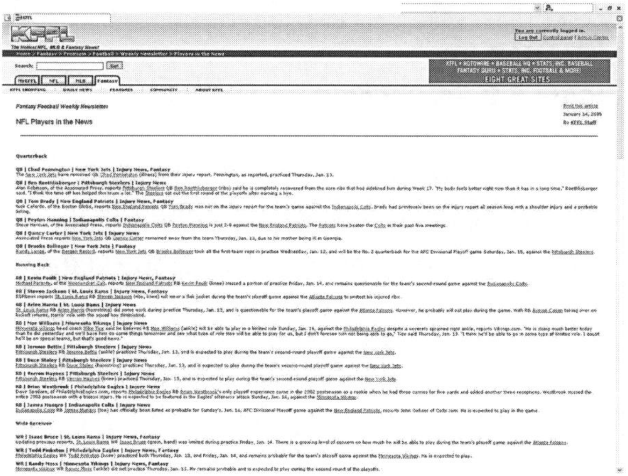

Figure 5.1.
KFFL

Figure 5.2. Talentedmrroto.com

news. KFFL and The Talented Mr. Roto are two examples of the myriad of resources available to guide participants' strategies. These packages include daily updates, chats, mailbag features, and statistical breakdowns designed to give the purchaser an edge over the competition.

A listing of fantasy game information and magazines is available in Appendix II.

Other Costs

Regardless of the amount of money spent on magazines, draft tools, and commissioner services, most private leagues require an entry fee on top of each manager's re-payment of the site access fee. The inclusion of an entry fee, normally doled out as prizes, serves to keep all managers interested and active in the proceedings.

Most leagues keep things simple, charging somewhere on the scale from $10 to $100 plus the appropriate portion of the registration fee. The prizes are normally doled out for first, second, and third place, and occasionally the victor of a head-to-head matchup between the two teams lowest in the standings will receive their entry fee back.

A subsection of leagues also uses a bidding process for waiver claims to sweeten the pot and force participants to truly ponder a player's worth instead of the constant add/drop process that prevails in leagues that omit this setup. The bidding process is simple. Managers must submit a bid in dollar increments from $1 to some predetermined maximum (or in some cases, no maximum). Over the course of the season, these small transaction fees can add up to make for a very sizable pool and will certainly keep teams focused and the message boards lively until the final snap of the season.

The prizes available for capturing the league championship vary greatly. Participants in free fantasy contests may not receive prizes at all, save for bragging rights. The trophy or other trinket received by the champion serves as the physical embodiment of the bragging rights.

To that end, commemorative trophies, plaques and items of clothing such as hats and T-shirts are the norm. Recently,

Jostens, a longtime distributor of high school and college class rings, entered the market with a stylish line of rings for fantasy owners. Figures 5.3 illustrates two of the popular prize options available to commemorate a league title. A trophy with an engraved nameplate remains the industry standard, while the wearable and omnipresent ring presents a subtle reminder to all league members of who's boss. It serves to stoke the competitive fires heading into the next season. Appendix II offers a listing of companies that offer a variety of prizing options.

Figure 5.3. Examples of fantasy sports league prize options are the FantasyTrophy.com trophy (left) and the Josten's fantasy football championship ring.

A new trend in the industry revolves around high-stakes games, where the cash prizes dwarf the regular salaries of the participants. WCOFF (World Championship of Fantasy Football), Fantasy VIPs, and the NFFC (National Fantasy Football Championship) are three games that require a heavy outlay of cash in order to participate. These contests appeal as much to the participants' egos as much as they do to their wallets. Entry fees run upward of $1,000 with prizes ranging from $5,000 for an individual league champion to $100,000 for the overall winner. Therefore, registration in these leagues is not for the faint of heart and requires a wealth of knowledge and dedication.

The atmosphere in these high-stakes games rivals that of the NFL draft in that the conference room essentially mirrors the war rooms of NFL teams, with chatter over the pick that was and the one that is to come.

Season Timeline

Ask any NFL player or coach about his plans for the off-season, and you're likely to get a chuckle and the response, "What off-season?" While it's not necessarily the same for fantasy owners, the off-season is decidedly shorter than it used to be. Fantasy owners now anxiously watch the off-season free agent activity of the entire league as opposed to only reviewing their favorite team and its division rivals.

The true beginning to the fantasy season occurs as early as March, when the initial round of free agent signings occurs. Eager fantasy participants update their year-end cheatsheets to account for the changes and the impacts to teammates new and old.

The NFL Draft occurs at the end of April and starts the speculation of roles and achievements for the new class. They also begin to appear in early cheatsheets within online sites.

The first magazines and books hit the stands in early July, offering cheatsheets, a review of the off-season activity for those fans who spend their sports minutes on baseball, basketball, hockey, or any other of thousands of pursuits.

By the end of July, the first fantasy drafts begin to take place in conjunction with early training camp battles and reviews.

Naturally, momentum builds as the preseason wears on, injury reports are absorbed, and depth charts are solidified. The final week of August represents peak draft season, as most managers seek to get the draft completed ahead of a Labor Day week vacation, which leads into Week 1 of the season.

ROSTER CONFIGURATION

There are two basic roster configurations utilized within the vast majority of fantasy football leagues. The main difference between the most common setups is the amount of flexibility afforded the participant in filling each of the roster spots.

The first of these configurations, shown as Basic Roster Configuration I in Table 5.1, represents the classic offensive formation utilized in the NFL of the past. In this setup, a player from each of the offensive positions (as well as multiple running backs and wide receivers) must be taken to complete a roster.

The requirement of three wide receivers (WR) forces participants to extend their research beyond the first and second options on NFL rosters. Since each team has to fill a six-man bench, as many as 60 to 70 wide receivers will be taken on draft day (three starters per team plus an average of two on each team's bench).

Similarly, the tight end (TE) position creates an interesting draft-day dilemma. Participants must determine how valuable those top-tier performers at tight end are relative to wide receivers, running backs, and quarterbacks in the early rounds of the draft.

Kickers and team defenses are typically among the last players selected in the draft, with a few notable exceptions. There will be several top performers at each of these positions that separate from the pack in the points column. This goes back to the tiering style of draft preparation outlined in Chapter 9.

Table 5.1. Fantasy football Basic Roster Configuration I

Basic Roster Configuration I	
Position	**Expected Contribution**
1 Quarterback (QB)	Passing Yards, Passing Touchdowns, Rushing Yards, Rushing Touchdowns
2 Running Back (RB)	Rushing Yards, Rushing Touchdowns, Receiving Yards, Receiving Touchdowns
3 Wide Receiver (WR)	Receiving Yards, Receiving Touchdowns
1 Tight End (TE)	Receiving Yards, Receiving Touchdowns
1 Kicker (K)	Point After Touchdown Conversions, Field Goals
1 Team Defense (DEF)	Interceptions, Fumble Recoveries, Defensive Touchdowns, Sacks, Safeties
6 Bench (BN)/Any Player	Any of the above dependent on the position chosen to fill the role
15 Total Players	

The second standard roster configuration, designated as Basic Roster Configuration II in Table 5.2, offers participants more flexibility when selecting players for their starting lineups. The change here is that the third wide receiver position required in the Basic Roster Configuration I is now designated as a "flex" position. In leagues using this "flex" position, participants can choose to fill that particular roster spot with either a running back or wide receiver.

This increased flexibility impacts draft strategy as it relates to the scoring categories and point modifiers assigned therein. Of course, the number of league participants also greatly impacts these decisions. In a 12-team league, participants are required to start a total of 24 running backs. That leaves eight NFL starters available for selection. As few as four teams will be compelled to start a third wide receiver in this "flex" position.

Table 5.2. Fantasy football Basic Roster Configuration II

Basic Roster Configuration II		
P Position	**Eligible Positions**	**Expected Contribution**
1 QB	Quarterback	Passing Yards, Passing Touchdowns, Rushing Yards, Rushing Touchdowns
2 RB	Running Back	Rushing Yards, Rushing Touchdowns, Receiving Yards, Receiving Touchdowns
2 WR	Wide Receiver	Receiving Yards, Receiving Touchdowns
1 RB/WR	Running Back OR Wide Receiver	Rushing Yards and Rushing Touchdowns or Receiving Yards and Receiving Touchdowns
1 TE	Tight End	Receiving Yards, Receiving Touchdowns
1 K	Kicker	Point After Touchdown Conversions, Field Goals
1 Defense (DEF)	Defensive Team	Interceptions, Fumble Recoveries, Defensive Touchdowns, Sacks, Safeties
6 Bench (BN)	Any Player	Any of the above dependent on the position chosen to fill the role

In both systems, the inclusion of bench positions allows participants to protect themselves with the backups or replacements for their key players. It also permits participants to speculate about players whom they think will assume larger roles during the season.

SCORING CONFIGURATION

Just as leagues determine their starting roster positions, they also face a myriad of options when choosing scoring categories and point modifiers. The information in Table

5.3 details the standing scoring categories utilized within leagues and the main categories used by those leagues including individual defensive players. The scoring categories and their respective point modifiers apply to all active players on the roster. If a wide receiver throws a touchdown pass, he receives the appropriate points for the feat. Similarly, if a backup quarterback is forced to serve as the kicker, he would receive points for the accomplishment. In order to conserve space, game providers will typically denote these unusual activities with some designation, typically an asterisk (*).

Table 5.3. Fantasy Football Standard Scoring Categories

Fantasy Football Standard Scoring Categories	
Scoring Category	**Definition**
Passing Yards	The distance gained following the completion of a forward pass.
Passing Touchdowns	Earned by completing a forward pass to a receiver that is advanced into the opponent's end zone.
Rushing Yards	Distance gained following a hand-off or pitch behind the line of scrimmage.
Rushing Touchdowns	Earned by carrying the ball into the opponent's end zone.
Receiving Yards	Distance gained following the completion of a forward pass.
Receiving Touchdowns	Earned by carrying the ball into the opponent's end zone after catching a forward pass.
Two-Point Conversion	Rushing or catching a pass in the opponent's end zone from three yards out following a touchdown.
Fumble Lost	When an offensive player drops the ball and it is recovered by the opposition.
Interception	When a pass attempt is caught by the opposing defense instead of the intended receiver.
Field Goal	A kicked ball that travels through the goal posts at either end of the field. It is worth three points in the NFL, but values vary according to distance in fantasy football.

Table 5.3. Fantasy Football Standard Scoring Categories

Fantasy Football Standard Scoring Categories (continued)	
Scoring Category	**Definition**
Point After Touchdown (PAT)	A kick following a touchdown from the opponent's three-yard line. It is worth one point for a successful conversion.
Return Touchdown	The advancement of a kickoff or punt to the opponent's end zone.
Blocked Kick	Tipping or batting a field goal or point after touchdown attempt to force a miss.
Sack	Tackling the opposing quarterback behind the line of scrimmage on a passing play.
Safety	Tackling the opposing ball carrier within their end zone. It is worth two points to the team's score. This also occurs on passing plays when an offensive lineman is called for holding in the end zone.
Points Allowed	A tally of the number of points allowed by a team's defense.
Tackles	Stopping the advancement of a ball carrier by bringing them to the ground.
Forced Fumbles	Whether through a hit or stripping the ball away, forcing the ball carrier to lose possession. The play must end with the player's team gaining possession.
Passes Defended	Successfully batting away an attempted forward pass and is typically awarded to defensive backs.

It is interesting that the Points Allowed category is defined differently by some Web sites and game providers. Some providers count all points scored against the team against the defense regardless of how they were earned. If a team lost 31-21, then all 31 points would be counted against the defense.

Other sites consider the source of the points. If a team earns six points as the result of a quarterback throwing an interception that was subsequently returned for a touchdown, then those points are not counted against the defense. Generally speaking, these sites consider only those plays in which the team is trying to stop the opposition from scoring at the start of the play.

Consult your provider's help or rules section about this type of play as you configure the league. Not only does it possibly change the draft rankings of team defenses slightly, but it is also a potential problem if the league assumes one setting and the site handles it differently. Don't wait for the first interception of the year to be returned for a score to send your league into a frenzy.

Standard Point Modifiers

During the league configuration process, the league commissioner will have the opportunity to select the point modifiers for his or her chosen scoring categories. Table 5.4 illustrates the two most popular sets of point modifiers used in fantasy football leagues.

The point modifiers for defensive and kicking activities normally only change based on an individual league's preference in order to more significantly reward fewer points allowed or longer field goals. In general, these modifiers go untouched during the configuration process.

The main difference between these columns is to regulate the performance of quarterbacks relative to the performance of other positions, particularly when it comes to touchdowns.

Table 5.4. Standard fantasy football point modifiers

Standard Point Modifiers		
Scoring Category	**Point Modifier (I)**	**Point Modifier (II)**
Passing Yards	1 point per 50 yards	1 point per 25 yards
Passing Touchdowns	6 points	4 points
Rushing Yards	1 point per 20 yards	1 point per 10 yards
Rushing Touchdowns	6 points	6 points
Receiving Yards	1 point per 20 yards	1 point per 10 yards
Receiving Touchdowns	6 points	6 points
Interceptions	-2 points	-1 points
Return Touchdowns	6 points	6 points
Two-Point Conversions	2 points	2 points
Fumbles Lost	-2 points	-2 points
Field Goal 0-39	3 points	3 points
Field Goal 40-49	4 points	4 points
Field Goal 50+	5 points	5 points
Point After TD (PAT)	1 point	1 point
Missed Point After TD	-4 points	-4 points
Missed Field Goal 0-39	-3 points	-3 points
Missed Field Goal 40-49	-2 points	-2 points
Missed Field Goal 50+	-1 point	-1 point
Sack	1 point	1 point
Interception	2 points	1 point
Fumble Recovery	2 points	2 points
Touchdown	6 points	6 points
Safety	2 points	2 points
Blocked Kick	2 points	2 points
Zero Points Allowed	10 points	10 points
1-6 Points Allowed	7 points	7 points
7-13 Points Allowed	4 points	4 points
14-20 Points Allowed	1 point	1 point
21-27 Points Allowed	0 points	0 points
28-34 Points Allowed	-1 point	-1 point
35+ Points Allowed	-4 points	-4 points

PLAYOFFS

The regular season in most fantasy football leagues ends after Week 14 or 15. The final weeks of the NFL season (typically Weeks 15 and 16) are reserved for the fantasy playoffs. Because only 12 NFL teams participate in the real-life playoffs, it would not be prudent to extend the fantasy league's playoffs into the NFL playoffs. The use of the actual NFL playoffs would require a new draft and roster shuffle, which would not reflect the activities and accomplishments of qualifying teams during the season, nor would it account for many of the top fantasy performers from the regular season.

A larger debate occurs with regard to whether Week 17 of the NFL season should be used to decide a league title. In Week 17, those teams whose playoff berths have been secured often limit the participation of star players. As a result, fantasy playoff participants are forced to guess whether the star that led them to the title game will actually see the field.

The camps are split down the middle on this particular issue. Those in favor of using Week 17 argue that an NFL season is an NFL season, and that since those games count in the standings, they should be used in fantasy football leagues and be integrated as part of a participant's overall strategy. They center their argument on the fact that teams take to the field without injured stars throughout the regular season. Therefore, the Week 17 dilemma of whether a player will or will not suit up for his team's game based on the standings should be treated in the same manner as the fantasy participant navigates through the weekly injury reports.

The other side argues that the competition should be decided when all of a team's best players are on the field. They define Week 16 of the season as the true finale, where all teams are "trying" and a true league championship can be decided.

 As league commissioner, do not assume this decision away. The issue of the league schedule and playoffs should be decided well ahead of the draft to allow managers to factor playoff schedules into their decisions.

The preceding material provides the foundation, the veritable building blocks on which to build a successful league. Chapter 6 examines additional roster and configuration options available to commissioners.

6 Expanding the Settings

- ◆ Additional Roster Positions
- ◆ Special Teams
- ◆ Additional Scoring Categories
- ◆ Fractional Points

As fantasy football participants become more comfortable with general game play and the ebb and flow of a season, there is often the temptation to tweak the standard settings put forth by the provider in the subsequent season. The level of customization allowed by each provider varies greatly. As I wrote in Chapter 4, the commissioner should spend some time doing a compare and contrast between the contending sites before committing the group's time and precious dollars.

The areas of the league configuration most often customized are the available roster positions, scoring categories, and point modifiers. The commissioner and the league's members should strongly consider the level of dedication to the league and the complexity added by introducing new elements to the configuration.

ADDITIONAL ROSTER POSITIONS

There are several additional roster positions available for selection beyond the traditional roster configuration set forth in Chapter 5. The purpose of including these positions is two-fold. First, their inclusion offers participants greater flexibility when setting their lineups. Second, they serve to create a greater emphasis on draft strategy and execution, which forces league participants to fully invest in the league from the beginning.

WR/TE Flex

A growing number of leagues are choosing to eliminate the straight tight end position and have instead turned to the WR/TE position. This position allows participants to fill an active slot with either a wide receiver or tight end. The adoption of this roster spot came largely in response to the dearth of talent at the tight end position during the late-1990s. The position was dominated by two players, Tony Gonzalez and Shannon Sharpe, who posted numbers far exceeding those of any other player at the position. The remaining players chosen at the position offered little contribution on a weekly basis.

Most would argue that position scarcity stands as one of the prominent predraft planning considerations. After all, that perceived scarcity is what separates players at the other positions into tiers for selection. The point has become moot with the redefinition of the tight end's role for many NFL teams over the last three to four years. A number of teams now use the TE as a primary receiving option. Last year, tight ends on 10 teams recorded at least 60 receptions. Another dozen players at the position caught at least 32 passes (two per game).

However, there still are a number of teams that will utilize the tight end only in the "red zone," the area inside the opponent's 20-yard line driving toward a score. Or worse yet, they rely on one tight end for the majority of catches and yards, but often utilize a second tight end deep in opponent's territory. In 2005, 56 different tight ends scored at least one touchdown.

For a small percentage of leagues, swaying the week's results on the strength of a single play to a seldom-used receiver leaves them uneasy, and for that reason, they include the flex position.

WR/RB Flex

The other flex position currently being used allows the participant to choose between starting a third running back or wide receiver. As stated in the introduction to this section, the inclusion of this position forces one to rethink his or her draft strategy for the early rounds. For most, the decision to hoard running backs springs immediately to mind. Others may look at injury histories of feature running backs versus wide receivers and decide that, while receiver performances are less predictable than those of starting running backs, the addition of another elite receiver trumps the selection of a middle- or lower-tier third back.

The debates that rage about how the role should be filled and the wrinkle it provides to the draft make it worthy of consideration.

IDP (Individual Defensive Players)

The use of individual defensive players (called IDP in the industry) is continually increasing in popularity. The proliferation of highlight shows and videotapes available for rental or sale that glorify big hits on receivers or quarterbacks have made once anonymous defensive players household names. Ed Reed, Ray Lewis, Brian Urlacher, Warren Sapp, the late Reggie White, and legendary defensive back and special teams contributor Deion Sanders stand as examples of players who have shone under the media spotlight.

Historically, defensive units have been linked together by a nickname that describes the entire team regardless of the status of each individual player. The "Purple People Eaters" of the Minnesota Vikings, "The Fearsome Foursome" of the Los Angeles Rams, and the "No Name Defense" of the last undefeated team in NFL history, the 1972 Miami Dolphins. In 1985, the "Monsters of the Midway" (the Chicago Bears) dominated the New England Patriots in Super Bowl XX.

The two most prevalent defensive roster positions available for selection are defensive linemen and defensive backs. For fantasy football purposes, the more publicized and well-known linebackers (hard-hitting tacklers who play in the middle of the defensive scheme) are usually included with the defensive lineman position. Some fantasy gaming sites will separate these positions.

The most difficult choices to be made with the inclusion of individual defensive players are those concerning which scoring categories and point modifiers will be used. Scoring for these positions becomes far more complicated than that of defensive teams. The individual accomplishments of tackles, assisted tackles, and passes defended for defensive backs must be considered and point modifiers assigned. More easily identifiable categories such as sacks and interceptions are also used. Leagues using individual defensive players for the first time typically make the mistake of assigning too heavy a weight to the accomplishments of the defensive players. As a result, many of the weekly head-to-head matchups become overly dependent on the scores of those defensive players.

To properly weight the scoring categories, the league should discuss defensive players in relation to the top players at other positions. For example, owners should debate the value of Donnie Edwards' high tackle total against the touchdowns of Peyton Manning. Discussing this issue and serving up hypothetical situations based on previous performance will help to cut off any issues that should arise from an improperly weighted system.

Team QB

A growing number of fantasy football participants are turning to the concept of the "Team Quarterback" after watching their starting QB get helped off the field one too many times. In this system, participants draft the quarterback position by team. So, instead of calling out the name of Peyton Manning on draft day, the participant will select "Indianapolis QB." With this selection, they receive all scoring associated with the player performing as the quarterback for Indianapolis, regardless of whether it is Peyton Manning, his backup Jim Sorgi, or whoever else may occupy the role of quarterback on the play.

Not all services currently offer this roster position. Once you determine whether your preferred service offers this position, find out how it accounts for trick plays. That is to say, find out whether a ball thrown by a running back, wide receiver, or other player who isn't typically under center is counted for the "Team QB" position.

The inclusion of this roster option allows participants to breathe easier on a Sunday when their normal starter has the tag of "game-time decision" attached to him. There's perhaps no feeling worse in fantasy football than finding out that your starter is a late scratch for that game due to injury, illness, or some other cause. In the traditional system that utilizes the individual quarterback, the participant receives zero points for the position unless he or she makes a preemptive move based on the questionable status of the player. With this roster position in place, the participant receives the statistics earned by that player's replacement.

Additionally, the "Team QB" position serves to protect the participant against an in-game injury that forces the starter to the sidelines early. The number of quarterbacks that take every one of their respective team's significant snaps can be counted on one hand. Between tweaked ankles or hamstrings, hand, elbow, or shoulder injuries, or the occasional crushing blow, the majority of quarterbacks miss some time each year. This position offers an in-roster insurance policy.

SPECIAL TEAMS

The term "special teams" refers to any players who are in on plays that involve kicking the ball. Kickoffs to begin each half of play, kickoffs following touchdowns or successful field goals, the point-after-touchdown attempt, and punting the ball back to the opponent after failing to earn the yardage necessary to continue a drive comprise the full set of special teams play. Points for special teams play have traditionally been assigned to either individual players or team defenses. Points for successful conversions of point-after-touchdown attempts and field goals clearly go to the kicker. The discussion among fantasy football participants regarding special teams is where to assign the points earned for kickoff and punt return yards and touchdowns.

In some instances, leagues award points to both the individual players and team defenses. A point of contention surfaces as to whether the double counting of the scoring play should occur. That point can be easily contested, as every passing touchdown registers points for the both the quarterback and receiver responsible for the score.

Other leagues award points only to the team defense, as a number of punt and kickoff returners do not factor into the normal offensive game plan and therefore do not normally justify a draft selection.

Still other leagues award points only to the individual player, regardless of where he appears on the roster. Unfortunately, for those leagues using defensive teams instead of individual defensive players, there is a chance that those plays will go unaccounted for in the league's scoring should the return man's primary position be on the defense.

As most leagues use the team defense position as part of the roster configuration, the simplest way to handle this setting is to make special teams part of the team defense. In this way, the accomplishments of all special teams are rewarded. No owner will replace a wide receiver or running back on the off chance that a player returns a kickoff or punt for a touchdown. Certainly, those events are rare, but they do happen and should therefore be reflected in fantasy football scoring.

ADDITIONAL SCORING CATEGORIES

Each game provider will offer a number of scoring categories beyond the traditional configuration offered in Chapter 5 to recognize on-field accomplishments. Some leagues use completions and attempts to further highlight quarterback play. Others use rushing attempts or receptions to mark the number of times that a running back or wide receiver is utilized in the offensive scheme and reward durability.

Leagues using these categories will generally include more experienced fantasy participants who seek to acknowledge the difference in offensive schemes and recognize the value of individual players that might not translate directly in the box score. In these leagues, the fantasy status of efficient quarterbacks such as Troy Aikman, Steve McNair, and Tom Brady is elevated.

That is to say, by including a point per reception, wide receivers who are frequent targets and running backs who can catch the ball out of the backfield have increased value. The consistent performers at wide receivers are not devalued by the presence of a long-pass threat who catches one pass for a touchdown. The inclusion of this category accounts for the "why" of a scoring drive in addition to the "how."

For quarterbacks, the inclusion of completions or completion percentage rewards a quarterback who effectively leads his team up and down the field as opposed to the huge fantasy total that can be put up by a quarterback on the wrong side of a lopsided score.

Remember, the addition of another scoring category or roster position increases the time that each league participant needs to commit to research. Additionally, more categories and roster positions make the fantasy matchup more difficult to follow while watching the real games. That can, in turn, make the fantasy contest less appealing to new participants.

FRACTIONAL POINTS

The debate of whether to utilize fractional points within leagues resides primarily in those scoring categories dealing with yardage (rushing yards, receiving yards, passing yards). At issue is the painful situation when a player fails to achieve that extra yard or two to earn another point.

For a simple example, suppose the league rewards participants with one point for every 20 rushing yards. In a particular game, a running back rushes for only 19 yards. How many points does he receive?

If the league does not award fractional points, the running back receives zero points for his efforts.

If the league does award fractional points, the running back receives 0.95 points for his rushing efforts (.05 x 19 = .95).

In leagues that eliminate fractional scoring, a player's accomplishments are always rounded down to the point level attained. In this case, the player did not reach the threshold necessary to earn one point. As a result, he earns zero points for the rushing effort.

Too often, participants are under the impression that the use of fractional scoring is implicit and challenge the league after a close loss (a win if fractional scoring were in place). This situation creates tension in the league and unnecessary grief for the commissioner. Be sure to verify how your league's chosen site addresses this concept and then discuss how its application affects your league.

As fantasy games evolve to meet consumer demand to mirror real life wherever possible, the number of scoring and roster options is sure to expand. The preceding material offers information and advice on handling those most prevalent as you enter the 2006 season. If your league is adventurous, roam the available options during the configuration process. Just be sure to have Plan B available within your chosen site should the results of experimentation fall short of expectations.

In the next chapter, I review the different styles of fantasy football games currently available for consumption as you prepare to commit to a league or competition this fall.

7 Game Styles

- ◆ Pick'Em
- ◆ Salary Cap
- ◆ Simulation
- ◆ Full Fantasy
- ◆ Stock Market

The fantasy football landscape continues to evolve and offer new technology by which to analyze players and teams, execute drafts, and evaluate roster moves during the season. For all the changes to the actual in-game components and experiential side of the equation, the fantasy football world continues to be dominated by four main styles of games. The full fantasy games are clearly the most mainstream and popular entries, with Pick'Em, salary cap, and simulation contests offering different ways by which to analyze and enjoy the action. However, there is a fifth gaming style now available that converts a player's contributions into a stock price to be traded on a fantasy market. The following material lays out the options available to fantasy owners for the 2006 season.

PICK'EM

There are primarily two types of Pick'Em-style contests available. The first style takes on the basic format of selecting winning teams from the full slate of NFL games. The second style forces participants to look at the full season and adopt a strategy for selecting a single winning team each week in order to extend their playing time.

Traditional

The most elemental fantasy football game available is the quick and simple Pick'Em game. Participants in these contests need only choose winning teams for each week's NFL games using one of several scoring configurations (straight up, point spread, or confidence points).

Straight up: This scoring style requires participants to simply select a winner.

Point spread: Point spreads are created by sports books and organizations such as the Associated Press to create balance in the wagers placed on a specific contest. Without the spread, participants form quick decisions on each contest and quickly run through the games. Making a correct selection in games using the point spread requires a more thorough review of past performances, injury statuses, and trends.

A minus (-) sign next to the team in the listing of games means the team is favored to win. In determining wins and losses with regard to the spread, the team must win by more than the listed number in order to "cover" the point spread and earn the participant a winning selection. If the team wins by less than that number or loses outright, then the selection is marked as incorrect.

Confidence points: In these contests, participants must ascribe a numerical value to each of the week's games based on how confident they are of the outcome. The values to be assigned depend on the number of games played in a given week. If there are 16 games on the docket, then participants must assign values from 1-16 to each game. Therefore, for a week in which all teams are playing (16 games), the maximum number of points to be assigned is 136 (16+15+14+etc.). Each value can be assigned only once, with a participant's proverbial lock of the week being assigned the maximum value and their most questionable the lowest the value of one.

Groups that combine straight up or point spread scoring with the wrinkle of confidence points add an element of skill that makes the game more captivating and requires additional research and analysis to successfully complete.

The traditional straight up Pick'Em contest for the NFL is certainly no simple task given the league's effort to achieving parity. A sample Pro-Pick'Em selection page is displayed within Figure 7.1.

Survivor

The survivor Pick'Em game is even easier to process than the Pro Pick'Em game, which requires the selection of the full slate of games. In these contests, participants select a single winning team each week. However, a single misstep forces them out of the competition. Additionally, participants who choose successfully cannot repeat the selection of a single NFL team. That is to say, if a participant uses New England in Week 1, they cannot select the Patriots again during that contest. For as long as they choose correctly, they will need to select a different team each week.

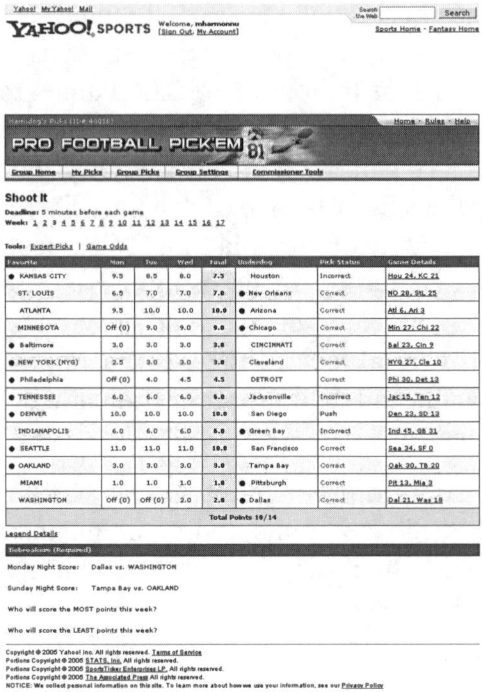

Yahoo! My Yahoo! Mail

YAHOO! SPORTS Welcome, mharmonnu [Sign Out, My Account]

Search the Web Search

Sports Home - Fantasy Home

Home - Rules - Help

PRO FOOTBALL PICK'EM

Group Home | My Picks | Group Picks | Group Settings | Commissioner Tools

Shoot It

Deadline: 5 minutes before each game

Week: 1 2 3 4 5 6 7 8 9 10 11 12 13 14 15 16 17

Tools: Expert Picks | Game Odds

Favorite	Mon	Tue	Wed	Final	Underdog	Pick Status	Game Details
● KANSAS CITY	9.5	8.5	8.0	7.5	Houston	Incorrect	Hou 24, KC 21
ST. LOUIS	6.5	7.0	7.0	7.0	● New Orleans	Correct	NO 28, StL 25
ATLANTA	9.5	10.0	10.0	10.0	● Arizona	Correct	Atl 6, Ari 3
MINNESOTA	Off (0)	9.0	9.0	9.0	● Chicago	Correct	Min 27, Chi 22
● Baltimore	3.0	3.0	3.0	3.0	CINCINNATI	Correct	Bal 23, Cin 9
● NEW YORK (NYG)	2.5	3.0	3.0	3.0	Cleveland	Correct	NYG 27, Cle 10
● Philadelphia	Off (0)	4.0	4.5	4.5	DETROIT	Correct	Phi 30, Det 13
● TENNESSEE	6.0	6.0	6.0	6.0	Jacksonville	Incorrect	Jac 15, Ten 12
● DENVER	10.0	10.0	10.0	10.0	San Diego	Push	Den 23, SD 13
INDIANAPOLIS	6.0	6.0	6.0	6.0	● Green Bay	Incorrect	Ind 45, GB 31
● SEATTLE	11.0	11.0	11.0	10.0	San Francisco	Correct	Sea 34, SF 0
● OAKLAND	3.0	3.0	3.0	3.0	Tampa Bay	Correct	Oak 30, TB 20
MIAMI	1.0	1.0	1.0	1.0	● Pittsburgh	Correct	Pit 13, Mia 3
WASHINGTON	Off (0)	Off (0)	2.0	2.0	● Dallas	Correct	Dal 21, Was 18
Total Points 10/14							

Legend Details

Tiebreakers (Required)

Monday Night Score: Dallas vs. WASHINGTON

Sunday Night Score: Tampa Bay vs. OAKLAND

Who will score the MOST points this week?

Who will score the LEAST points this week?

Copyright © 2005 Yahoo! Inc. All rights reserved. Terms of Service
Portions Copyright © 2005 STATS, Inc. All rights reserved.
Portions Copyright © 2005 SportsTicker Enterprises LP. All rights reserved.
Portions Copyright © 2005 The Associated Press All rights reserved.
NOTICE: We collect personal information on this site. To learn more about how we use your information, see our Privacy Policy

Figure 7.1. Yahoo! Sports Pro Pick'Em selection page

Once a single participant remains, they are declared the victor and a new contest begins the following week. All group members will then be able to make selections once again using any NFL team.

Salary Cap

Salary cap contests appeal to the armchair general managers and owners. This setup allowed participants to take on the role of team owner and assemble the best squad possible within a budget. In this game, there are no drafts or mad dashes to the available player lists to beat the other league managers to a new player. Rather, participants review their player's performance against their salary cap and their available cap space to make moves to improve their team.

Participants can choose from all NFL players to stock their team. However, they must fill their entire roster, so the strategy of selecting the four or five highest priced players and leaving the lower-scoring slots of tight end, kicker, or team defense empty is not available. And naturally, the algorithm that sets player salaries forces participants to create a mix of superstars, middle-tier performers, and lower-end players to fill out a squad.

These games are simpler to enter, as all scoring and roster configurations are dictated by the provider. This allows a single algorithm to run the entire game. Figure 7.2 demonstrates a traditional salary cap fantasy football roster page.

Figure 7.2. Salary cap fantasy football roster page

SIMULATION GAMES

Simulation games are growing in popularity. In these contests, participants choose their ideal team either through a draft or the previously described salary cap method.

The majority of the work in this style of game is done before the first simulation is run. Once their squad is assembled, participants choose coaching strategies for both offense and defense, covering different downs and distances, and utilizing different standard formations. Figure 7.3 displays the roster selection process of a simulation game.

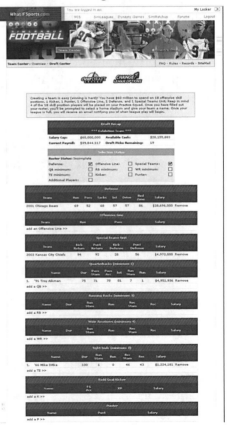

Figure 7.3. What If
Sports roster page

After the coaching strategy has been assembled, the participants then begin a schedule of games against other league members, generally executed one per day. Using an algorithm which takes into account all settings chosen by the two coaches, the computer completes a game and a winner is decided.

Each participant is then apprised of the results of the match-up, as well as any injuries that occurred. They can then adjust their rosters and depth charts, acquire new players, or make changes to the game plan before the next match-up.

FULL FANTASY

Full fantasy football games receive the bulk of attention from television networks, magazines, and web sites. They are called "full" games in that participants own every piece of the action from the initial draft to all subsequent actions on the waiver wire or trading floor.

These games start with a replication of the glorious event that is the NFL entry draft. Whether the league members meet at a designated space to truly mimic its real-life counterpart or complete the activity online, each league member has the opportunity to draft their own squad of players. Full accounts of the different types of draft options and participation strategies for each are developed in Chapter 8.

League members have greater control over how their individual league will operate in this type of game than any other. Besides the decision of how to draft, the league must come to a consensus on which scoring type, roster, and scoring configurations to use, and what point values will be ascribed to each category. Figure 7.4 illustrates a sample roster page in a full fantasy game.

Scoring Styles

Full fantasy football game participants choose between two basic scoring styles. The rotisserie scoring style, heavily prevalent in fantasy baseball, basketball, and hockey leagues, is non-existent in this sport. Fantasy football leagues are restricted to fantasy point and head-to-head scoring.

Fantasy Point Scoring

A small percentage of full fantasy leagues ignore the typical head-to-head format described below and operate their leagues according to total fantasy points earned. In this

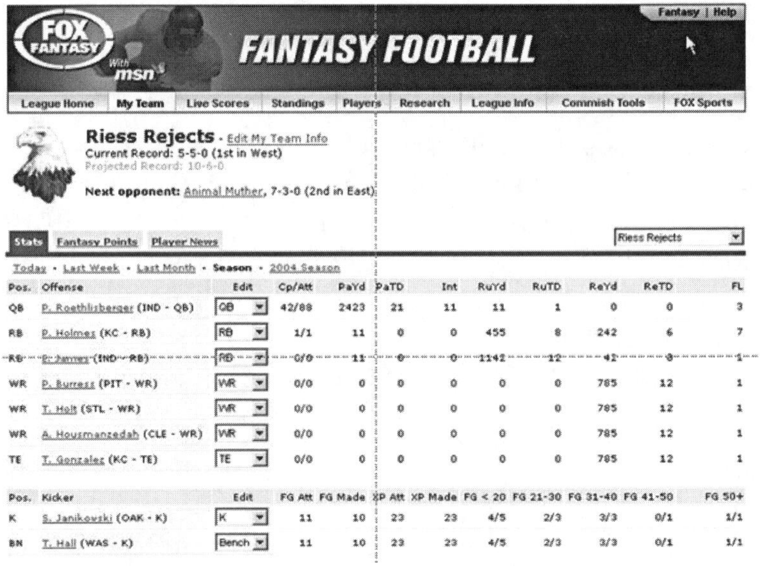

Pos.	Offense	Edit	Cp/Att	PaYd	PaTD	Int	RuYd	RuTD	ReYd	ReTD	FL
QB	P. Roethlisberger (IND - QB)	QB	42/88	2423	21	11	11	1	0	0	3
RB	P. Holmes (KC - RB)	RB	1/1	11	0	0	455	8	242	6	7
RB	P. James (IND - RB)	RB	0/0	11	0	0	1142	12	42	0	1
WR	P. Burress (PIT - WR)	WR	0/0	0	0	0	0	0	785	12	1
WR	T. Holt (STL - WR)	WR	0/0	0	0	0	0	0	785	12	1
WR	A. Housmanzedah (CLE - WR)	WR	0/0	0	0	0	0	0	785	12	1
TE	T. Gonzalez (KC - TE)	TE	0/0	0	0	0	0	0	785	12	1

Pos.	Kicker	Edit	FG Att	FG Made	XP Att	XP Made	FG < 20	FG 21-30	FG 31-40	FG 41-50	FG 50+
K	S. Janikovski (OAK - K)	K	11	10	23	23	4/5	2/3	3/3	0/1	1/1
BN	T. Hall (WAS - K)	Bench	11	10	23	23	4/5	2/3	3/3	0/1	1/1

Figure 7.4. FOX Sports Fantasy Football

style of league, the competition doesn't get bogged down by an unfortunate scheduling blip that saw your team outscore all others in the league by 60 points except one; the team you just happened to be matched up against. Here, it's all about point maximization for an entire season without worrying about playoff contention.

Leagues using fantasy point scoring are ordinarily tied to the Salary Cap games described above. Point modifiers are assigned to each of the scoring categories, and player salaries rise and fall according to a player's performance against the rest of the league. In those leagues, the proper management of cap space allows participants to purchase bargain players and watch their values rise, utilizing the new cap to buy better players, accrue more points, and so on.

Head-to-Head Scoring

The majority of fantasy football leagues utilize head-to-head scoring. At the core, head-to-head scoring is the same as straight fantasy point scoring, as all teams seek to maximize the points put forth by their active rosters. The points scored by active players are added together for each matchup, and wins, losses, and ties are assigned accordingly.

In this type of contest, however, the results of the head-to-head matchup dictate the success or failure of a team rather than a straight point tally. Therein lays the glory and frustration of the head-to-head structure. An ordinarily high-scoring team can have one average week at a critical juncture of the schedule that devastates its championship dream. The excitement and draw of fantasy football is that the action in the game is, at times, as unpredictable as the real thing.

Unlike the straight fantasy point game where competition among the lower-tier teams can drop off, the head-to-head style allows struggling teams to play the "spoiler" role. Even if a series of mishaps and injuries conspire to send them to the bottom of the standings, any team can pull a big upset if the stars align properly. As the movie title states: *Any Given Sunday.*

An example of a fantasy football matchup page is available in Figure 7.5. Pride forces them to stay active in the hope of pulling off the monster upset.

Week 16
Dec 21 - Dec 27

Operation Domination vs. NO LUCK

Operation Domination (11-4-0)					NO LUCK (9-5-8)				
Pos	Player	Opp	Status	Pts	Pos	Player	Opp	Status	Pts
QB	D. Culpepper (Min - QB)	GB	L. 34-31	24	QB	B. Volek (Ten - QB)	Den	L. 37-16	-2
WR	Ro. Williams (Det - WR)	Chi	W. 19-13	1	WR	E. Kennison (KC - WR)	Oak	W. 31-30	3
WR	L. Evans (Buf - WR)	@SF	W. 41-7	17	WR	B. Stokley (Ind - WR)	SD	W. 34-31	12
WR	D. Jackson (Sea - WR)	Ari	W. 24-21	5	WR	D. Driver (GB - WR)	@Min	W. 34-31	14
RB	La. Johnson (KC - RB)	Oak	W. 31-30	17	RB	L. Tomlinson (SD - RB)	@Ind	L. 34-31	20
RB	S. Morris (Mia - RB)	Cle	W. 10-7	3	RB	N. Goings (Car - RB)	@TB	W. 37-20	7
TE	C. Cooley (Was - RB,TE)	@Dal	L. 13-10	1	TE	A. Gates (SD - TE)	@Ind	L. 34-31	8
K	S. Graham (Cin - K)	NYG	L. 23-22	6	K	J. Elam (Den - K)	@Ten	W. 37-16	13
DEF	New York (NYJ - DEF)	NE	L. 23-7	1	DEF	Baltimore (Bal - DEF)	@Pit	L. 20-7	5
Total				75	Total				88

Figure 7.5. Head-to-head matchup page

STOCK MARKET

A recent addition to the fantasy sports world is a stock market-style game from ProTrade.com that allows participants to buy and sell shares of athletes as they would a share of stock in a company on the NYSE or NASDAQ. Player values are determined using an advanced on-field performance algorithm that goes beyond traditional box score metrics.

Player values rise and fall based on participant reaction to performance. If the player goes through an extended streak of sub-par performances, then participants will look to sell off their shares of a particular player, sending his market

Figure 7.6. ProTrade.com home page

value down. Conversely, a hot streak will send a player's value soaring as participants seek to ride the streak.

The use of metrics such as down and distance performance, passing efficiency, the effectiveness of possession receivers, and many others, forces fantasy participants to watch games in a new way to find bargains beyond the top line performers as you would on the market.

In the next chapter, I explore the different draft methods available to participants of full fantasy games. As the fantasy draft marks the beginning of a five- or six-month investment of time, money, and emotion, it's a decision in the league formation that shouldn't be taken lightly.

8 Draft Types

- ◆ Auto-Pick
- ◆ Live Online Draft
- ◆ Live Offline Straight Draft (In-Person)
- ◆ Live Offline Auction (In-Person)
- ◆ Live Online Auction
- ◆ Determining Draft Order

The determination of the league's draft type ranks among the most important decisions to be made. It serves as the kickoff to the action and sets the tone for the season to follow. A well-executed draft helps to get managers excited about the action and lets that momentum carry over into an active, competitive, and fun-filled league. If the draft fails, it's possible that the league dies that evening, as one or more managers may abandon their squads.

In fact, some participants spend more time poring through statistics and materials than they did in school. Others relish in the fact that for the period between the draft and the first game of the season, they can pat themselves on the back for executing a superior draft.

The challenge is to find the draft system that speaks to the needs of the group and to assess the availability of all participants to devote the time necessary to complete the selection process.

- Is everyone located in the same office, dorm, or house?

- Are your league's managers spread across the same general region, or do time zones play into the decision process? That is to say, do you need to account for the fact that some of your managers out East are attending to the bedtime of either their children or themselves when those in the West are just leaving the office?

Fortunately, fantasy football participants have the ability to choose among several draft options. This chapter introduces the five styles of drafts available for selection: Auto-Pick, Live Online, Live Offline (In-Person), Offline Auction, and Online Auction. In the following pages, we will discuss the basic structures of each draft type and offer the advantages and pitfalls as well. We'll also examine fair ways by which to determine draft order.

Remember to involve all league members in the decision-making regarding the details of the draft. There's no point in risking the health of the league (or relationships, for that matter) when it's so easy to get everyone invested in its success.

AUTO-PICK

The auto-pick draft is a prevalent option within many online sites. It allows the game provider's computers to process the draft without the involvement of the league members. This type of draft is most popular among first-time players who are first getting acclimated to fantasy football and how the process works. It is also used frequently by managers joining "public leagues," whereby the individual is randomly assigned to a league. Since nobody in public leagues knows one another, the need for an interactive draft as would occur in the live or offline formats is lessened.

The auto-pick draft offers the advantage of allowing managers to spend as little or as much time as they wish creating a personalized ranking list ahead of the draft. It's a process that can be executed over a longer period of time at the leisure of the participants instead of getting 10-12 people to commit to a specific time, place, or date. This draft style also protects owners from overlooking a player's availability due to distractions. It also provides an easy out for the owners of underperforming players, as they can blame the provider's ranking algorithm.

Conversely, part of the fun of fantasy football is controlling all aspects of the team. The auto-pick draft requires not only the preparation time to create your rankings, but also the time to enter them into the system. Then there's no chance to react to a player's selection. If the algorithm determines that your team has already selected the requisite number of running backs, then there is no opportunity to adjust for the occasion where a player slips in the draft. Finally, there's less affinity with the team because it wasn't drafted in-person. As such, early struggles are more apt to lead to team abandonment.

Negotiate ample time with the league members to reconfigure the default rankings to your liking before the "draft ready" button is pressed. If you don't, it's possible that the provider hasn't updated properly to reflect depth chart changes or injuries.

LIVE ONLINE DRAFT

Most fantasy gaming sites offer the ability to conduct the draft online via their individualized application. In these systems, managers can make their selections, review the picks of other participants, and scout remaining players. There's also a chat function to truly make the draft "live," as managers get the opportunity to react to each selection. Figure 8.1 demonstrates a typical draft applet from Mock Draft Central.

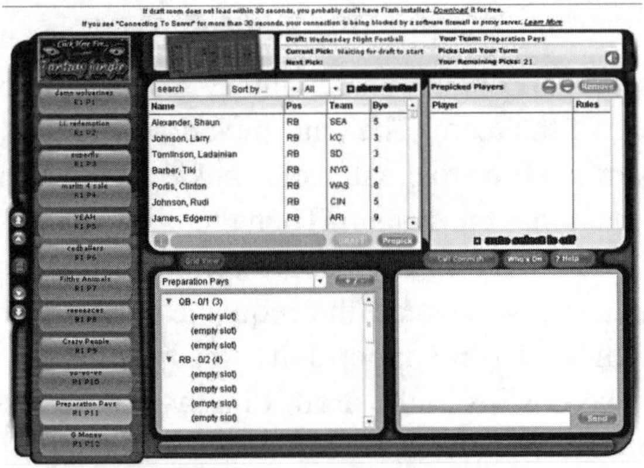

Figure 8.1. Mock Draft Central live draft applet

This type of draft allows managers to access the system from anywhere, which makes it an efficient process. The game provider typically has one or two options available regarding the time allowed per pick. The league's managers will need to debate the merits of having more or less time to make a selection. In either event, drafting live provides a full sense of ownership that the auto-pick style doesn't, as each selection decision was made by the manager.

There are two main issues that can negatively impact a live draft. The first of these involves the previously mentioned problem of availability. In order to process a draft, all 10-12 managers need to commit to a single time amid family and work commitments. If one manager fails to appear for the draft, his or her team is done based on the manager's prerankings or the default computer rankings. In many instances, the manager will be unhappy with the draft results.

The other concern that comes into play is that of technical issues. There may be compatibility problems based on operating systems or missing applications. Additionally, those managers attempting to access the league from work (it happens more than you might believe) may be blocked by a corporate firewall. Again, if they're unable to participate, the personal stake in the league is lowered.

LIVE OFFLINE
STRAIGHT DRAFT (IN-PERSON)

The live draft done in-person mimics the online format with one major additional benefit and one crushing drawback. The most positive aspect of this style is that each manager gets to feel as though he or she is a member of an NFL management group, even if only in the fictional world. Each selection is announced live in front of the group, and like the NFL Draft where Jets fans cheer or jeer a selection, the other members of the league get to provide that instant feedback here. Typically, draft selections are placed on a large draft board so that all league members can track the players who have been chosen.

The major drawback is that a representative for each team *must* attend the draft. Otherwise, the potential exists for hurt feelings and the possible disintegration of the league. Basically, if a manager has to miss the draft, he or she should be required to send a proxy or an extremely detailed step-by-step list and appropriate rankings on how to draft the team. Failure to do so puts the league commissioner and the other members of the league in an awkward position.

OFFLINE AUCTION

This is without question the most time consuming of all fantasy football draft styles. I've personally participated in auction drafts that lasted in excess of seven hours. League members assemble at a predetermined area such as someone's home, the meeting room at work, or in some instances, a rented ballroom. That's right. Some participants build this up to a level that rivals the actual NFL Draft. Once all members arrive for the draft, they are holed up in a room for hours.

Each manager is allocated a certain amount of money by which to bid on players to fill his or her roster. Before the draft, a nomination order is determined. This is the order in which individual players will be put up for bidding. For instance, "I'd like to nominate Peyton Manning for $5." The bidding on Manning then proceeds, with all interested managers responding to the auctioneer's request for another bid. Once sufficient time has passed since the last bid (normally a number of seconds), that player is marked "Sold!" and the next player is nominated.

As in the offline live (straight) draft, a manager must be present for each team, and it adds the wrinkle of the need for an impartial nonleague member to serve as auctioneer. Remember, the commissioner also fields a team, and as such, cannot perform double duty.

Save time by establishing a minimum price for top performers. Since there is no chance that Larry Johnson or Shaun Alexander will be sold for $1, it's a waste of everyone's time to have the bidding start there. Arrange an opening bid that is roughly half of the expected value. If there are no takers, you can always lower it. But there's no need to waste time. This process will be long enough.

As you participate in the draft, mind both your virtual wallet and those of your competitors. Those who burn through money too quickly usually either haven't given the draft much thought, or they've got somewhere to be. In either event, if one or more of the league's owners operate in this fashion, you will be able to find forgotten stars at a bargain later in the draft.

Keep track of every participant's budget and roster composition. You'll be in a better position to track where potential bargains and bidding wars are being set up for later in the draft process.

ONLINE AUCTION

The auction draft process has recently been streamlined with the advent of a tool whereby leagues can complete this process online. Figure 8.2 shows the Fantasy Auctioneer draft applet. The same bidding process exists here as it does for in-person drafts of this ilk. However, the online application allows the commissioner to set a time limit by which the next bid on a player must be made and allows only a small amount of time before the next player must be nominated. It's very difficult to enforce a time limit in person, but here, it's automatic. The strict time limit on bidding will help cut the time of a normal in-person auction in half.

Figure 8.2. Fantasy Auctioneer online auction draft

Moving the auction draft online allows participants to better track league spending and roster status. It offers the same flexibility as the online straight draft, whereby managers can participate from anywhere with the additional GM responsibility of controlling dollars.

DETERMINING DRAFT ORDER

With the exception of those leagues using auction drafts, virtually all fantasy football leagues utilize a winding draft order. Put simply, the team with the first pick in the draft doesn't select again until the last pick of the second round. This type of draft is commonly referred to as a "serpentine draft" in industry publications, in that the order curls back like a snake.

Heading into the 2006 season, trading of draft picks is highly irregular on sites. Usually the league commissioner and managers have to track any such deals and make adjustments to rosters post-draft.

The easiest way to determine draft order is by drawing cards of a single suit (assuming you have 13 or fewer managers), with the high card receiving the first pick, the next highest card the second, and so on. Some leagues will literally pick names from a hat. In the end, it doesn't matter, so long as all league members agree with the method.

Chapter 9 provides tips on preranking players and executing a successful draft.

9 Draft-Day Preparation and Execution

- ◆ Plan the Work
- ◆ Be Prepared
- ◆ Chart the Draft's Progress
- ◆ Bye Weeks
- ◆ Auction Tips

The draft is the seminal event in the fantasy football season. Participants spend the summer months poring over cheatsheets, player and team notes, and advice from fantasy experts to ready themselves for the three hours that will shape their friendships and overall attitude for the subsequent six months.

Okay, so perhaps I overstated the importance of this event to the majority of the fantasy population. However, there is a small percentage of owners who embody the preceding paragraph.

For those first entering the world of fantasy football or looking to shake off a bad 2005, this chapter was written to get you prepared to dominate draft day 2006.

PLAN THE WORK

Managers spend hour after hour fretting about statistics splits, situational stats, and tracking every off-season move. Position-by-position rankings are constantly reconfigured to account for the latest news report, mind-blowing pre-season performance, and sometimes reading between the lines of a coach's press conference. After all, it's rare that two columnists see players in precisely the same light.

Once the analysis has dictated the order of the top 10 or 12 (or however big the league is), fill it in on your cheatsheet in pen. In many instances, managers discover their draft position only minutes before the commissioner calls for the first pick. There's no time for reconsideration or shifting based on a last-second look at a magazine. A panic pick here could set the tone for a bad day.

The first round of the draft should go by quickly and painlessly. In general, managers unanimously agree on the top 10 players. The order will be shuffled, but more or less, the names are a given. Round two should go down nearly as quickly because the excitement of the event has yet to die down and the shouts of "is (insert player name here) gone?" are still a couple of rounds away. The real challenge of staying true to this precept begins in the third round. As early as the third round, managers begin waffling on their instincts and draft strategy and shift their draft priorities.

One principal reason for this shift is a panic that occurs when a player's name comes up earlier than expected (commonly referred to as a "reach"). At least one manager then begins scrambling through their pages to find that line of text or magic number that makes the pick more obvious. Most managers will get themselves righted quickly and dismiss the selection, but there's always one that remains on the edge.

Stick to your list. If you've done your due diligence, the "reach" pick was probably just that. It's part of the beauty of fantasy football. Everyone has his or her own opinion as to how players and teams will perform in the year to come.

A second reason for this shift in strategy is the preoccupation with the literal pile of resources brought to the table. After all, there are as many as 23 other selections to go before you're on the board again. If you spent ample time pouring over statistics to create your list, then you factored the data into your decisions. Leave the magazines alone. Put the printouts away. It's akin to that last-minute scramble in high school or school on test day while the professor is literally handing out the test — it's not going to help. In fact, this activity is more likely to jumble your brain and force you to miss out on the other draft activity. It also makes you the candidate to be the first to blurt out the name of a player who's already been selected. That leads to derision from the other managers and more frustration. It's a vicious circle.

There are primarily three ways by which to construct an effective preranking list for the big day. They are outlined in the following sections in the Good, Better, Best format.

Good: Overall Preranking List

Online game providers and magazines provide the ubiquitous all-encompassing ranking list before each season. The list will extend to include as many players as its authors deem relevant, often stopping at a convenient round number. I've included an Overall Top 400 and lists for each individual position in the Appendices section.

The default rankings are constructed in one of two manners. In the first, the list is fully generated by way of a complicated formula that weights players' contributions to each of the scoring categories. In the second style, a group of editors and writers sits and argues through the night on the placement of players using past performance and expected returns as a guide.

However, the deeper you run down the list, the more similar players seem to become, particularly when it comes to third-string running backs, quarterbacks, or wide receivers deeper on the depth chart. Certainly, some teams are clearly better than others, but once a team gets to its third option, the problems have typically compounded and the overall team performance suffers. One need only look to the performances of the New York Jets or Green Bay Packers of 2005 to see this principle in action.

If there are players of similar value on your cheatsheet and one particular issue forced you to rank one ahead of the other, make a note of it next to the player. In the heat of the draft, you don't want to scramble to your files or magazines. You made the sheet. Make it efficient.

This type of ranking system is a good starting point to create a vision of relative value, but the process needs to be refined before entering the draft war room. Table 9.1 provides a snapshot of an all-inclusive ranking list.

Table 9.1. All-inclusive ranking list

Rank	Player	Pos	Rank	Player	Pos	Rank	Player	Pos
1	Larry Johnson	RB	11	Steven Jackson	RB	21	Randy Moss	WR
2	Shaun Alexander	RB	12	Steve Smith	WR	22	Thomas Jones	RB
3	LaDainian Tomlinson	RB	13	Carnell Williams	RB	23	Reuben Droughns	RB
4	Peyton Manning	QB	14	Julius Jones	RB	24	Anquan Boldin	WR
5	Edgerrin James	RB	15	Chad Johnson	WR	25	Larry Fitzgerald	WR
6	Tiki Barber	RB	16	Marvin Harrison	WR	26	Antonio Gates	TE
7	Clinton Portis	RB	17	Deuce McAllister	RB	27	Willie Parker	RB
8	LaMont Jordan	RB	18	Tatum Bell	RB	28	Jamal Lewis	RB
9	Rudi Johnson	RB	19	Torry Holt	WR	29	Ronnie Brown	RB
10	Terrell Owens	WR	20	Willis McGahee	RB	30	Tom Brady	QB

Note that in his process that the sheet includes players of all positions. This is a good starting point and should accompany you to the draft. However, it can cloud the next obvious selection in your strategy as the draft runs into its middle rounds.

Better: By Position

Once the overall ranking list has been completed, it's time to build a second spreadsheet and deconstruct it to a more granular level. By switching out the extensive list to a position-by-position approach, it becomes easier to reevaluate an individual player's value. If taken on a larger scale, would an emerging training camp battle at running back affect how you'd evaluate starting quarterbacks and when to select them? Most likely, it won't have an impact. However, when taken down to the position level, that sudden shakiness in a player's status might shift him down one, two, even 10 slots on your draft board.

The overall board becomes somewhat clunky in this type of situation. It's a great reference tool to remind you of overall valuation, but the key is finding value at each individual position.

Though players are less likely to be swapped on the gridiron, turned ankles and frayed rotator cuffs know no boundaries. These events may cause a dramatic shift in the player's rank. Again, if using a bulky list, how do you gauge the rise and fall of players impacted by the move? Remember, for every player lost to injury or trade, another steps up to assume a new role, thereby requiring the reevaluation of his value. Certainly, if a player is lost for the season, he simply is dumped onto your "Do Not Draft" list. But you do need to address his replacement. The position-by-position ranking system better addresses managers' needs to adjust rankings accordingly.

This type of cheatsheet also helps managers more effectively track draft results, particularly for those positions such as tight end, kicker, or defense for which each manager will select only one player. For instance, if eight of the other 10 managers in your league have selected a tight end, then you can safely draft players at another position, as the difference between the ninth and tenth players at the position normally will not be terribly large. Table 9.2 provides a glimpse at the make-up of a position-by-position ranking sheet.

Position-by-position ranking will make your draft-day more effective and enjoyable, but there's another step in the process to make this a fool-proof production.

Table 9.2. Position-by-position ranking sheet

Rank	Quarterback	Bye Week	Rank	Running Back	Bye Week	Rank	Wide Receiver	Bye Week
1	Peyton Manning	6	1	Larry Johnson	3	1	Terrell Owens	3
2	Tom Brady	6	2	Shaun Alexander	5	2	Steve Smith	9
3	Matt Hasselbeck	5	3	LaDainian Tomlinson	3	3	Chad Johnson	5
4	Donovan McNabb	9	4	Edgerrin James	9	4	Marvin Harrison	6
5	Carson Palmer	5	5	Tiki Barber	4	5	Torry Holt	7
6	Daunte Culpepper	8	6	Clinton Portis	8	6	Randy Moss	3
7	Marc Bulger	7	7	LaMont Jordan	3	7	Anquan Boldin	9
8	Trent Green	3	8	Rudi Johnson	5	8	Larry Fitzgerald	9
9	Jake Delhomme	9	9	Steven Jackson	7	9	Santana Moss	8
10	Kurt Warner	9	10	Carnell Williams	4	10	Hines Ward	4

Best: Tiered By Position

The straight list approach fails to distinguish where the separation occurs between the third and fourth or even eighth player on the list. This tiered-by-position approach provides managers with the same benefits as the standard position-by-position method but adds the new wrinkle of statistical separation. And it required considerably more time and patience.

Naturally, it will be difficult to determine what that exact cutoff point should be for each tier. Like I mentioned earlier, the deeper you get into the overall rankings, the more subtle will be the difference in the players' contributions. The key to this method is to effectively sort out the players in the upper tiers, and then through a combination of statistics and gut instinct, to note those players on the rise at a certain position who may not be fairly represented by prior stats and to shuffle those players whose numbers showed signs of tailing off. It's part art and part science, to be sure.

The ranking process can be done based on the single category that defines a player's place at his position. For instance, touchdowns can be used for quarterbacks. It would be far more accurate if players are evaluated using all of the scoring categories selected for use within the league. If the league uses the same settings year to year, then it's easy to cheat and use last season's point totals. Barring the aforementioned issues of retirement (Jimmy Smith in Jacksonville) and injury (Ahman Green in Green Bay), you can approximate the year-to-year performances of most players.

But remember the old adage about player histories that appears in the fine print of every ad hailing a firm's prowess in picking winning stocks or football games: past performance is not indicative of future results.

In some instances, the separation will be obvious. For instance, when you seek to rank quarterbacks prior to your fantasy football draft, Peyton Manning stands alone. The debate begins at the second tier with Tom Brady, Donovan McNabb, and Matt Hasselbeck all worthy of consideration among others. Therein lies the fun of the numbers game. Table 9.3 offers a sample of the tiering system for three key fantasy football positions.

Table 9.3. Tiered position-by-position ranking sheet

Rank	Quarterback	Bye Week	Rank	Running Back	Bye Week	Rank	Wide Receiver	Bye Week
1	Peyton Manning	6	1	Larry Johnson	3	1	Terrell Owens	3
			2	Shaun Alexander	5	2	Steve Smith	9
2	Tom Brady	6	3	LaDainian Tomlinson	3			
3	Matt Hasselbeck	5				3	Chad Johnson	5
			4	Edgerrin James	9	4	Marvin Harrison	6
4	Donovan McNabb	9	5	Tiki Barber	4	5	Torry Holt	7
5	Carson Palmer	5	6	Clinton Portis	8			
6	Daunte Culpepper	8				6	Randy Moss	3
7	Marc Bulger	7	7	LaMont Jordan	3	7	Anquan Boldin	9
			8	Rudi Johnson	5	8	Larry Fitzgerald	9
8	Trent Green	3						
9	Jake Delhomme	9	9	Steven Jackson	7	9	Santana Moss	8
10	Kurt Warner	9	10	Carnell Williams	4	10	Hines Ward	4

Take your rankings list out as far as you deem necessary to get through all rounds of the draft. Remember, it's better to toss away the final page of preparation than to select a player at random off the magazine you unearthed from your briefcase.

BE PREPARED

It's easier said than done with the mountains of information that become available weeks before your draft. Press access to every training camp session leads to a lot of stories being reported that are actually non-stories. It's always good to check multiple sources when possible.

Of course, depending on when your draft occurs, there will be the occasional instance where a player literally gets hurt as the clock strikes zero for your selection. Adjust as necessary, but 99.9 percent of your research and information will be locked in before you enter the room.

- Be rehearsed
- Be thorough
- Be confident

Be Rehearsed

Fantasy Web sites and magazines on the newsstand post countless drafts done by a collective of industry experts at different stages of the off-season. You would be amazed at how different these drafts look over a short period of time. Trades of established veterans to clear paths for the "next big thing," free agent acquisitions to shore up the heart of a lineup, and sometimes just the replacement of one owner in the group all contribute to this phenomenon.

Therefore, I would suggest viewing, and even participating, in one or more drafts in anticipation of "THE" draft. "THE" draft refers to that league in which you participate with friends and co-workers that means endless derision as a result of a feeble showing. There are subscription services such as Mockdraftcentral.com and Mockdrafts.com that allow managers to experience, for a fee, ad nauseam, the excitement of a live draft. These services appeal to the hardcore fan who seeks to gain a better understanding of the psychology of the average participant in anticipation of "the big day." The repetition of the draft process certainly exposes the participant to ample scenarios from which they will be able to anticipate likely runs and reaches on the big day. Of course, there are always some members in the group who do not take the process seriously and use this session to practice their chat and messaging skills. As such, take it for the learning process it is and try to find positives.

If you join an actual league with the primary purpose of draft practice, be sure to actively participate in the league. Remember, nine or eleven other participants are playing that league for a championship. Your inactivity will ruin the experience for the group.

Be Thorough

As I mentioned above, managers must, at the very least, rank an adequate number of players to fill all rosters with a bit of slack on the end. Too often, I've witnessed managers leave themselves short at the wide receiver and running back positions. Each manager drafts a minimum of three of each with four or five being far more likely. As such, that means that 60 or more wide receivers will be selected among 12 teams. Ranking fewer than 60 in this example leaves the manager subject to an inferior selection when he or she randomly selects a name. A general rule of thumb is to rank two to three times the number of starters that must be fielded at a particular position. This covers all starters, backups, and leaves some wiggle room in case of hoarding by one or more managers.

There are a number of Web sites and products that offer extensive previews of each player and team in advance of the season opener. A listing of available resources is available in Appendix II. I offer rankings and analysis for players at each position in Chapters 27 through 33. Online reports are updated regularly in advance of the season to keep managers apprised of position battles, changes to depth charts, and injuries.

Be Confident

When a manager is on the clock, it is important to demonstrate confidence and mastery of the task at hand. Running the clock down to the final seconds in a straight draft serves to agitate the other members of the league. Waiting until the "going twice" portion of an auction process allows the other managers to perceive the offender as disorganized and panicked, meaning that the other managers will conspire to squeeze every dime out of their budget.

 "A cluttered desk indicates a cluttered mind" or something to that effect. Basically, bring only what you need to accomplish the task. Any other pages or information serve only to distract you from the task at hand.

In addition to their homespun prerankings and cheat sheets, managers now have a number of tools to use in-draft to keep them on task. One such tool by Draft Dynamix is illustrated in Figure 9.1. These tools are designed to allow managers to enter their league's settings and point modifiers. As the manager updates the list to note a player's selection, the values of the remaining players adjust automatically based on a patented algorithm. The advent of these analytical tools takes much of the guesswork out of the process for the fantasy novice.

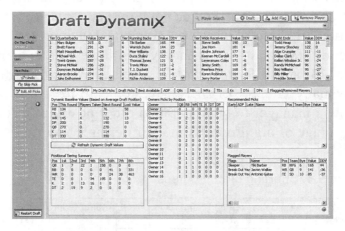

Figure 9.1. Draft Dynamix draft tool

CHART THE DRAFT'S PROGRESS

In addition to your cheatsheets, bring a sheet to the draft that displays the roster positions to be used in your league and create a grid with each team at the top. I know, I said to limit the paper on the table; but trust me, this will help.

As the draft progresses, mark the slot for the appropriate position under each. For the sake of example, I've filled in several rounds worth of selections. Table 9.4 offers an example of a draft tracking sheet. Note that in the Bench section for Team 1 that I included the position of the first Bench player. This will be important as the draft progresses into the middle round and the backup quarterbacks begin to come off the board.

It's unquestionably a simple process, but when combined with your tiered ranking sheet, it truly gives you the best handle on the draft at a given point in time. This process is particularly helpful in determining how long one can wait to draft players at the secondary positions. That is to say, RB, QB, and WR slots will be filled early. But charting how many TEs, Ks, or DEFs have come off the board will allow a manager to build depth at other positions or take advantage of big drop-offs in their tiering system.

Table 9.4. Charting draft progress

Position	Team 1	Team 2	Team 3	Team 4	Team 5	Team 6	Team 7	Team 8	Team 9	Team 10
QB					x			x		
RB	x	x	x	x	x	x	x	x	x	x
RB	x	x	x	x	x	x	x	x	x	x
WR	x		x			x	x		x	x
WR										
WR										
TE		x								
K										
DEF										
Bench 1	x RB									
Bench 2										
Bench 3										
Bench 4										
Bench 5										

"Never put all your eggs in one basket."

Many times managers enter the season with insufficient depth at key positions, leaving themselves vulnerable to the specters of injury and lackluster performance. Remember, one vicious hit or bad plant that rips a knee or ankle can disrupt not only the performance of your favorite team, but can be crushing to the fantasy experience. It rarely pays off to draft one dominant player at a position and fail to acquire a serviceable backup.

But note that I wrote "at key positions." First-time managers often fall prey to the thinking that they must cover each and every position with a backup. To put things into perspective, only 13 starting quarterbacks appeared in each of their team's 16 games in the 2005 season (41 percent). Injuries, poor play, and the raising of the white flag, also known as "rebuilding," rolled up to force piles of missed time at the position. Similarly, only nine feature backs played in all 16 games (including Larry Johnson of the Chiefs, who wasn't the full-time starter to begin '05), with others missing one or more games to injury, suspension, and demotion.

Hoarding players at these key positions will serve to protect you from the inevitable injury and will make you an active player in the trade market when desperation hits other managers who were more shortsighted.

Flexibility

Many fantasy participants approach the draft table with a rigid strategy in place. As I have already stated, it is important to have a strategy and stick to it ... except when you don't. There will inevitably be one or more points in the draft where a selection comes off the chart. Sensing he or she is missing a trend or other issue, the manager immediately preceding you may bypass the next obvious selection and either follows the previous selection with another player at the position or an equally curious move. Often these selections can be attributed to outdated information or the fear that a run at a particular position will leave him or her exposed later in the draft. As such, a player is drafted who sits further down your cheatsheet.

Whatever the cause, these selections present a long-term opportunity. The employment of the tiered position-by-position ranking system outlined earlier in the chapter may reveal that there will be a significant drop-off in talent at the position following the selection of this player. Coupled with being an active participant in the overall draft and not just your own picks, you've been tracking the selections and needs of your opponents. This process allows you to further analyze the significance of the pick. If several of the league's teams have not yet drafted a player from that position, you stand to significantly weaken them at one starting position with your selection of this individual.

BYE WEEKS

The notion of adjusting draft selections to account for Bye Weeks is somewhat overblown to me. While it's clear that overloading a roster with players that share a Bye Week almost predicts certain doom for that particular week, the fantasy football season extends at least 13 weeks plus playoffs. There are, however, two situations that must be monitored in reviewing Bye Weeks during the draft.

As such, if using your tiered approach mandates the selection of a second starting running back with the same Bye Week as your first, make the selection. For the other 13 weeks, you will bask in the reflected glory of their brilliance. However, when you next address the position, you'll obviously have to find a starting running back with a different Bye Week. Likewise, you'll need to make a difficult decision for your fourth RB slot between another starter for the Bye Week or a handcuff for your normal starter (see Chapter 18).

The other situation where the Bye Week must be considered is the selection of a backup quarterback. Teams generally carry two to three quarterbacks, and backups generally come off the board in rapid succession. As such, it is imperative to secure a solid backup with a different Bye Week. If you choose to carry a third viable QB option, you're likely leaving yourself exposed at RB or WR.

AUCTION TIPS

The auction draft stands apart from all other processes (see Chapter 8 for full accounts of the different available draft types). In this type of draft, the adherence to a predetermined strategy and gasp, budget, are essential for fielding a competitive team. Given the fact that the auction draft process ordinarily takes much longer than the other available options and that historically these required meeting rooms and the gathering of all league participants in one place, most new participants are introduced to the hobby via the live and auto-pick varieties.

Fantasyauctioneer.com (a screenshot of this application is provided in Figure 9.2) is the first product to bring the excitement and true GM experience to the Web with its innovative auction draft software package. This unique product allows league members to participate in the auction process from anywhere in the world. The software also completes the difficult task of tracking each individual's available funds.

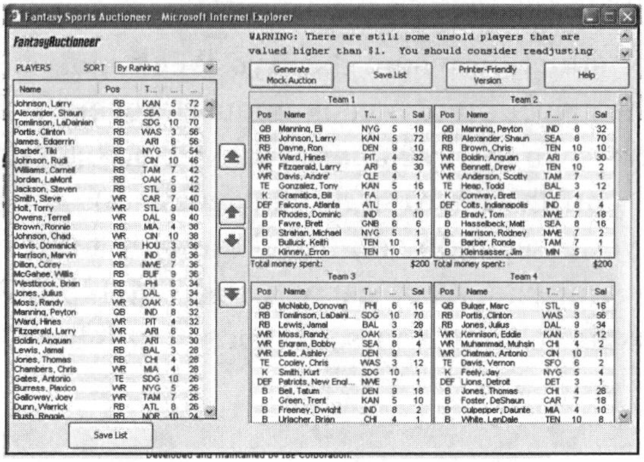

Figure 9.2. Fantasyauctioneer.com

Most fantasy magazines and information hubs offer auction values based on the traditional league configurations that have been tweaked with their own formula. Naturally, these serve only as a guide, because the regional flavors and managerial biases enter into the actual draft process. If you're drafting in New York, then it stands to reason that players from the Giants and Jets will be valued somewhat higher than they should.

The key to the auction process is being disciplined. Most managers approach the auction like they do pay day. They overspend for the first appealing item out of the gate.

The player normally acknowledged as the most valuable in the league (Larry Johnson or Shaun Alexander) will be nominated early to set the bar. Historically, it takes roughly 35 percent of available funds to acquire their services. With that said, the first 10 to 12 players off the board generally carry large price tags. In fact, some second- or third-tier players nominated during this process may get bid to levels far exceeding your target price. Let them go.

The early nominations in an auction draft will carry huge price tags. Be patient with your funds, and let the early fever pitch die down a bit.

In fantasy football, 45 percent of the budget is typically allocated toward the acquisition of running backs, 20 percent to quarterbacks, 25 percent to wide receivers, and 10 percent to round out the squad. These figures may adjust dramatically from position to position depending on whether the manager wishes to possess Peyton Manning (or insert your favorite player here) at any cost. Remember, the relative value of each position adjusts according to your league's scoring and roster configuration. Be mindful of the league settings as you create your values.

Be cautious about developing a pattern of nominating players and then bidding aggressively each time. Vary your entry to the bidding cycle as you fill out your roster. The other players will pick up on any patterns and will suck your wallet dry in short order.

Managers who show discipline early are rewarded later in the draft as funds begin to dry up. There's no getting around the need to pay top dollar for players at positions where talent is scarce. It's all about supply and demand. A tight end such as Antonio Gates or Tony Gonzalez will carry a premium. Most teams will be stocked with a few superstars at big price tags and lower-priced players to round out the roster. The key to a successful auction draft is to find value in those forgotten players.

The next chapter brings us to the playing season and tips and strategies for navigating your way to the league title.

10 In-Season Roster Management

- ♦ Monitoring the Waiver Wire
- ♦ Trades
- ♦ Shoring Up for the Stretch Run

The challenge of successfully navigating a fantasy season is remembering the old adage that you're participating in a marathon and not a sprint. For many fantasy football players, the season begins and ends with the draft, and they simply shuttle players in and out of their lineup without considering other options available to them.

This chapter offers tips for in-season activity to keep your team in the hunt for a championship run.

MONITORING THE WAIVER WIRE

During the season, fantasy owners obviously need to address injury and performance concerns. In most leagues, players are subject to the waiver process after the first kickoff of Sunday games. As such, owners can make the minimal investment on a Monday morning to evaluate whether emerging talents on the waiver wire are more solid long-term investments than those players currently occupying their bench positions.

Remember, the use of the waiver wire is as much an offensive strategy at it is a defensive one. An opportunity may present itself whereby a player can be added who would be a huge benefit to another league competitor. Acquiring this player not only gives you added depth, but weakens your opponent.

Obviously, the biggest issues to address on the waiver wire involve potential long-term injuries and eroding playing time. Remember to check your league's configuration to determine how the available players list is handled. That is to say, some leagues only allow managers to acquire players during a specific period during the week, and then all free agents are frozen for the duration of the week. This is especially important to note for the quarterback and running back positions, as a coach may announce a change on the depth chart, or updated injury information during the middle of the week may reveal more dire results that leave you without a viable option. Don't get caught in the switches.

TRADES

Trades are often talked about in fantasy football circles, but are seldom executed. One of the largest problems facing managers is that nobody wants to make the deal that ultimately catapults another manager to the league championship. As such, many fair deals will be passed upon for fear of receiving the equivalent of a coach's dunce cap.

The thing to remember if you should pursue the trade route is that proposing unfair and lopsided deals will serve to poison the league's atmosphere and likely thwart your ability to strike a deal with another member of the league.

Propose win/win deals. Slamming another player's team, intentionally or inadvertently, with an unfair deal is bad form and doesn't serve any true purpose. The best trades occur when both sides are able to upgrade an area of need.

Naturally, one or more managers in the league will post to the league's message board to complain about the performance of one or more expected stars. Again, while the opening is there to try and lowball the other manager, there will still be an attachment to the player, particularly if he was a high draft pick. Approach the deal by trying to determine the team's needs and then work from your depth and areas of strength.

I'm not saying that you need to take the back seat in the deal or that you necessarily have to give up more to procure the desired player. On the contrary, the whole point of the game is to find value to build a stronger team both at the draft and during the year. However, I do believe that the appropriate approach is to speak positively of the principal players involved. There's no need to bash the already bruised ego of an opponent whose draft selection has gone wrong.

SHORING UP FOR THE STRETCH RUN

Regardless of how well your team performs in the early weeks of the season, it is important to keep one eye on the road ahead. Evaluate the rosters of the players on upcoming opponents and where Bye Weeks may impact their overall performance. Combined with frequent monitoring on the waiver wire, this process will put a manager in the best position to succeed.

Additionally, preseason rankings are heavily based on past performance. As the season progresses, managers should be sure to review the NFL schedules for their league's playoff weeks. If a highly ranked team defense has been ravaged by injury, as happened to both Philadelphia and New England during stretches of 2005, there may be an opportunity to make a roster move to take advantage of this change. In Chapter 14, I offer a preliminary strength of schedule for each team's playoff weeks based on total defense statistics from the 2005 season.

The worst enemy of a fantasy owner, other than poor performance and injury, is inactivity. The game and players' roles within it change on a weekly basis. Managers must stay on top of these developments in order to stay ahead of the competition.

Chapter 11 looks into various resources available to help fantasy owners optimize performance on a weekly basis.

11 Overload the Internal Computer: News Watching

- ◆ Injury Reports
- ◆ Columns and Web Updates
- ◆ Magazines
- ◆ Local News, Nightly Wrap-Ups, Pregame
- ◆ Radio, TV, and Webcasts

Fantasy football participants rely heavily on their gut instincts to make lineup changes and waiver wire acquisitions. Some will make casual glances to notices on player pages and quickly review short notes that address larger injury issues. They provide quick glimpses into the matchups ahead and baseline information on which to draw a conclusion. Fantasy game providers will signal the arrival of news with an icon on the roster page, most commonly a red cross to signal an injury, or a notepad for any and all news. Figure 11.1 displays a sample news update.

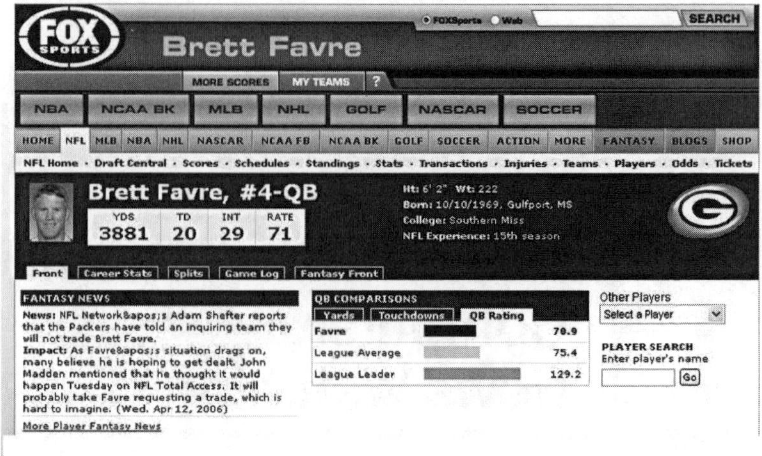

Figure 11.1. Fantasy football sample player note

For most of the fantasy football population, those snippets of information fail to satiate their curiosity and longing for opinions and stats to confirm or refute their own opinions on a player. Managers spend millions of dollars each year on periodicals, newsletters, and other reports designed to create an edge over the competition. Companies work to procure the best inside sources to tap into the locker room chatter and send managers into a frenzy.

The growth of the fantasy sports industry and interest in the mainstream media led to an explosion of small companies offering opinions and analysis about players and teams and attracted the interest of larger companies such as FOX, ESPN, and Yahoo!. Managers place the value of the words and advice of industry contributors (self included) somewhere between a sounding board and gospel.

Each fantasy football information provider approaches the game from a different angle. Some companies specialize in statistical and trend analysis. Others focus on systems and personnel. Still others spend their resources solely on finding the inside dish on player news including injury and team chemistry. It takes a potent combination of all available data and perspectives to successfully march to the league crown.

Injury Reports

Every time a microphone turns on during the football season, fantasy football managers hold their collective breath that their valued player is healthy, happy, and ready to contribute. They hang on every word, hoping for anything but euphemisms and innocuous chatter. Managers seek insights on lingering injuries and brewing position battles. With the NFL playing all but one game on a single day of the week, there's ample time for analysts to break down game footage and stats from every angle. Those with access to a television can literally watch each coach's press conference on Monday through ESPN.

Always check multiple sources regarding injuries. Too often, managers react based on the initial posting, only to find that an injury originally considered serious was misidentified. The Patriots are one team whose injury reports should be scrutinized closely, as they routinely list players as questionable or doubtful, only to have them line up from the first play from scrimmage.

Injuries to major stars will be the subject of ample reports on the Web and mentions on sports talk radio. For role players or secondary contributors, particularly as related to wide receivers or individual defensive players, fantasy football managers will need to dig a little deeper and scan more sources.

COLUMNISTS AND WEB UPDATES

Innumerable sites employ one of more columnists charged with keeping participants informed of the latest developments and analyzing stats and game film to provide strategy tips. The season never ends, with fantasy columnists looking ahead to the following season as soon as the final gun sounds at the Super Bowl. Columnists offer draft tips, preseason rankings, and shift to position battles and performance trends once the season is in gear. Figure 11.2 illustrates a representative offering of player rankings.

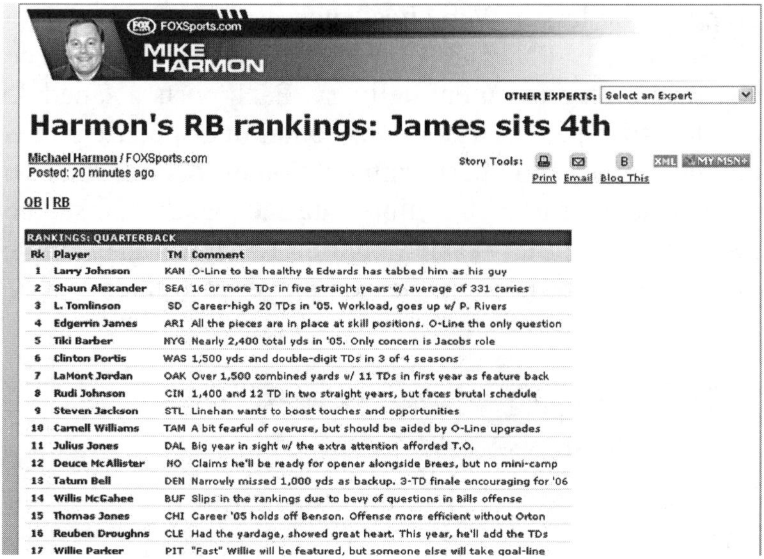
FOXSports.com
MIKE
HARMON

OTHER EXPERTS: Select an Expert

Harmon's RB rankings: James sits 4th

Michael Harmon / FOXSports.com
Posted: 20 minutes ago

Story Tools: Print Email Blog This

QB | RB

RANKINGS: QUARTERBACK

Rk	Player	TM	Comment
1	Larry Johnson	KAN	O-Line to be healthy & Edwards has tabbed him as his guy
2	Shaun Alexander	SEA	16 or more TDs in five straight years w/ average of 331 carries
3	L. Tomlinson	SD	Career-high 20 TDs in '05. Workload, goes up w/ P. Rivers
4	Edgerrin James	ARI	All the pieces are in place at skill positions. O-Line the only question
5	Tiki Barber	NYG	Nearly 2,400 total yds in '05. Only concern is Jacobs role
6	Clinton Portis	WAS	1,500 yds and double-digit TDs in 3 of 4 seasons
7	LaMont Jordan	OAK	Over 1,500 combined yards w/ 11 TDs in first year as feature back
8	Rudi Johnson	CIN	1,400 and 12 TD in two straight years, but faces brutal schedule
9	Steven Jackson	STL	Linehan wants to boost touches and opportunities
10	Carnell Williams	TAM	A bit fearful of overuse, but should be aided by O-Line upgrades
11	Julius Jones	DAL	Big year in sight w/ the extra attention afforded T.O.
12	Deuce McAllister	NO	Claims he'll be ready for opener alongside Brees, but no mini-camp
13	Tatum Bell	DEN	Narrowly missed 1,000 yds as backup. 3-TD finale encouraging for '06
14	Willis McGahee	BUF	Slips in the rankings due to bevy of questions in Bills offense
15	Thomas Jones	CHI	Career '05 holds off Benson. Offense more efficient without Orton
16	Reuben Droughns	CLE	Had the yardage, showed great heart. This year, he'll add the TDs
17	Willie Parker	PIT	"Fast" Willie will be featured, but someone else will take goal-line

Figure 11.2. FOX Sports' Harmon RB rankings

It's a mixed bag of information and entertainment. After all, the columns consist of news and advice to be used for a game … about a game. Some columnists rely on humor. Some play it straight and offer stats, and loads of them. Fantasy football enthusiasts enjoy both varieties and the entire spectrum in between.

The basic tenet to all information providers is that the fantasy football participant needed the information five minutes ago. As such, timely delivery of all information, whether by e-mail or a posting to a Web site, blog, or chat room, is paramount to building an audience. Some writers actively engage their audience via feedback forums and mailbag columns. Others list comments by readers who react to previously posted analysis. Local newspapers provide a great resource for team information from beat writers. Some even employ writers to address fantasy football specifically.

Some of the larger Web sites, such as FOX Sports, CBS SportsLine, ESPN, and Yahoo!, take a more structured approach to their content delivery. Each posts a schedule of when to expect new columns containing specific points of analysis. The compartmentalization of this information offers readers readily digestible data and makes their search for analysis infinitely easier. Figure 11.3 shows an example of fantasy analysis on off-season player movement.

Figure 11.3. FOX Sports' Roger Rotter QB movement

A number of content providers, most notably KFFL and RotoWire, offer some combination of daily and weekly updates via e-mail and PDF files available by subscription. These documents offer detailed breakdowns of each game, performance trends, injury updates, and game plan analysis. Fantasy football participants might see upwards of 25 pages of information to pore through in a given week! No participant can ever contend that he or she suffered from a lack of information.

MAGAZINES

Fantasy preview magazines generally hit the newsstands three to four months ahead of the first week of games and long before training camp. Position-by-position rankings and cheat sheets stand as the top two pieces for comparison. Companies also include individual player analysis and team breakdowns. Some companies will include some semblance of Web services with the purchase of their magazine.

Pick up one or more magazines on the newsstand. You'll need to supplement the information as the pre-season continues to account for injuries and coaching decisions during camp. Due to early press deadlines, some information will need updating as you approach your draft-day decision-making.

Oftentimes, I see participants arrive to a draft armed with a mountain of magazines. They pull a list of rankings from one of the magazines to make that their guide. As emphasized in the previous Savvy Tip, a number of factors may have changed since the publication of the magazine. A player may have been hurt or fallen out of favor with the coach, or worse yet, the magazine's rankings are based on a scoring system completely different from that of their league. The rankings and opinions provided via a magazine or Web site should serve as the basis for your decisions, but ultimately, you're the manager and need to formulate your own opinion. Figure 11.4 illustrates a representative fantasy football magazine cover.

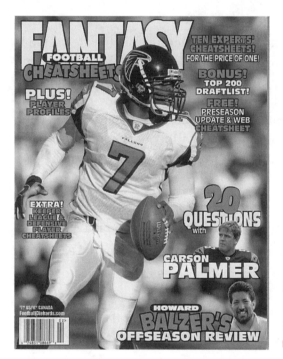

Figure 11.4.
Fantasy Football Cheatsheets
magazine cover

It's sometimes difficult to separate players, and the full ranking process and countless revisions will take time and effort. But as Tom Hanks said in *A League of Their Own* (yes, it's a baseball movie, but it still works), "It's the hard that makes it great."

LOCAL NEWS, NIGHTLY WRAP-UPS, PREGAME

If you load your team with hometown heroes, then five minutes of sports on the local evening news might get you the information you need to make your lineup changes. The additional access afforded to local media outlets will provide greater insight to the clubhouse than national telecasts. Figure 11.5 displays a directory of online editions for newspapers all over the country.

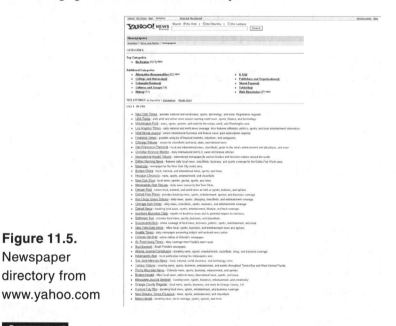

Figure 11.5.
Newspaper directory from www.yahoo.com

Add the directory to your list of bookmarks, and make the local newspaper one of the required stops on your quest to find updated information.

Since most participants will draft players from all over the league, information from local sources will need to be supplemented with a viewing of ESPN's *SportsCenter* and a segment or two of sports radio. Be sure to have a computer or mobile device with you whenever possible as you listen or watch, as there may be injury news that requires immediate action.

Finally, the NFL pregame shows offered by each broadcasting network provide injury updates and analysis from top reporters such as FOX Sports' Jay Glazer or ESPN's Chris Mortensen. They offer up-to-the-minute injury notes as kickoff looms. The studio talent is comprised of top journalists and a bevy of NFL greats to break down matchups and strategy. If you can't commit to the full morning of pregame activity due to other commitments, try to catch the last 15 minutes. The whip-around segments to each stadium often provide last-minute nuggets of wisdom.

FANTASY RADIO, TV, AND WEBCASTS

The true demonstration of fantasy football's growth is its prominence in broadcast media. In addition to my columns on FOX Sports, I appear on countless radio stations during each football season offering sit/start advice, performance predictions, and trade help. There are a number of other analysts and columnists who do the same across the country. In fact, I'm told by many program directors that fantasy football segments bring the highest rate of listener participation, jamming phone lines well in advance of the fantasy segment of the show. Check out the Web site of your local radio station or jot down its phone number and ask about the availability of fantasy football segments on the station. My guess is that you'll find at least one block of time from Thursday morning to kickoff dedicated to fantasy football talk.

Entering the 2006 season, fantasy football content is prevalent across a myriad of broadcast outlets.

- In addition to my radio appearances, I regularly appear in video segments for the FOXSports.com Web site. I address viewer feedback, offer matchup advice, and predict the week's best and worst performers.

- Matthew Berry of Talentedmrroto.com offers a weekly call-in show for AM 710 in Los Angeles.

- FOX Sports has offered a weekly *Ultimate Fantasy Football Show* with former NFL stars Warren Moon and Erik Kramer for two seasons. The panelists answer viewer questions, make predictions for the week and target their "Fantasy Stud" for that week's contests.

- Eric Karabell of ESPN hosts a weekly call-in show and participates in online chats, as does his colleague Scott Engel.

- John Hansen and Adam Caplan offer a weekly program on Sirius Satellite Radio.

- Brandon Funston appears on Yahoo! Sports' *SportStream* product, offering roster advice and tracking trends.

- FOX Sports, CBS, and ESPN each offered a fantasy football mock draft and preview show using on-air talent such as Terry Bradshaw, Howie Long,

Jimmy Johnson, Mike Ditka, Dan Marino, and many others. According to reports, executives at each network were so impressed with the viewer response that those specials will return to the airwaves ahead of the draft season for 2006.

Get your DVRs ready!

12 Ask the Experts

- ◆ General Questions
- ◆ Savvy Tips
- ◆ Sleepers and Flops

The fundamental truth in operating a business holds true for the fantasy sports industry as well. Adapt to the changes in the landscape and embrace technological advancements, or find yourself on the sidelines. The growth of the fantasy sports industry in the past decade can be credited to the entrepreneurs at start-up companies and, in some cases, larger enterprises (CBS Sportsline, ESPN, etc.), who took the fascination with players and statistics to create a game within the game. The other big industry push occurred when the major media outlets and the leagues themselves began to promote fantasy sports content and products.

Like any investment in time or money, participants in fantasy football game seek out the advice of industry professionals. Each representative writer, analyst, and talk show host has developed his or her own voice and philosophy with regard to player rankings and a team's ability to generate points, and metrics by which to make such observations. Some rely on humor to make their point, while others stick to the numbers in the box score. The variations of style and approach are just as important as the content therein in keeping fantasy football participants engaged, informed, entertained, and coming back for more.

Six of the industry's leading analysts and game producers generously gave of their time and experience to discuss their involvement in the industry and provide a series of Savvy Tips to aid both new and longtime players to become more familiar and confident heading into 2006 drafts. Of course, no poll of the industry's leaders would be complete without predictions, so each participant offers Sleeper and Flop picks for the coming year.

To a man, they seek to clear up any confusion about the passion of fantasy football participants and those involved in running these sites. They echo my sentiment put forth at several points in this book regarding the knowledge base necessary to be competitive within fantasy football leagues and the fact that fantasy football involvement doesn't compromise your fandom, but rather that it enhances it.

The participants in this discussion are:

- Matthew Berry of TalentedMrRoto.com and Rotopass.com
- Roger Rotter of FOXSports.com
- William Del Pilar of KFFL.com
- Peter Schoenke of RotoWire.com
- Rick Wolf, EVP of Rotoworld.com, AllstarStats.com, Sandbox.com

- Jeffrey Thomas of SportsBuff.com and president of the Fantasy Sports Trade Association

GENERAL QUESTIONS

1. What products and services does your company offer?
2. How long have you been involved in the industry?
3. What first attracted you to the industry?
4. What is your favorite aspect of your job?
5. What is the hardest aspect of your job?
6. How much time do you spend watching or reading about football during the season?
7. What do you believe to be the most common misconception about fantasy football and its participants?
8. Where do you see the industry in five years?

SAVVY TIPS

1. What's the first piece of advice you'd offer to first-time players?
2. How about first-time commissioners?
3. What's the biggest mistake that fantasy football owners make?

4. Where do you begin the ranking process, and why?

5. Who should be the number one fantasy football selection this season, and why?

SLEEPERS AND FLOPS

1. Please offer one sleeper pick for this season and explain why you believe it so.

2. Please offer one bust selection for this season and explain why you believe it so.

Matthew Berry
TalentedMrRoto.com

General Questions

What products and services does your company offer?

We offer everything you need to win your league, no matter what sport. We feature an award-winning staff that has won more awards and gotten more nominations from the Fantasy Sports Writers Association than any other site. TalentedMrRoto.com offers news, advice, analysis, stats, rankings, at least seven new articles daily, a message board where every post is answered by an expert, guaranteed; draft kits, nightly chats with experts, and unique statistical tools to analyze lineups and free agent acquisitions for every sport, especially fantasy football.

How long have you been involved in the industry?

I've been involved since 1999.

What first attracted you to the industry?

It was my big passion and hobby. I spent more of my free time on fantasy sports than anything else.

What is your favorite aspect of your job?

Giving advice, dealing with readers and subscribers on the site, writing... playing the game at the highest levels in expert leagues.

What is the hardest aspect of your job?

The typical business part of it is the most difficult, from dealing with payroll, tech issues, personnel problems on the site, and most frustrating, when other sites in the industry rip us off, which happens, unfortunately, a lot more often than you'd think.

How much time do you spend watching or reading about football during the season?

I spend probably 50 to 60 hours a week. Seriously, we live, eat, sleep, and breathe it.

What do you believe to be the most common misconception about fantasy football and its participants?

Obviously, the "stat nerd" aspect leaps to mind first. Also, there is a general feeling that fantasy guys don't know "real" football. Fantasy players understand and have a better appreciation of football than "regular" fans.

Where do you see the industry in five years?

I think fantasy will be even bigger. It is becoming more mainstream. You'll see more of the "big" companies get into the fantasy space and the "mom and pop" type companies will become fewer. I think you will see more programming and media directed specifically at fantasy players and it will become even more prevalent in sports and everyday life.

Savvy Tips

What's the first piece of advice you'd offer to first-time players?

Resist the urge to overcoach. Pay attention, read a lot, and play your best players, and things will work out okay. You're bound to make mistakes — we all do — so when it happens, don't beat yourself up. Just move on.

How about first-time commissioners?

Have a very specific and clear constitution that spells out the rules before the season. Be consistent in your dealings with all owners. Know that it is a difficult job and that complaints go with the territory. If it comes down to it, be harsher rather than more lenient. It will go a long way to establishing yourself as a strong voice in your first year.

What's the biggest mistake that fantasy football owners make?

Overcoaching and getting cute with their rosters, like benching a stud player even though he has a favorable matchup.

Where do you begin the ranking process, and why?

With projected yardage and touches. TDs are generally hard to predict. When a team gets to the red zone, it wants anyone — a TE, a fullback, whoever — to get in. Think about Mike Sellers of the Redskins last year who is a perfect example. (Sellers had 12 receptions and carried the ball once, and scored eight touchdowns for Washington.) You can get a pretty good handle on yardage and times they touch the ball. So I start there. And once you have those numbers, you can start extrapolating what those touches and yardage can translate to in terms of fantasy points.

Who should be the number one fantasy football selection this season, and why?

Larry Johnson because he was the number two RB last year and he only played half a season.

Sleepers and Flops
Please offer one sleeper pick for this season and explain why you believe it so.

Deep, deep sleeper, but I like Zach Hilton of New Orleans at TE. He averaged seven receptions his last two games. Drew Brees likes to look for his TE and I think defenses will be so focused on Reggie Bush/Deuce McAllister out of the backfield that Hilton will have a lot of space in the middle of the field. He's a guy you can find in the very last round who I think will have six TDs or so.

Please offer one flop selection for this season and explain why you believe it so.

Reggie Bush in New Orleans because he will split carries with Deuce McAllister and it remains to be seen if he can handle the NFL pounding for a lot of carries. He'll be good, but he will go much higher in the draft than he should because of his name.

Roger Rotter
FOXSports.com

General Questions

What products and services does your company offer?

FOXSports.com offers a suite of fantasy and simulation games, along with a deep selection of original fantasy editorial.

How long have you been involved in the industry?

I've been in the industry going on 10 years.

What first attracted you to the industry?

The chance to help others field their own winning team is most appealing. Additionally, I enjoy providing insight for football owners with stats, analysis, and observation.

What is your favorite aspect of your job?

I get to help fantasy owners win titles.

What is the hardest aspect of your job?

Ensuring the predictions ring true.

How much time do you spend watching or reading about football during the season?

I spend probably 60 hours per week following the action.

What do you believe to be the most common misconception about fantasy football and its participants?

That they stop becoming fans when fantasy actually helps them become more knowledgeable fans.

Where do you see the industry in five years?

Evolving to simulation games where football fans exercise more control over their own team's performance.

Savvy Tips

What's the first piece of advice you'd offer to first-time players?

Learn by trial and follow your instincts.

How about first-time commissioners?

Ensure a fair league.

What's the biggest mistake that fantasy football owners make?

Trading away a star for multiple mediocre players

Where do you begin the ranking process, and why?

Look at last year's production and determine who is most likely to improve or decline.

Who should be the number one fantasy football selection this season, and why?

Larry Johnson. He'll be the featured back for the entire season in Kansas City after finishing as fantasy's third-best back in half of a season last year.

Sleepers and Flops

Please offer one sleeper pick for this season and explain why you believe it so.

Chester Taylor: The release of Onterrio Smith and the departure of Michael Bennett likely makes the former Ravens backup the featured runner in new coach Brad Childress' offense at Minnesota. Taylor will play a role similar to all-around back Brian Westbrook, whom Childress showcased in Philadelphia. Adding one of the league's top guards, Steve Hutchinson, will help Taylor find running room as well.

Please offer one flop selection for this season and explain why you believe it so.

Ron Dayne: As owners can expect DeShaun Foster to endure his fourth season-ending injury in five seasons, they will also likely see Dayne crumble under the weight of the duties of a starting running back. He's rarely been used as the featured back and never carried more than 13 times last season. He's bound to be inconsistent. Last season, though he averaged a hefty 7.4 yards in three games, he posted a lowly 2.6 yards in his other five contests.

William Del Pilar
KFFL.com

General Questions

What products and services does your company offer?

KFFL offers free NFL and MLB news (best in the industry) while also providing fantasy football and baseball content. KFFL specializes in being an insider to the fantasy football industry.

How long have you been involved in the industry?

Since 1998 (individually), and KFFL has been in existence since 1996.

What first attracted you to the industry?

While it was not just one thing, the overall thrill of being in a new era (the Internet) and combining that with a hobby I loved was exciting. Being one of the first on the Internet helped tremendously and the passion in the beginning helped to carry us during the early years.

What is your favorite aspect of your job?

Seeing what I do come to fruition whether it's the rankings or an article. Seeing the hard work in print is always exciting.

What is the hardest aspect of your job?

The hardest job is actually maintaining my fantasy teams. Due to work and the popularity of it all, I find myself in too many leagues. That, and actually separating the business from the fantasy side of things, is tough because the business side is so serious.

How much time do you spend watching or reading about football during the season?

During the season, I literally live and breathe football. I would say I'll easily spend 70 hours per week. Remember, this is what I do for a living!

What do you believe to be the most common misconception about fantasy football and its participants?

The most common misconception about fantasy football is that it's made up of statistical geeks. It's just the opposite. It's an extension of coming closer to a sport we all love. It's a game the casual player can get into and enjoy with the serious player. That's why it's growing so fast.

Where do you see the industry in five years?

I think it will only get bigger and better. Just as it has happened in the NFL and MLB, you'll see other sports gain popularity because of the fantasy element attached. While some will try and fail, it will be a fun ride.

Savvy Tips

What's the first piece of advice you'd offer to first-time players?

Seriously, I tell them to know the rules before they draft. I tell them that in order to help them understand the importance of correlating who the best players in each specific scoring system are. Jokingly, I always tell them not to be homers!

How about first-time commissioners?

I tell first-time commissioners that you can't be wishy-washy. You have to make a decision based on what's best for the league. If you do that, you will always have the league's support. You will always have a few jerks; but for the most part, you'll be fine. If you do make a decision from a selfish perspective and you get caught, it will always follow you in that league.

What's the biggest mistake that fantasy football owners make?

Being homers is the worst mistake I see made. However, *newbies* are much more savvy — in this Internet age — because they'll try to draft the stud of their favorite team. Sometimes they may overpay, but they'll get their player.

Where do you begin the ranking process, and why?

I begin the ranking process as soon as the NFL draft is over, and it starts out with a simple depth chart for all 32 teams. From there begins the process of breaking the players down by position and then rolling the sleeves up and getting to work. This process takes weeks!

Who should be the number one fantasy football selection this season, and why?

The 2006 season will bring us RBs LaDainian Tomlinson, Shaun Alexander, and Larry Johnson as the top three running backs, and I would not hesitate to pick Tomlinson. He's still the safest pick, but if I was daring and a complete risk taker, I would take Johnson. I view Alexander as number three because I don't think the other two backs have the wear and tear that he had last season.

Sleepers and Flops

Please offer one sleeper pick for this season and explain why you believe it so.

I like WR Terry Glenn as the No. 3-type fantasy receiver that is always a must play. In other words, I think he'll be productive weekly to make you happy and have enough big games to help give you the necessary edge in points to capture those close wins. I think Glenn is a sleeper due to the arrival of Terrell Owens, who will demand double coverage.

Please offer one flop selection for this season and explain why you believe it so.

As far as a 2006 flop, I would say one player to look for a dip could be someone such as WR Torry Holt. Holt's new head coach, Scott Linehan, has produced some outstanding offenses, but he's also done it with the likes of WR Randy Moss, Cris Carter, and most recently Chris Chambers — big, physical players whose athletic abilities helped create if not make the big play. Holt is a finesse player. Will Linehan's offense help or hurt Holt? I think I'll let someone else take that risk before me.

Peter Schoenke
RotoWire.com

General Questions

What products and services does your company offer?

RotoWire.com features 24/7 player news and information with a real-time draft kit. Our NFL Commissioner service will also run your league.

How long have you been involved in the industry?

I've been in the industry since 1997.

What first attracted you to the industry?

I was a baseball stat head after reading Bill James, Pete Palmer, and other SABRmetric authors, so I started with fantasy baseball as most people did in the 1980s. Fantasy football soon gained popularity, and I was quick to play it as well. I was also a big fan of following the NFL draft, so fantasy was a great outlet to mimic a real NFL general manager.

What is your favorite aspect of your job?

It's still as much fun now as ever when a big news item breaks and you start to contemplate all the fantasy implications. Despite participating in about 30 fantasy leagues a year, drafting players is still a rush each season.

What is the hardest aspect of your job?

The fact that fantasy football is a 24/7 business. There's news at every hour, and our site needs to be running at all times.

How much time do you spend watching or reading about football during the season?

Pretty much nonstop. It's easier to quantify the hours I'm not researching or watching football. I do play other fantasy sports, so late summer/early fall is very busy with baseball winding down and the NHL and NBA starting their preseasons.

What do you believe to be the most common misconception about fantasy football and its participants?

That fantasy football fans don't know football and only care about a few narrow stats. Sure, some fantasy players don't realize the stats in fantasy don't fully match up to the real game (i.e., a player like Troy Aikman wasn't a great fantasy player), but most know the game better than the average fan with knowledge of rosters beyond their own teams.

Where do you see the industry in five years?

Fantasy football moved into the mainstream earlier this decade once the league and major media sites embraced the concept instead of fearing it as a form of gambling. Fantasy football players watch more football on television and attend more games. They consume more of the NFL's product. That should only help keep both games growing strong.

Savvy Tips

What's the first piece of advice you'd offer to first-time players?

Study the rules of the game. It may seem simple, but even if you know football you may not have a feel for a player's fantasy value. Troy Aikman was a Hall of Fame quarterback, but he wasn't a great fantasy player since he was more about quality than quantity in his passing stats. Sometimes minor rules (such as a point per reception for running backs) can cause dramatic changes in a player's fantasy value in different formats.

How about first-time commissioners?

Keep it simple. Make the categories basic and minimize any other rules. More rules and categories usually equal less fun.

What's the biggest mistake that fantasy football owners make?

Overvaluing rookies and not knowing the rules/scoring system.

Where do you begin the ranking process, and why?

My first step is to study the depth chart of every team. What new players have starting jobs after the draft or off-season moves? Then I look at each player's team context to figure out how his historical patterns of statistics may change this season.

Who should be the number one fantasy football selection this season, and why?

I think Larry Johnson, LaDainian Tomlinson, and Shaun Alexander are clearly a tier above everyone else. If Priest Holmes doesn't come back this season, then I think Johnson is No. 1 on my board. Otherwise, you can make a good argument for any of those three as the top choice.

Sleepers and Flops

Please offer one sleeper pick for this season and explain why you believe it so.

Whoever wins the Indianapolis running back job between Dominic Rhodes and rookie Joseph Addai should have a lot of upside, as opposing defenses will probably dare the Colts to prove they can run the ball without Edgerrin James.

Please offer one flop selection for this season and explain why you believe it so.

Daunte Culpepper is coming back from three torn knee ligaments. Since he relies so much on his legs for his fantasy value, he may not offer those rushing yards and touchdowns to offset his turnovers even if he's ready to start the season.

Rick Wolf
EVP of RotoWorld.com,
Allstarstats.com,
Sandbox.com

General Questions

What products and services does your company offer?

The sites with which I am affiliated offer a wide range of options. I have listed the services provided by each site in the following:

- Rotoworld.com Products: Free player news, depth charts, transactions, injury reports, columns, features, and stats; Draft guides (free and pay) in nine sports; Season Pass — e-mail scheduled content to your inbox or wireless device

- Allstarstats.com Products — League Manager products for NHL, NBA, MLB, NFL

- Sandbox.com Products: SandboxPlus — 25 Sports Games in nine sports for $4.95/month; SandboxNews — coverage and personal news products in nine sports including draft guides and in-season tools for $4.95/month

How long have you been involved in the industry?

I've been in the fantasy world for 16 years. I was on the development team on Baseball Manager, the first online fantasy baseball game in 1989, and was the 16th employee at CBS SportsLine.com in April 1995; Allstar Stats EVP in January 2002.

What first attracted you to the industry?

It was luck. It just happened to me. I was asked by Harold Topper, my boss at PRODIGY, to play in a rotisserie league as his partner. That league was the second Allstar Stats league with Mike Oliveto and Rich Pike as owners in the league. They owned Allstar Stats, but still had day jobs. Pike worked with me at PRODIGY and played on my softball team. After winning the PRODIGY Rotisserie League, Topper picked me to lead a development team for the first online fantasy baseball game, Baseball Manager, in 1990.

Topper accepted a job in 1995 to be vice president of product development for CBS SportsLine USA and asked me to come along to direct the products and markets. I went. He left in controversy 90 days later. I made a gut-wrenching decision to stay and accept the challenge of overseeing all products and services. The rest is sports Internet history.

What is the hardest aspect of your job?

Really, it is no different than any other business. It has good and bad things and they are generally the same as being in the stock market. The worst thing about my job is the fact that it never shuts off. There are only two days a year where there are no American sporting events — the day before the MLB All-Star game and the day after the MLB All-Star game. Every other day of the year, there is something going on in sports. Most sporting events are nights and weekends, so you have to be ready to be interrupted at other people's normal down time.

What is your favorite aspect of your job?

The same thing I hate, I love. It never shuts off. I always feel vital. I love working with intense sports fans as colleagues and as customers. They know so many great stories and are so intense about their teams. It has energy about it that other jobs don't have. The stock market has that edgy intensity, but selling insurance, cars, or widgets just doesn't match the day to day enthusiasm and passion that people involved in this hobby possess.

How much time do you spend watching or reading about football during the season?

I spend at least a couple of hours a day, even in the off-season. I enjoy the NFL Draft a lot.

What do you believe to be the most common misconception about fantasy football and its participants?

Many people believe that fantasy players do not love football. They only love the numbers and winning their league. Fantasy football heightens the viewing experience of *every* game. It makes every down more fun. It takes your knowledge to another level as to what makes up every play. Fantasy football players enjoy the game more and appreciate the game more.

Where do you see the industry in five years?

Within five years, 60 to 70 percent of football fans will be playing some kind of fantasy. It will make the games better. There will be fantasy events at every bar, tavern, pub in America. American football will be watched around the world because people in other countries will be playing and loving to watch the games. People will discuss their fantasy teams like they discuss the Dallas Cowboys, and everyone will relate to it.

Savvy Tips

What's the first piece of advice you'd offer to first-time players?

Play for fun, not to win. Get involved. Enjoy watching the games more and play even if you think you don't know a lot. You do not have to win or be ultracompetitive to have a blast with fantasy football.

How about first-time commissioners?

Be fair, firm, and nice with all decisions. Make decisions and *never* leave it up to a vote. It undermines the decision. My fifth year as commissioner of the LAP (Lawyers and Pretty boys), I had a situation. I accidentally added a player (Randall Cunningham) to more than one team, and no one noticed until the week was over. The owners went nuts. I assumed I would just back out the transactions and redo the scores, but then which QB do I give to the team that doesn't get him since it would not have one?

The league voted to have both players keep him. Cunningham went nuts the last five weeks of the season, carrying both teams to the Fantasy Bowl. The whole league was a mess about it for about five years. Everyone felt cheated. The team that won felt like it wasn't a real win. The team that lost felt like it played without a QB. The 10 other teams felt that they lost because the two teams with Cunningham knocked them out. It was a disaster. MAKE A DECISION...DON'T TAKE VOTES.

Also, indecision is a decision to do nothing. Make a quick decision on things that need to be decided and be fair and never look back.

What's the biggest mistake that fantasy football owners make?

I have found that year after year I can trade a *big* name player for a better player because the name player always gets interest. Also, starting guys because they have the right name instead of better players or better matchups. They say, "Always start your studs." I couldn't agree less. Do the homework and make a decision that is not based on the fact that the guy's name is Moss.

Where do you begin the ranking process, and why?

I start the ranking process with the offensive line changes in football and rank the O lines. After that you can determine who will protect the QB and make lanes for RBs. Then, I go to schedule and rank the team defenses and create the strength of schedule not based on winning percentage from the previous season, but projected defense for the coming year. Then, I create the Strength of Schedule Fantasy Playoffs (SOSFP — weeks 14-16). Based on that I can start ranking on talent, schedule, and how they will help me in my fantasy playoffs should I be lucky enough to make it there (14 for 15 years in the playoffs in the LAP league).

Who should be the number one fantasy football selection this season, and why?

This depends on your scoring system. In general, though, since most leagues have two RB spots and they give a lot of points for receptions, LaDainian Tomlinson should be the first pick in just about every draft. If you play *only* TDs, then you have to go with Shaun Alexander.

Sleepers and Flops

Please offer one sleeper pick for this season and explain why you believe it so.

It is hard since the scoring system is important and the moves are not completed, but based on what we know now:

- **QB: David Carr** — Add the experience of Eric Moulds (tight routes, understanding breaks and defenses, and good mentor) to pure talent in Andre Davis and you have a pair of WRs that will make him great. Dominick Davis will keep defenses honest, and Carr is ready to break out.

- **Deep sleeper: Philip Rivers** — LaDainian Tomlinson can catch out of the backfield and score from anywhere…those will be credited as long TD passes even though it was a screen and a run. This will pad his stats as it did for Drew Brees.

- **RB: Willie Parker** — Hard to call a 1,200-yard runner a sleeper, but his lack of TDs because of the presence of the Bus, Jerome Bettis, makes him appear lower on a lot of cheat sheets making him come to you on the way back in the second round. 1,500 yards and 10 TDs from your second RB is a sleeper pick in my opinion.

- **Deep Sleeper: Chester Taylor** — Starting RBs in West Coast offenses get a lot of catches and run for a lot of yards and TDs. Brad Johnson isn't Joe Montana, but he will get it done, and Taylor will get a lot of fantasy points.

- **WR: Ernest Wilford** — He had seven TDs last year and didn't even get the start until late in the season. Fantasy footballers know who he is, but he will take his game to 1,200 yards and 10 TDs making him a fantasy stud.

- **Deep Sleeper: Samie Parker** — Extremely steady the last five weeks of the season.
- **Eric Parker from San Diego** — Signed a big new deal. They think he is the real deal and he knows how to work with Philip Rivers. Also, always been a big Tyrone Calico fan. Is this the year he breaks out?

Please offer one flop selection for this season and explain why you believe it so.

Lamont Jordan will not withstand a second season of pounding in Oakland. He already wore down late in the season. Jordan is destined for mediocrity.

Jeffrey R. Thomas
Founder & CEO, SportsBuff.com;
President, Fantasy Sports Trade
Association

General Questions

What products and services does your company offer?

Pay and free fantasy sports contests, specializing in salary cap-style contests.

How long have you been involved in the industry?

Founded Sports Buff in 1993.

What first attracted you to the industry?

I was searching for new business opportunities in the early 1990s and started competing in fantasy football leagues. There were very few companies operating nationwide or regional contests, and contest automation was limited or nonexistent. We created the first unlimited trade, 24/7 automated voice system for fantasy sports. In those offline years, it was a major competitive advantage.

What is your favorite aspect of your job?

This industry is incredible. I don't know of many other industries that have created similar opportunities for small entrepreneurs. I'm a huge sports fan, but a businessman first. Combining both has been a dream. It's also great to do something unique. I was playing golf while on vacation in the Bay area and was randomly paired up with a couple of guys from the area. After a few holes, they asked about my career and I said I play games for a living, explaining the fantasy sports biz. They were very complimentary and seemed impressed that I had been in the industry for more than a decade. A couple of holes later, I asked them what they did. One was a successful attorney and one was the president of Guinness. Wow! The president of Guinness? For a beer-loving guy from Wisconsin, getting a little respect from the prez... well, it made my day.

What is the hardest aspect of your job?

Continuously competing with companies that have larger budgets and larger distribution channels.

How much time do you spend watching or reading about football during the season?

I spend most of my time running the business and very little time writing articles or making recommendations.

Because this started as a hobby, I try to compete in our contests and others, so I continue to be a fantasy fan. To keep up, I probably spend eight to 12 hours watching and reading during the football season. Sunday is a workday.

What do you believe to be the most common misconception about fantasy football and its participants?

The media likes to talk up the geek factor because it's sexy and makes a better story. It's a stereotype that is fun sometimes, but I wish writers and broadcasters would ease up a bit and look at the real people playing fantasy football. We try to do this by writing personal stories about our contestants and by producing videos and making them available on the site. The average fantasy football player is married, 37 years old, and earns more than $80,000 per year. They are super fans and super consumers.

Where do you see the industry in five years?

My first thought is that I hope to make a positive impact as the president of the FSTA for the next three years. We have a great organization and the new board of directors is active and has been very helpful. Innovation is leading the way, with new supporting products and services leading the way. I think geography is also going to play a huge role in fantasy sports, on two levels. First, local games and events and contests will grow as local sponsors learn about the power of fantasy football. The industry could grow 50 percent just in local contests and services in the next five years. And second, the larger companies will expand globally, and we'll see global consolidation. I recently received an e-mail from a company starting a fantasy cricket game in Africa and saw a press release for fantasy badminton in India.

Savvy Tips

What's the first piece of advice you'd offer to first-time players?

Don't listen to the first person that tells you what "fantasy football" is. Talk to several about the types of fantasy football they play. There are many types of games and leagues out there — free, pay a little, pay a lot, large, small, with drafts, without drafts, salary cap style, with big prizes, with no prizes, and many others. Some people are discouraged because they think they have to recruit 10 friends and then prepare for a five-hour draft. That's just not true. You can play in a salary cap game against fun people from across the country and easily pick your players online without a draft. Or you can be in a free league with an automated draft, ranking your players and letting the computer pick your team.

How about first-time commissioners?

Don't get nuts with crazy rules or scoring systems. Use a fairly standard scoring system and learn... you can always make changes in year two.

What's the biggest mistake that fantasy football owners make?

In a salary cap-style system, rules are very important. In a league-style system, rules are very important. What is the exact scoring system? Many owners compete and pick players based on generic rankings, or they pick favorite teams or favorite players. Focus on the details. A top player in a game that counts touchdowns only is a lot different than a top player in a system that counts receptions and yards.

Where do you begin the ranking process, and why?

See above... rules and scoring system. Generic rankings sell magazines, but don't win leagues.

Who should be the number one fantasy football selection this season, and why?

The first pick in the 2006 Sports Buff Fantasy Football draft is LT (LaDainian Tomlinson). I've never been a Shaun Alexander guy and he won't repeat. Larry Johnson is interesting, but I'm not ready to take him number one this year. LT has the skills. Even in an average year, like the one he had in 2005, he can carry your fantasy team. He will post 2004 numbers again in 2006.

Sleepers and Flops

Please offer one sleeper pick for this season and explain why you believe it so.

I put up a sleeper rookie — Brandon Williams, the wide receiver in San Francisco. This kid can catch the ball all over the field. He will go over the middle, beat you deep, and return punts and kick-offs. Somebody in San Francisco did his research. Alex Smith (or QB of the day) will improve big time over 2005 with Vernon Davis and Brandon Williams.

Please offer one bust selection for this season and explain why you believe it so.

Tom Brady was a surprise as the number two quarterback in Sports Buff Fantasy Football last year, and he will struggle to be in the Top 15 this year.

In Chapter 13, I turn away from the leaders of the fantasy sports industry back to the sidelines. I will discuss the role of head coaches and their respective schemes and how the decisions made in the team practice facilities in the wee hours of the morning affect the fantasy fortunes of players.

13 Coaching Styles and the Impact on Your Squad

- ◆ AFC North
- ◆ NFC North
- ◆ AFC South
- ◆ NFC South

- ◆ AFC East
- ◆ NFC East
- ◆ AFC West
- ◆ NFC West

As owners complete the difficult task of preranking players for the draft, the strategy and history of NFL head coaches is often dismissed. "The proof is in the numbers" is only somewhat true. After all, the NFL is a game of inches. A more precise receiving route can result in a touchdown instead of an incompletion off the fingertips that leads to a field goal attempt.

In this chapter, I go inside the virtual huddle with each NFL head coach to break down his respective game plan and personnel decisions. To offer perspective of a particular coach's place in the game, there are references to past positions and colleagues. Getting inside the game plans aids owners in their quest to find the proverbial diamond in the rough.

AFC NORTH

Baltimore Ravens

Baltimore Ravens coach Brian Billick gained fame with the high-powered Minnesota offense before joining Baltimore in 1999. His offense in Baltimore has been predicated on a power running game with Jamal Lewis. The Ravens offense has taken heat the past several years, relying on the running game and generating little success passing. To that end, the Ravens have ranked in the top 10 in scoring only once in seven years (eighth in 2003).

The Ravens have consistently ranked among the top defensive units in the game. The Ravens added Haloti Ngata to the defensive line in this year's NFL Draft to plug the center of the field and allow the linebackers to rush to the ball uncontested by blockers. With a full season of health, there's no reason to believe that the star-laden Baltimore defense won't be among the most dominant fantasy defenses this season.

Cincinnati Bengals

Marvin Lewis and the Cincinnati Bengals have assembled one of the most talented groups of skill-position players in the game on offense. Carson Palmer led the NFL in passing TDs in his second season as the starting quarterback. The Bengals rely heavily on the legs of Rudi Johnson to open the game for Palmer and the passing game. Cincinnati ranked 11th in the NFL at 119 rushing yards per game. Johnson shoulders a heavy load weekly and gets rewarded by handling goal-line carries himself.

The Bengals run defense suffered in 2005, when it ranked 20th in yards allowed and surrendered one TD per game. To address that issue, the Bengals drafted Frostee Rucker and Domata Peko and acquired former Bills DT Sam Adams. Cincinnati led the NFL with 31 interceptions, but registered only 28 sacks. Marvin Lewis and team management beefed up the defensive line this off-season, which will allow linebackers Odell Thurman, David Pollack, and Brian Simmons to be more active in blitz packages. The Bengals boast strong CB play from Deltha O'Neal and Tory James, which will allow Lewis to be more creative in his coverage calls.

Cleveland BrownsRomeo Crennel and the Cleveland Browns struggled to find the end zone in his first season in Cleveland, ranking last in points scored at 14.5 per game. There was no consistency in the passing game to complement Reuben Droughns' 1,200 rushing yards, and 1,000-yard receiver Antonio Bryant was left virtually on an island. The trade that sent Trent Dilfer to San Francisco solidifies Charlie Frye as the No. 1 QB. The Browns figure to steal a page from the New England Patriots' (Crennel's former employer) playbook and integrate a short passing game that features Droughns heavily out of the backfield.

The Browns ranked in the bottom 10 in rushing yards per game (93) despite Droughns' 1,200 yards. They received little input from frequently injured backups William Green and Lee Suggs. The history of injuries and inconsistency from this pair leads me to believe that the Browns will actively seek out another veteran back this summer.

Cleveland had only one true receiving option last year in Antonio Bryant. Bryant left for San Francisco and was replaced by Joe Jurevicius, who turned in a huge 10-touchdown season in Seattle. Jurevicius will be joined by second-year man Braylon Edwards in the starting lineup. Edwards showed great potential as a deep-ball threat and game-changing receiver before being lost to injury. The key to the Browns' success in the passing game rests with 2004 No. 1 pick Kellen Winslow Jr., who expects to contribute at a high level this year after two injury-riddled seasons.

New England was a perennial powerhouse against the run during his tenure. Despite a boatload of injuries that forced 10 different starting lineups in 2004, the Patriots still ranked sixth against the run at 98 yards per game and allowed only nine rushing TDs. The main feature of the Patriots defense was that they disguised coverages very well, offering cornerbacks and safeties opportunities to make big plays off of interceptions. The Patriots built their defense to "out-quick" opponents, which frequently led to large sack totals and errant throws.

Pittsburgh Steelers

The Steelers finally earned a Super Bowl win for longtime coach Bill Cowher in 2005. The Pittsburgh offense has been known for three things during Cowher's 14-year run as head coach. First, the execution of a sound ground game is paramount. Since Cowher assumed the head coaching duties in 1992, the Steelers have amassed more rushing yards than any other team in the NFL, and they've tallied nearly 100 100-yard performances. Second, the team will be efficient in its approach and limit penalties and turnovers. Finally, there will be gadget plays in the mix. Long before

Antwaan Randle El was flinging TD passes on end-around calls, Kordell Stewart's alter ego, "Slash," was keeping defenses honest by lining up all over the field.

The Pittsburgh backfield will miss fantasy stalwart Jerome Bettis, but the run-heavy offense remains. Willie Parker can gain tough yards in between the tackles, and Verron Haynes and Duce Staley will offer support in short-yardage and goal-line situations. The threat of a strong running game opens things up for the passing game. Though Ben Roethlisberger isn't called upon to throw with great frequency, he picks his spots and makes great use of an efficient short passing game. Top option Hines Ward runs great routes and catches the ball in stride to make big gains, and the Steelers found a playmaker in TE Heath Miller last season. The Steelers almost lost coordinator Ken Whisenhunt to a head coaching position after the Super Bowl win. He instead returned to the team for 2006. Though Randle El left for Washington in free agency, expect more trickery in the passing game with Whisenhunt's return. His return ranks among the most important off-season moves made by any team in the NFL.

Cowher began his NFL coaching career in special teams and ultimately moved to defensive coordinator. His intense coaching style translates to aggressive play on the field with unique blitz packages and stunts. The Steelers defense is predicated on stuffing the run. Using large and quick nose tackles such as Casey Hampton, the Steelers have allowed an average of 94 rushing yards per game over the past 14 seasons. The defensive line in this scheme effectively closes and holds gaps while allowing linebackers such as Joey Porter and James Farrior to make plays. The Steelers have allowed an average of 193 passing yards per game in Cowher's 14 years at the helm.

NFC NORTH

Chicago Bears

Lovie Smith of the Chicago Bears has full confidence in his young and athletic defense. As such, the offense in his two years in Chicago has relied heavily on the running game. Part of that can be attributed to the instability at QB and lack of big playmakers in the passing game. A full season with either Rex Grossman or Brian Griese might help to balance the equation.

In each of Smith's last three NFL stops (including the current Chicago run), he's had a running back capable not only of picking up yards on the ground but who also factored heavily in the passing game. Thomas Jones had a career year in 2005 after being left unopposed in camp due to Cedric Benson's failure to sign a deal. Barring a deal later in the summer, look for a split of the workload this season with Benson fully integrated into the system.

The Bears hope to find out whether Rex Grossman can be their quarterback of the future this summer. He's lost virtually all of the last two seasons to injury. Grossman offers an ability to go downfield that has been lacking. Grossman's injury last year forced rookie Kyle Orton into action. Orton has the arm to make deep throws, but it's clear that Smith wasn't ready to put the ball in the rookie's hands. As such, Muhsin Muhammad was limited and players such as Bernard Berrian went underutilized.

Smith employs an aggressive defensive philosophy that relies heavily on playmaking linebackers. Under Smith's guidance, Hardy Nickerson and Derrick Brooks became dominant NFL players in Tampa Bay. He went to St. Louis and turned Leonard Little into a star despite playing primarily only on passing downs. Football fans recognize Brian Urlacher's ability, but each member of the unit has improved immensely under Smith.

The Bears ranked 11th in rushing yards allowed in 2005 at 102 per game. Most impressive was that opponents gained only 3.7 yards per game on the ground and scored only nine rushing touchdowns. Alex Brown and Tommie Harris have become adept at clogging the rushing lanes, which allows Urlacher, Lance Briggs, and Hunter Hillenmeyer to make hits at the line of scrimmage. The Bears return all 11 starters this season on a defense that allowed only 12.6 points per game in 2005.

Detroit Lions

New Detroit Lions coach Rod Marinelli knows defense, but hired former St. Louis Rams guru Mike Martz to turn around an offense rich in talent but lacking in production. Joey Harrington was dealt to Miami, leaving Jon Kitna and Josh McCown to battle for the top spot. Whoever wins the job can point to Martz's successes with Kurt Warner and Marc Bulger and feel confident about his ability to produce.

Martz ran to great success with a similar cast in St. Louis. These quarterbacks have experienced a little more fanfare than Warner or Bulger had before their breakout seasons, but ultimately it's the same story of a veteran player looking for a chance. The thick playbooks (receiver Mike Williams estimated Colin Cowherd's ESPN Radio show that they were four to five times thicker than last year's) are filled with wrinkles to thwart every coverage scheme and require precision and crisp execution. The receiving corps is working hard to learn the intricacies of the scheme, salivating over the possibility of putting up numbers similar to those achieved by Rams receivers.

Marinelli's defensive units in Tampa Bay ranked in the top 10 in total defense in nine of his 10 seasons. The Buccaneers racked up an incredible 416 sacks, 328 of which were achieved by the defensive line, a total that ranked first in the NFL. He emphasizes technique and, as Lions players have learned quickly in mini-camp, discipline and hard work. The huge sack totals of the Buccaneers alluded to earlier will be difficult to reach in short order, as the Lions don't have a premier defensive end to rack up double-digit totals. In fact, the Lions ranked 24th in the category last year with 31.

Green Bay Packers

Mike McCarthy assumes the head coaching job in Green Bay after serving as the offensive coordinator for the 49ers last year. With the exception of last season's struggles by Alex Smith and the 49ers offense, McCarthy has had great success in each of his prior assignments. He entered the NFL as an offensive assistant for the Chiefs in 1993 and was elevated to QB coach in 1995. McCarthy previously worked with Brett Favre as QB coach in 1999 before joining the Saints as offensive coordinator for four seasons. In his third year in New Orleans, the Saints ranked third in the league in points scored with 432.

Packers fans and fantasy owners can be encouraged by the patches of brilliance from Aaron Brooks and the Saints offense during McCarthy's four years in New Orleans. Note that I said patches. Though the overall rankings in terms of yardage and points might have been high, there were also a number of high turnover efforts. The return of Brett Favre means that the passing game will yield at least 3,000 yards. Their success in 2006 will be predicated on keeping wide receivers healthy and finding some consistency on the offensive line. If not, Favre will begin flinging downfield to nobody in particular again, and that's not good for anybody, including fantasy lineups.

McCarthy has been around defenses that utilized strong linebacker play and a heavy pass rush. The Saints ranked second in the NFL in sacks over the past decade, and Kansas City was led by Derrick Thomas during McCarthy's tenure. As such, the Packers addressed the middle of their defense in this year's draft. A.J. Hawk and Abdul Hodge were added to the linebacking corps to work alongside Nick Barnett. The athletic trio will always be around the ball and will clean up the efforts of Aaron Kampman and Kabeer Gbaja-Biamila (KGB) up front. Kampman provided a career-high 6.5 sacks last season and KGB added his customary 8 sacks.

Minnesota Vikings

Brad Childress joins the Minnesota Vikings after a tremendous run as coordinator with the Eagles. Under his guidance, the Eagles ranked in the top 10 in terms of point production three times in six years. Childress inherits a backfield stocked with talented runners. The Eagles utilized multiple RBs during his tenure, often relying on players such as Brian Westbrook as much in the passing game as they did in the running game. In 2003, Westbrook teamed with Duce Staley and Correll Buckhalter as part of a three-headed attack. That season, the Eagles ranked 11th in points scored. New acquisition Chester Taylor will own the featured role with 15 to 20 touches per game, but Mewelde Moore and Ciatrick Fason also figure to receive touches. All backs will be aided immensely by the acquisition of lineman Steve Hutchinson from Seattle. At the core of the passing game is the simple precept of efficiency. Childress wants to limit turnovers and take what the defense gives him. Veteran QB Brad Johnson is the perfect quarterback to run Childress' efficient ball-control offense.

On the defensive end, the Vikings secondary was opportunistic in 2005, ranking third in interceptions. The high turnover wasn't enough to overcome bad field position, as they still ranked 19th in points allowed at 21.5. The Vikings were unable to sustain a pass rush, accruing only 34 sacks. Their run defense ranked 19th at 115 yards allowed per game and surrendered 14 touchdowns. Minnesota has worked diligently the last two seasons to build a defensive presence, adding players such as Kenechi Udeze, Erasmus James, and Chad Greenway to complement a core of strong veteran players. Pat and Kevin Williams are effective in plugging running lanes, but they'll need stronger efforts from the linebacking corps to stop the big play.

AFC South

Houston Texans

Gary Kubiak joins the Houston Texans after achieving incredible success in Denver. His offenses have always been predicated on balance between the run and pass. The blocking scheme in the Denver running attack is a thing of legend, elevating five different rushers over the heralded 1,000-yard mark in the last 11 years. In fact, the system has produced a 1,000-yard rusher in 10 of the last 11 seasons. The running game commands respect and therefore opens holes in the passing game. The passing game flourished in the mid-90s with John Elway, experienced great heights again with Brian Griese in 2000, and made a new player out of Jake Plummer. Kubiak will look to apply that scheme to the Houston offense to make Domanick Davis and more importantly, David Carr, more efficient and effective players. Former Packers coach Mike Sherman is onboard as coordinator.

The Denver system rewards runners for their patience and instantly turns the feature back into a fantasy star. While the system may work magic, teams still need talented linemen to run it. The Texans selected two linemen in the middle rounds of the 2006 NFL Draft, but it will be at least another season before the Texans will be able to fully implement that part of the playbook. Kubiak preaches ball control, efficiency, and quick decision-making for his quarterbacks. In Denver, Jake Plummer has been sacked half as many times as he had been in Arizona. The tight end plays a major role in this system, as the quarterback is taught to go through his reads quickly in order to avoid negative plays. Additionally, though the QB does take an occasional shot downfield, the system works off of a short passing game. Therefore, Domanick Davis and tight end Jeb Putzier figure to loom large in the passing game.

The Broncos relied on speed at linebacker, strong cover cornerbacks, and a big rush from Trevor Pryce to reach the pinnacle of the sport. Kubiak knows that the Texans' defense he inherited is far from equipped to repeat those successes. With that said, Kubiak made the point loud and clear about the need to improve the defensive side of the ball with the selection of Mario Williams at No. 1 overall. Robaire Smith and second-year player Travis Johnson do an adequate job of stuffing the middle, but the Texans lacked the playmakers in the linebacking corps to finish plays. The Texans are banking that the pressure applied by Williams will help to pinch the edges and force a cutback to the middle of the field. Dunta Robinson has the ability to become a strong cornerback in the league, and Phillip Buchanon needs to adopt the cornerback mentality. That is to say, past mistakes or errors in coverage need to be forgotten as quickly as they occur. The Texans will also look to find better ways to utilize the talents of Antwan Peek and Jason Babin to make them more consistent contributors. Babin may be used as a speed rusher to piggyback on Williams' efforts.

Indianapolis Colts

Tony Dungy-coached teams through the years have several things in common. His teams are disciplined, well prepared, and perennially rank among the least penalized in the league. The pinball-like totals of the past couple seasons are well documented, and the receiving corps returns intact (except Troy Walters). The big question relating to the Colts' offense in '06 is how balanced the play calling will be in the absence of Edgerrin James.

The Colts set everything up these past years with the strong-willed running of Edgerrin James. He averaged 28 touches through the regular season in 2005 to complement that fine passing attack. Dominic Rhodes has starred in the past, rushing for over 1,100 yards in his lone season as the featured back. He'll face competition in camp from rookie Joseph Addai, who possesses much the same running style as the departed James.

The page just turns to a blank sheet for this juggernaut. The improvement of the defense didn't force the Colts to keep their collective foot on the throttle throughout each game. As such, Edgerrin James' numbers ballooned and there were several games during which Peyton Manning did not throw a TD pass. James's departure would suggest that Manning takes the game back into his hands for the early part of the season until he grows fully comfortable with Dominic Rhodes or Joseph Addai.

Regardless of the huge numbers put forth by the Indianapolis offense, Dungy is still a defensive man at heart. After all, he did play defensive back at the professional level. To boil his career accomplishments in the regular season down to one line, Dungy's teams between Tampa Bay and Indianapolis own a record of 87-22 when they've scored at least 17 points. When the personnel is in place to do so, Dungy believes in aggressive play and trying to force the action. During his tenures as coordinator in Minnesota and later as head coach in Tampa Bay, his defenses regularly ranked among the leaders in sacks and interceptions. In the last two seasons, Dungy has been able to take more chances in his defensive calls with the knowledge that the offense can score anytime, anyplace.

The Colts ranked in the middle of the pack against the run in 2005, allowing 110 yards per game and nine total touchdowns. With the amount of pressure put on by the Indianapolis offense, opposing running games are predominantly nonfactors in most contests, but pick up hunks of yardage once the game has been decided. Corey Simon and Montae Reagor effectively plug the middle and divert attention away from the rush of Dwight Freeney and Robert Mathis, who produced 22.5 sacks in 2005. That type of pressure forces many an ill-fated pass from opposing quarterbacks and allows several other members of the defense to make enough plays to earn a Pro Bowl berth (LB Cato June and DB Bob Sanders).

Jacksonville Jaguars

The last several years of Jaguars history have been marked by a heavy reliance on the legs of Fred Taylor and timely catches by Jimmy Smith. The changing began this off-season when Smith retired after 13 NFL seasons and the oft-injured Taylor refused to attend mandatory meetings in early May. Since Jack Del Rio's arrival, the Jaguars have begun to stockpile young talent at wide receiver and running back. While these players contributed to the team's success last season, they're being called upon to lead in 2006.

The legs of Fred Taylor have defined the franchise in the past several seasons. He's topped 1,000 yards in five of his eight NFL seasons, but he's also missed 30 complete games and parts of numerous others with various leg ailments. As a result, there are currently three talented backs on the roster behind him, including 2006 draft pick Maurice Drew. Taylor reportedly looked sharp in mini-camp in early May, but then refused to participate in additional team drills. There's a possibility that he ends up in another uniform in 2006, leaving Greg Jones and Maurice Drew to split time at tailback.

Smith's retirement leaves a capable but inexperienced trio of receivers and a rookie TE to handle the receiving chores for Byron Leftwich this year. Matt Jones is only in his second full season as a receiver, but his lanky frame and athleticism make him a red zone force. Ernest Wilford exploded on the scene last year with seven touchdowns, but looks to make a huge leap in his receiving yards and receptions this year in Smith's absence. Former first-round selection Reggie Williams will also elevate his role this season. TE Marcedes Lewis has tremendous hands and size and will cause matchup problems in coverage.

The former Pro Bowl linebacker Del Rio takes pride in the dominance of his own linebacking corps of Pat Thomas, Daryl Smith, and tackling machine Mike Peterson. A strong presence in the middle has been the foundation of his defensive structure since his first coaching assignment in New Orleans. Del Rio served as linebackers coach for three seasons under Brian Billick in Baltimore from 1999-2001, and the defense ranked second overall in three straight years. In 2002, Del Rio served as coordinator for the Panthers and improved their defense from 31st overall to second.

Teams coached by Del Rio typically rank among the best against the run. The brilliance of the Super Bowl team in Baltimore is well known. His 2002 Panthers did not allow a single 100-yard rusher until Week 17. The Jaguars allowed 106 rushing yards per game in 2005, but only surrendered four rushing touchdowns. The presence of Marcus Stroud and John Henderson in the middle forces the action to the edges, where Reggie Hayward and an aggressive linebacking corps finish the play.

The Jaguars ranked seventh in the NFL with 184 passing yards allowed per game. They tallied nearly as many interceptions as touchdowns allowed, and a strong pass rush and timely blitzing yielded 47 sacks (tied for third). Jacksonville has a budding star in Rashean Mathis at one corner and former Vikings standout Brian Williams has been brought in this off-season to secure the other.

Tennessee Titans

Jeff Fisher's Tennessee offense is predicated on sustaining a power running game and controlling the clock. The Titans rarely throw the ball deep downfield. Instead, they work methodically down the field with a power running back and utilize the short passing game. In particular, the TE position has long been a huge factor in the Titans attack.

The Titans employ a multiple back system that allows them to keep players fresh for the fourth quarter and runs clock. Chris Brown and Travis Henry have been an effective duo, but both are frequent visitors to the injury report. Therefore, coordinator Norm Chow pressed to select former USC pupil LenDale White in the second round. This trio should fit Fisher's preference for a consistent ground game and take the pressure off of the passing game.

Last season proved to be the year of the tight end for the Titans, as Ben Troupe and Erron Kinney combined to catch 110 passes. The Titans receiving corps was young and inexperienced behind Drew Bennett last year, which forced Steve McNair and Billy Volek to turn to the TEs perhaps more often that they'd anticipated. The Titans added former Patriots star David Givens to aid the development of talented second-year players Roydell Williams and Brandon Jones and offer another solid route runner for whoever lines up under center.

Fisher's defensive philosophy rests on building a unit with a dominant pass rusher, speedy linebackers, and strong cover cornerbacks. At the heart of his system stand two defensive tackles whose sole task is to plug gaps to push action to the edges. The Titans defense is currently in rebuilding mode with the loss of prominent names of the past and an influx of first and second-year players. The Titans have ranked in the top 10 in run defense in 9 of the last 11 seasons under Fisher. Young defensive tackles Albert Haynesworth and Randy Starks are charged with containing the interior of the line, which allows a quick linebacking corps led by Keith Bulluck to finish off the play. Haynesworth has been in the news of late for a charge of reckless endangerment. It does not appear that disciplinary action will be required.

Tennessee went through severe growing pains in 2005 with a young secondary. Though they ranked a respectable 17th in passing yardage allowed (201 yards per game) and received great pressure from Kyle Vanden Bosch, the Titans surrendered a league-worst 33 passing touchdowns against only nine interceptions. Fisher and company are counting on Adam "Pacman" Jones to grow by leaps and bounds in his sophomore season to return the pass defense to a competitive level. The Titans surrendered 28 or more points on nine occasions in 2005.

NFC SOUTH

Atlanta Falcons

Jim Mora effectively utilizes the 1-2 punch available to him in the form of Warrick Dunn and T.J. Duckett. The Falcons ranked first in the league in rushing production last season. The success of the running game effectively dictates all play calling for the Falcons. QB Michael Vick has established a strong rapport with TE Alge Crumpler, but the Falcons will need more efficiency with the young wide receiving corps.

Warrick Dunn remains the top option in Atlanta. Though his TD was low, Dunn offered over 1,400 rushing yards last year. T.J. Duckett finished drives off in the vulture role, and barring a shift in scheme or a deal to another team, he figures to occupy the same role this season. He will face some competition from rookie Jerious Norwood, who looked sharp in Atlanta's mini-camp.

In years past, the receiving corps consisted almost entirely of tight end Alge Crumper. However, Vick worked extensively with receivers Roddy White and Michael Jenkins throughout the off-season, trying to work through the kinks which limited his effectiveness last season. By all reports, Vick is throwing with purpose and showing great touch in deeper routes.

In his previous job, Mora was a successful defensive coordinator with the 49ers. He led San Francisco to a top 5 finish in total defense in his final season before accepting the Falcons head coaching job. Mora's chief talent was in recognizing the talent in young, unproven players and getting them into the proper schemes. He has long been a proponent of stuffing the run to set up long passing downs. His final two 49ers teams finished in the top 10 in terms of rushing defense. The ability to stifle a team's run game early sometimes forces them to offer up their entire playbook early to get some positive contribution from the passing game. Kerney and Abraham will keep the edges contained, and some combination of blitzes will allow the Falcons to stuff the run at the line. The addition of Abraham to the defensive line bolsters the pressure on opposing quarterbacks and limits their time to act, thereby setting up big play opportunities for the defensive backs. The duo of Abraham and Kerney will be a most daunting task for opposing coordinators to navigate.

Carolina Panthers

Panthers coach John Fox prefers a balanced attack on offense, and likes to control the clock and momentum with a sustained ground game. That isn't to say that he doesn't like the deep patterns and game-changing ability afforded him by Steve Smith, but given the choice, he'll work the clock and pound on the opposition. The Panthers have employed a split workload over the past several seasons of part design and part necessity. The running back position has been hit so hard by injuries in the past so as to necessitate the location of six or more viable RB options during the course of the year. DeShaun Foster enters the year as the premier back, but will no doubt cede carries to DeAngelo Williams and/or Eric Shelton.

The passing game received a boost with the addition of Keyshawn Johnson from the Cowboys. Johnson offers smart, precise route running and will draw attention over the middle. His presence opens the edges for Steve Smith and Drew Carter to dominate. Jake Delhomme generally plays it safe with shorter, more efficient routes, but he also has the arm to make the deep toss.

Fox has effectively navigated his team through several periods or personal trials and battled piles of injuries to key starters to regularly post top 10 defensive marks. His 2005 unit ranked in the top 10 in all defensive categories, led by the great efforts from pass rusher Julius Peppers. The Panthers ranked fourth in the NFL in rushing defense in '05, limiting opponents to a smallish 3.6 yards per carry and 91.6 yards per game. In theory, they should be even better in 2006 as they welcome back Kris Jenkins from injury. The defensive end combination of Peppers and Rucker effectively keep all running plays contained on the interior line and let Dan Morgan, Thomas Davis, and company do their job. The pass defense ranked ninth in the NFL at 191 passing yards allowed per game. The intense pressure from Peppers and Rucker served to frustrate opposing quarterbacks and set up the defensive backfield for numerous turnover opportunities.

New Orleans Saints

Sean Payton served as the Assistant Coach/QB Coach/Passing Game Coordinator for Bill Parcells and the Cowboys for the past three seasons. He is known as an innovative play-caller who quickly recognizes gaps in coverages and adjusts game plans accordingly. Payton's hiring by the Saints marks his first head coaching job at the NFL level. In Dallas, the ground game with Julius Jones, and Eddie George before him, set up the success enjoyed by Vinny Testaverde, Quincy Carter, and Drew Bledsoe. Parcells is a big believer in the power ground game. As such, Payton was sometimes limited in his scheming by the conservative Parcells. Look for more three wide receiver sets (including Reggie Bush split wide) in New Orleans. Each starting quarterback under Payton's tutelage in the past six years has thrown for at least 3,000 yards. His use of the tight end as a viable receiving option serves to extend drives and puts the QB in the best position to succeed.

Payton has coached alongside the 3-4 defense for years and will likely seek to employ a similar system in New Orleans. They have two strong defensive linemen in Will Smith and Charles Grant, but still need to build out the linebacking corps and defensive backfield. The Saints struggled against the run in 2005, surrendering 134 yards (4.3 yard per carry average) and one rushing TD per game. The interior line struggled and failed to hold their gaps. Smith and Grant offer good pressure on passing downs, but the Saints found themselves in many 3rd-and-short defensive calls. They'll need better containment from Johnathan Sullivan and Brian Young inside to force the run outside and into their playmakers. They ranked third in pass defense at 178 yards per game, but that stat is deceiving because of the porous run defense.

Tampa Bay Buccaneers

Few remember that Jon Gruden began his career as a receivers coach. The famous scowl and Tampa Bay's place as a perennial defensive powerhouse certainly cloud the issue. What cannot be denied, however, was the impact Gruden had on the offense in Philadelphia (fourth in rushing and first in passing). Of course, he would later find success with Rich Gannon and the explosive Raiders offense in his first head coaching job. With that said, the coach has not been able to avoid controversy in his relationships with wide receivers. Two high profile receivers, Keyshawn Johnson and Keenan McCardell, have left the team in recent years under less than amicable circumstances.

At the heart of Gruden's offense sits the power running game. He declared he would run top draft choice Carnell Williams until he couldn't run any more. And, it was true. Williams carried a heavy workload until an injury sidelined him. Fan favorite and goal line vulture Mike Alstott also returns for one more season. Gruden figures to hand the ball to Williams upward of 25 times per game if he can.

The Buccaneers will enter the season with Chris Simms under center. Joey Galloway clearly remains the top target but there is some discussion as to whether Michael Clayton or Edell Shepherd will be the No. 2 option. TE Alex Smith has proven to have good hands and a willingness to absorb a hit. I suspect that the Buccaneers continue to utilize a short middle passing game with the occasional deep ball in the direction of Clayton or Shepherd.

Gruden prefers to apply pressure to opposing quarterbacks and force the action. It all begins with a big push up front, and Gruden was fortunate to have both Simeon Rice and Warren Sapp when he first joined Tampa Bay. The constant pass rush forced the opposition into rushed decisions, as evidenced by the turnover rate achieved annually by the Buccaneers defense.

The Buccaneers strength against the run begins with Anthony McFarland and Chris Hovan in the middle. Tampa Bay ranked sixth in the NFL in rushing yardage allowed due to the presence of these forces up front. They occupy offensive lineman, allowing Derrick Brooks to finish the play. The pressure applied by Simeon Rice (14 sacks in 2005) allows the Tampa Bay secondary to make plays on the ball. A variety of blitz packages and a trio of athletic linebackers who excel in pass coverage limit the options for the opposition.

AFC EAST

New England Patriots

Bill Belichick of the New England Patriots has picked up the label of "genius" for his ability to work with team management to acquire quality players who fit into the system. Belichick's offense is predicated on tremendous preparation and efficiency, limiting mistakes, and spreading the ball around.

The Patriots have featured a single power back each year during Belichick's tenure. Antowain Smith shouldered the load for three seasons (2001-03) before Corey Dillon joined the team. Dillon averaged nearly 20 touches per game last year before missing the final four games due to injury. Kevin Faulk and Patrick Pass remain available as receiving threats out of the backfield and will factor in on passing downs. Most interesting is the selection of Laurence

Maroney. He shone brightly in Minnesota and will be a force in his first NFL season. As Dillon has been slowed by injury in two of the last three seasons, the Patriots have nabbed their player for the future.

The Patriots have implemented a system by which Tom Brady spreads the ball to multiple targets. It emphasizes efficiency and taking the holes offered by the opposition. Brady has mastered the system, often connecting with six or more targets during the course of the game. While a single wide receiver rises to the top (Deion Branch, David Givens, and so on), the tight end is featured prominently.

New England utilizes a 3-4 (three defensive linemen and four linebackers) defense, relying heavily on reactive linebackers. Injuries decimated the Patriots in 2005, forcing Bill Belichick and company to get creative with their player personnel. Wide receiver Troy Brown appeared in the defensive backfield, and Tedy Bruschi missed half the year after suffering a minor stroke. The Patriots enter 2006 healthier and with reinforcements on defense, looking to ascend back to the top spots occupied in '03 and '04.

Miami Dolphins

Everything in Nick Saban's offensive attack with the Miami Dolphins begins with the power running game. Saban strives to control field position and time of possession. As such, his teams at Michigan State, LSU, and now in Miami featured strong offensive lines and frequent handoffs. The addition of Daunte Culpepper likely opens the offense up a bit more to make better use of Chris Chambers, Marty Booker, and Randy McMichael.

Saban simply wants to run the ball more than his opponent. The statistics bear out that the team that runs the ball more frequently wins the game. Ronnie Brown and Ricky Williams teamed to carry the ball over 25 times per game to great success last season. But with Williams suspended for the year, Miami will need to find a complement/backup for the 2006 season.

Saban seeks to exploit matchups. Chambers, Booker, and McMichael generally tower over opposing defenders and can work effectively downfield. That, in turn, opens the field for the running game and allows Miami to control the ball, and the clock. Saban expects disciplined ball free of penalties and turnovers. The acquisitions of Culpepper and Detroit castoff Joey Harrington leads me to believe that Saban sees something in their game tapes to indicate that they can play his style of football.

On defense, Saban likes to attack opposing quarterbacks, frequently calling for unique blitz combinations and forcing the action. During his tenure at LSU, the Tigers ranked among the NCAA's best in points and yards allowed. That success followed on the heels of his earlier triumphs as coordinator of the Cleveland Browns defense. In three years, he took Cleveland from last in points allowed to fewest in the NFL.

The Dolphins will rely on Keith Taylor and his 337-pound frame to clog the middle and command double-teams, allowing Taylor and Carter to apply pressure from the outside. The heady play of linebackers allows them to anticipate blocking schemes and finish off plays. No Saban team will ever enter a game unprepared. Saban knows how to disguise coverages and create schemes by which to get pressure on the quarterback. Having a linebacker like Zach Thomas to cover sideline to sideline certainly doesn't hurt his cause.

Buffalo Bills

New head coach Dick Jauron of the Buffalo Bills leaned heavily on the running game during his last head coaching job in Chicago. James Allen and Anthony Thomas ran effectively behind a strong offensive line and offered the Bears the ability to control the clock and field position. He will occasionally call for a shot downfield, which bodes well for those eyeing Lee Evans in this year's drafts.

Willis McGahee and recent acquisition Anthony Thomas will be called upon to shoulder a heavy load for the Bills. Thomas was the leading rusher for Jauron's final three seasons as the coach of the Bears with two 1,000-yard efforts. He offers solid insurance for McGahee. Jauron coached conservatively with the Bears, partially due to the personnel, but also because he believed in the strength of his defense to shut down opponents. I would expect the same pattern to develop here.

The Bills allowed 137.8 yards per game (31st) with 22 rushing touchdowns allowed in 2005. To address the situation, the Bill drafted two defensive tackles (John McCargo and Kyle Williams). The Bills are banking on a return to health for Takeo Spikes to anchor the middle of the field and for off-season acquisition Larry Triplett to stuff the run.

Buffalo has a veteran defensive backfield that will welcome the speed and playmaking ability of rookie Donte Whitner. Terrence McGee and Nate Clements are solid cover men, which will allow Troy Vincent and Whitner to gamble and make plays.

New York Jets

Eric Mangini takes on his first head coaching job and will likely employ an offensive system with the Jets that mirrors that of his former employer and new division rival New England Patriots. With Chad Pennington or Patrick Ramsey under center, the Jets will utilize a short passing game with multiple targets that will feed off of a strong running game.

Curtis Martin will return as the primary ball carrier, but the Jets got a glimpse of the future with the strong play of Cedric Houston down the stretch. Additionally, Derrick Blaylock returns from a season-ending injury to offer assistance as a receiver out of the backfield.

The additions of D'Brickashaw Ferguson and Nick Mangold will help solidify the offensive line and keep whomever lines up under center upright. One of the main issues in New York has been a lack of pass protection. The carousel of QBs last season limited the productivity of both Laveranues Coles and Justin McCareins. The ability to protect the QB will allow the Jets to set up a short passing game (with the occasional deep ball to Coles or Jerricho Cotchery) with McCareins and TE combo Doug Jolley and Chris Baker.

Mangini has extensive experience coaching defensive backs and working with head coaches to work players into a system. He was chiefly responsible for keeping the New England defense together as more players ended up on the sidelines due to injury. Mangini is credited with making Troy Brown an effective cornerback, and his rapport with the players and understanding of the game elevated him to Coordinator after Romeo Crennel left for Cleveland. The success of the New England defense was predicated on making their assignments and relying on the middle linebacker to read the offense. Jonathan Vilma will be called upon to elevate his game to another level here.

Dewayne Robertson is evolving into an effective run stuffer in the middle of the field. He effectively plugs the gaps. The Jets will bank on the implementation of the 3-4 defense and the athleticism of their linebackers to improve on the 29th-ranked run defense from 2005 (136.6 yards per game). The Jets added Kimo von Oelhoffen from Pittsburgh to play the DE vacated by John Abraham. He'll team with Shaun Ellis to provide pressure from the edge.

NFC East

New York Giants

The term "disciplinarian" immediately springs to mind at the mention of New York Giants coach Tom Coughlin's name. He makes no secret about his desire to play smart and aggressive football. During his long tenure in Jacksonville, Coughlin prided himself on his team's ability to take care of the football. In eight seasons at the helm (128 regular-season games), Coughlin's teams turned the ball over fewer than three times in 104 of those games. In fact, the Jaguars didn't commit a turnover in 25 percent of those games.

His offensive scheme relies heavily on the ability of the running back to shoulder a heavy load. Fred Taylor finished in the top 10 in rushing yards on three occasions under Coughlin, and finished in the top six in rushing TDs twice. In two years under Coughlin, Tiki Barber has finished in the top five in rushing yards in both seasons, ranked first in total yards from scrimmage both years, and finished in the top 10 scorers among running backs. Another stat in support of Coughlin's dedication to the run is his record with the lead heading into the fourth quarter. In his eight years in Jacksonville, the Jaguars compiled a record of 55-12 in those situations. Run down the clock and leave your opponent with few opportunities to beat them.

Most NFL fans would be hard pressed to recognize that Coughlin began his NFL coaching career as a wide receivers coach for the Philadelphia Eagles in the mid-1980s and served on Bill Parcells' staff in the same role from 1988-90. Coughlin knows how to throw wrinkles into plays to get his top receiver the ball as evidenced by the five times that Jimmy Smith finished in the top five in receiving yards during his tenure.

For all the offensive success in his past, Coughlin truly gets excited by good defensive play. The Giants enter 2006 with two of the best defensive ends in the game and a strong linebacking corps. Last season, opponents picked on the young and inexperienced secondary for 224 passing yards per game and 20 touchdowns. The Giants addressed that issue this off-season by changing personnel and bringing in veterans to play within Coughlin's system.

Dallas Cowboys

Dallas Cowboys coach Bill Parcells once famously benched Phil Simms in 1983 for Scott Brunner. That experiment didn't last long as Simms was reinstalled at QB for the Giants, and Parcells' winning ways began. Parcells has long used the formula of combining a power running game with a veteran quarterback. Unlike many of his peers in the coaching game, Parcells doesn't shy away from veteran players and relies on his reputation and achievements to wrangle in potential "distractions." Parcells keeps players he knows and trusts on his rosters. Drew Bledsoe, Keyshawn Johnson, and Terry Glenn join Curtis Martin as players who have played for Parcells in more than one city.

Wherever he has been, Parcells has always worked with a power ground game. Ottis Anderson helped lead the Giants to the Super Bowl. Curtis Martin began his incredible run of 10 consecutive 1,000-yard seasons with Parcells. He coached Martin for two years in New England and two years in New York with the Jets.

In five seasons with Parcells, Bledsoe has averaged 37 passing attempts per game. Parcells typically utilizes the TE position, as evidenced by the success of Jason Witten, Ben Coates, and Mark Bavaro during his years in Dallas, New England, and New York (Giants), respectively. The QB in Parcells' offense also spreads the ball around and limits mistakes.

Parcells utilizes the 3-4 defense and builds his unit starting with the linebacker position. In each stop during his coaching career, Parcells has had at least one dominant linebacker to lead the charge, be it Lawrence Taylor or Willie McGinest. He's still awaiting that breakout performer in the Dallas linebacking corps now that tackle machine Dat Nguyen has retired.

Washington Redskins

Joe Gibbs' offense with the Washington Redskins has always had a power running game as its foundation behind a huge offensive line. The names of Joe Jacoby, Mark May, and Russ Grimm are forever cemented in Redskins lore, as they formed the nucleus that led the Redskins to multiple Super Bowl appearance.

Gibbs' first season back from a self-imposed exile (and foray into NASCAR) was doomed in the preseason as tackle Jon Jansen was injured and missed the entire year. As a result, the ground game with new RB Clinton Portis sputtered and the team failed to gel. The return of Jansen to anchor the line in 2005 saw Portis return to his Denver form and opened the passing game for Mark Brunell.

Like his counterparts Parcells and Coughlin, Gibbs starts everything with the run. However, Gibbs has been an innovator in the passing game, utilizing small, quick receivers in three-receiver sets to spread the field. It opens rushing lanes for running backs and offers seams to turn short passes into big gains. The system also recognizes mismatches and opportunities afforded by use of the fullback position. Chris Cooley and Mike Sellers combined to score 14 total touchdowns in '05. The additions of Antwaan Randle El and Brandon Lloyd will give Gibbs the opportunity to re-create the "Smurfs" package of the '80s.

The Redskins built their defense on a strong secondary with young and athletic linebackers. They have two of the hardest hitters in the game in Adam Archuleta and Taylor, meaning that no receiver will go over the middle without hearing footsteps. The off-season acquisition of Andre Carter signals a desire to get up the field and after quarterbacks. Washington still awaits any fallout from the off-the-field issues of Sean Taylor. Cornerbacks Carlos Rogers and Shawn Springs maintain man coverage, leaving the linebacking corps to make plays.

Philadelphia Eagles

After years of dominating the NFC, the Philadelphia Eagles were hit hard by injuries in 2005 to slip to 6-10 and out of the playoffs. Andy Reid's offense utilizes the short passing game and forces the primary back (Brian Westbrook of late) to excel in catching the ball out of the backfield. Of course, much to the chagrin of fantasy owners, running backs during Reid's seven years in Philadelphia have often split time. He exploits matchups and situations, and works to keep his backs fresh.

Donovan McNabb might be happy to see Terrell Owens in another uniform this season, but it remains to be seen if the receivers left behind will be able to make up for his production. McNabb returns from hernia surgery with his mobility limited, so it will be imperative for his receivers to run crisp and precise short routes.

As much as the offense was plagued by injuries, the defense was positively decimated. The Eagles allowed 1.5 passing touchdowns and over 200 passing yards per game. To address that issue, Darren Howard was brought in from New Orleans to play right end opposite Jevon Kearse. That combination should be able to apply pressure to the quarterback and make things easier for Sheldon Brown and Lito Sheppard.

The Eagles will try to stuff the run with Mike Patterson and Darwin Walker up the middle. Walker was one of many Eagles hit by injury in '05. They have an active linebacker corps in Dhani Jones, Jeremiah Trotter, and Shawn Barber. All three players cover ground and can help seal against the big play.

Lito Sheppard was limited to 10 games in the secondary. His absence was just one of the many hits delivered to the Philly defense last season. The return of a healthy Walker helps to draw attention in the middle and leaves either Howard or Kearse to battle single coverage. Those matchups should help to force errant throws and allow the Philly DBs to contain coverage.

AFC WEST

Denver Broncos

The brilliance of the Denver offensive scheme under Mike Shanahan has been well chronicled, and the effectiveness of the running game is a thing of fantasy legend. In his last 14 years of coaching, Shanahan's offenses have ranked in the top four on 10 occasions and the running game, no surprise, has produced more yardage than any other team in the NFL. Additionally, the Broncos have averaged over 25 points per game over the past decade.

The running game has produced a 1,000-yard rusher in 10 of the last 11 years, turning unheralded players into superstars (Olandis Gary, Reuben Droughns). It's not a matter of whether the Denver running back will find success. It's merely a matter of whose name is on the jersey. Last season, Mike Anderson led the attack with just over 1,000 yards and the speedy Tatum Bell just missed the mark. The blocking game creates gaping holes and rewards patient backs. Critics may deride the methods and question the legality of the blocks on occasion, but nobody can deny the effectiveness. Check out Chapter 15 for a more detailed look at this incredible fantasy football trend.

For all the press that the Denver running attack receives — and deservedly so — the passing attack also thrived under former coordinator Gary Kubiak. Naturally, having Hall of Famer John Elway at the controls in the late-1990s didn't hurt, but the team has continued its success with quarterbacks Brian Griese and Jake Plummer. Shanahan preaches patience and execution. As such, quarterbacks in the system achieve a high completion percentage while limiting turnovers. Jake Plummer has been a much more reliable and efficient quarterback since joining the Broncos, learning to trust a system as much as he does his right arm.

The Denver defense has also enjoyed tremendous success under Shanahan, having ranked in the top 10 in each of the last three seasons. Like the precision of the offense, defense under Shanahan is all about executing assignments. Players know their roles and play within the system.

The key to the defense's success is shutting down the running game. The Denver defense has ranked in the top 10 against the run in eight of the past 10 seasons. Denver allowed 85 rushing yards per game (second) and only 10 touchdowns on the ground in 2005. The efficiency of the Denver offense often puts opposing teams into passing situations early in games. As such, the team typically ranks in the lower half of the NFL in passing yards allowed but cinches up in the red zone to stop scoring threats. From 2002-04, the Broncos ranked in the top 10 for fewest passing TDs allowed. Last season, an inconsistent pass rush (only 28 sacks) put additional pressure on the secondary and forced the Broncos down the rankings to 20th in passing touchdowns allowed.

Kansas City Chiefs

Kansas City Chiefs coach Herman Edwards loves to work the power ground game to wear down defenses, run clock, and put the game in the hands of his defense. At times, he has been criticized for perhaps being too conservative in his approach. Edwards relies heavily on a single-back offense and a short passing game with infrequent looks downfield. His basic approach to the game under Edwards will suit Larry Johnson just fine. Edwards works his tailback hard, which means that Johnson's high carry total from 2005 will be obliterated if he can stay healthy.

Trent Green quietly put up strong passing yardage last season, but his passing TDs dipped yet again. Health issues on the offensive line sabotaged the passing game early, as top option Tony Gonzalez was forced to stay in and block. Assuming that the aging offensive line can stay healthy, Gonzalez will be a bigger factor in the passing game this season. The presence of Samie Parker to complement Eddie Kennison in the intermediate and deep passing game should allow Green to produce in '06. After all, defensive coordinators are losing sleep trying to solve Larry Johnson.

As a former defensive back in the NFL, Edwards works tirelessly to prepare his secondary for the rigors of the season. Edwards is a coach who actually engages in drills to demonstrate proper technique and execution. The hands-on approach brings questions and bewilderment from those watching practices, but it helps Edwards connect with players and earns their respect. He preaches execution and stresses the need to finish plays and hawk to the ball.

Edwards inherits a defense that ranked seventh against the run at 98 yards per game with 11 touchdowns allowed. The addition of first-round selection Tamba Hali serves to provide another force on the end to contain the corners and allow the linebacking corps to excel. The run defense was solid, but the Chiefs' pass defense ranked 30th last season at 230 yards per game with 25 touchdowns allowed. Kansas City added veterans Patrick Surtain and Sammy Knight before the 2005 season, and while they were effective, an inconsistent pass rush except for Jared Allen left the cornerbacks on an island. As of mid-May, Edwards was in talks with Ty Law about the possibility of joining the Chiefs. Law played for Edwards last season and tallied 10 interceptions.

Oakland Raiders

After an 11-year absence from the sidelines as a head coach, the Oakland Raiders reached back to the past to rehire Art Shell. Shell entered the Hall of Fame in 1989 after a career as one of the most dominant offensive linemen ever. Therefore, it's easy to surmise that Shell's return to Oakland will stress pass protection and aggressive run blocking.

It would be easy to assume that the Raiders excelled in the running game last year based on LaMont Jordan's hefty statistics. However, they actually ranked 29th in the league at just 85.6 yards per game. As a team, the Raiders averaged only 3.8 yards per rushing attempt. Shell will force the action behind tackle Robert Gallery. The attention to blocking schemes and creating a more sustained running attack will then open the offense for Aaron Brooks.

The Raiders have the weapons to be among the league's top scoring offenses, provided that Brooks takes care of the ball and the receiving corps stays healthy. His 1993 Los Angeles Raiders team ranked in the top 5 in passing yardage, as Jeff Hostetler hooked up with Tim Brown and the speedy James Jett. A point of emphasis in this year's training camp will be pass protection, as the Raiders tied for ninth in the NFL last season with 45 sacks allowed.

Shell inherits a defense that is long on potential but short on experience. The majority of players have five years of experience or fewer. This is especially true in the secondary, where the most senior member has four years of experience. To that end, the Raiders turned to Michael Huff with their first selection in this year's draft.

The Raiders ranked 25th against the run in 2005 at 128 yards per game. Opponents were able to build sustained drives, rushing the ball nearly 32 times per game to wear down the Raider defense. Linebackers Kirk Morrison and Danny Clark performed well, but they can only cover so much ground. As mentioned before, the talent in the Raiders secondary is raw. Charles Woodson was the only experienced player last season, and he left through free agency. Cornerbacks Nnamdi Asomugha and Fabrian Washington will be subjected to trial by fire in this high-scoring division. Shell and his coaches will need to be creative in blitz packages to protect the young corners. They'll need to find a complement to sackmaster Derrick Burgess to accomplish the feat.

San Diego Chargers

San Diego Chargers coach Marty Schottenheimer emphasizes balance in his offensive attack, mixing the run game with an effective short and intermediate passing game. The ability to rely on LaDainian Tomlinson in the backfield certainly helps to minimize the risk of failure. In any event, the keys to the current Chargers offense are motion and spreading the field to allow receivers to operate in single coverage and exploit pockets in the zone. Drew Brees was particularly adept at picking out soft spots in coverage. It remains to be seen how Philip Rivers will perform in this system.

LaDainian Tomlinson absorbs hits and gains the tough yards, and can just as easily turn on the jets once he hits the second level of the defense. His inside-out running style has placed the Chargers in the top 10 in rushing yardage for four straight years. The lone concern is that the heavy workload of the past four years will begin to wear on him. There have seen signs late in each of the last two seasons that the hits had taken their toll.

The emergence of Antonio Gates truly opened up the offense in San Diego. His arrival took pressure off Tomlinson and the running game and turned Drew Brees into a star. The Chargers spread the field to allow receivers to operate in space, with Tomlinson always a capable safety valve. With Philip Rivers under center, I suspect that Tomlinson's work as a receiver increases this year to help open up the offense. The departure of Brees puts the focus of defensive coordinators back solely on stopping Tomlinson until Rivers' play warrants a change.

The Chargers have flourished on the defensive side of the ball with the implementation of Wade Phillips' 3-4 defensive scheme. They received tremendous contributions from rookies Luis Castillo and Shawne Merriman to complement All-Pro linebacker Donnie Edwards. San Diego ranked 13th in total defense last season and allowed 19.5 points per game.

The strong efforts of Castillo, Jamal Williams, and Igor Olshansky up front forced opposing rushers to test the middle of the field, where they were swallowed by the San Diego linebackers. San Diego ranked second in the NFL in rushing defense at 86 yards per game. The Chargers dominated opposing rushers, but found difficulty containing the pass. Opponents averaged 225 passing yards and 1.25 passing TDs per game. Of chief concern for Phillips and Schottenheimer was the fact that the Chargers collected only 10 interceptions despite an effective pass rush that piled up 46 sacks.

NFC WEST

Arizona Cardinals

Dennis Green's Arizona Cardinals offense ranked in the top 10 statistically last season despite obvious problems on the offensive line and decided lack of a running game. Even without any semblance of balance, the trio of Kurt Warner, Anquan Boldin, and Larry Fitzgerald put up phenomenal numbers. Boldin and Fitzgerald each reached 100 receptions and the Cardinals averaged nearly 300 passing yards per game.

Arizona made a big splash in free agency with the acquisition of former Colts superstar Edgerrin James. James thrived in the Colts' balanced attack, consistently eclipsing the 1,000-yard rushing barrier and offering a solid receiving threat out of the backfield. There are still some concerns about the offensive line, but the feeling in Arizona is that a premier back like James will make the situation workable.

Green has the type of high-powered offense to which he's grown accustomed. It's certainly a unit that should put up points by the barrel. Boldin is two years off of his big injury, and Fitzgerald continues to get better as he enters his third year. Warner has a full complement of receiving options once you include Bryant Johnson and 2006 draft pick, TE Leonard Pope. It's a unit that should produce, but will the expectations be set too high?

The Cardinals allowed 24.2 points per game in 2005. Though their offense is built to compete in games of that ilk, no coach wants to make a habit of it. Even Green, who went through years of that game style in Minnesota, would rather not have to go down that road. Part of the trouble last season was the absence of Bertrand Berry for half the season. His return and the continued development of players such as Karlos Dansby and Antrel Rolle will dictate how well this team progresses.

Arizona's run defense allowed a respectable 102 yards per game last season, but ceded 22 rushing touchdowns. The team acquired New York Giants DT Kendrick Clancy to help shore up the interior of the defensive line. This addition should improve the play of third-year starter Darnell Dockett and clear traffic for the linebackers.

Arizona ranked 12th in the NFL at 193 passing yards allowed per game, but still allowed 17 touchdowns. Opposing quarterbacks completed nearly 62 percent of their pass attempts. The return of Berry to his defensive end position should boost the pass rush and aid the cornerbacks in coverage. The Cardinals are banking on quick growth from 2005 draft selection Antrel Rolle.

St. Louis Rams

Like Dennis Green, new St. Louis Rams head coach Scott Linehan has his ties to the Minnesota Vikings organization. Linehan was the offensive coordinator for the Vikings during Daunte Culpepper's ridiculous 2004 campaign. He joined Nick Saban's staff in 2004 and immediately paid dividends. The Dolphins rose from 29th in total offense to 14th last season, and ranked among the leaders in a number of categories. They averaged 4.3 yards per carry (eighth), allowed only 26 sacks (fourth), and exploded for 26 plays that covered 25 yards or longer. The Dolphins averaged 26 points per game during their six-game winning streak to finish the year.

The Dolphins relied on power football under Nick Saban, and Linehan expects to implement the same approach here.

That strategy portends to a huge workload each week for Steven Jackson. Marshall Faulk will still see occasional work and serve as a receiver out of the backfield, but the offense will clearly go through Jackson. The Rams ranked 22nd in the league at 96 rushing yards per game. Jackson will easily surpass that mark this season.

The Rams ranked second in the league at 272 passing yards per game, despite losing starting quarterback Marc Bulger to injury in the middle of the year. St. Louis retains a deep receiving corps that stands at least four deep heading into training camp. Remember, all Vikings receivers shared the wealth in Culpepper's monster 2004 season. Additionally, the Rams made the move to bring in Gus Frerotte as insurance for Bulger. Frerotte passed for nearly 3,000 yards with 18 touchdowns. Even with the increased reliance on Steven Jackson, the passing game will remain potent.

As he built his coaching staff, new head man Scott Linehan honed in on former Saints head coach Jim Haslett for the job. Haslett's reputation as a stickler for discipline and technique sealed the deal. In short, the team went looking for someone to toughen them up and make them accountable. The Rams were tied for 30th in points allowed last year, and Haslett attributes much of the blame to poor tackling technique. That's the first order of business; simply buttoning up technique.

The Rams addressed the defensive personnel next. They landed four free agents (Will Witherspoon, six-time Pro Bowl DT La'Roi Glover, Corey Chavous, and Fakhir Brown) and then drafted three defensive players in April. St. Louis allowed a robust 134 yards per game (4.7 per carry) on the ground last season as well as 22 rushing touchdowns. The addition of Glover will help speed the development of Jimmy Kennedy on the interior. The two should be able to work in tandem to bring that rushing total to a more reasonable level.

St. Louis didn't find any solace in its pass defense, either. The Rams allowed 214 passing yards per game (23rd in the NFL) but surrendered an alarming 26 passing scores. These struggles occurred even with a pass rush that tallied 41 sacks. For all the changes, the Rams will still need tremendous development from cornerbacks Jerametrius Butler and Ronald Bartell to get a big payoff.

San Francisco 49ers

To no one's surprise, the 49ers offense struggled in 2005 for first-year coach Mike Nolan. They scored only 14.9 points per game and several quarterbacks, including No. 1 pick Alex Smith, combined to throw eight passing touchdowns. Nolan and the 49ers quickly jumped to hire Norv Turner as coordinator once he was relieved of duty in Oakland. Turner has experienced great success as a coordinator in each stop of his career and will immediately boost the status of the running game.

Frank Gore did well in his late-season audition to supplant Kevan Barlow as the top back in San Francisco. The running game produced a respectable 105.6 yards per contest. Naturally, after a season of misery as they experienced, the 49ers set about trying to shore up their passing game. The 49ers traded Ken Dorsey to Cleveland for former Super Bowl winner Trent Dilfer. They had previously signed 1,000-yard receiver Antonio Bryant after losing emerging star Brandon Lloyd to free agency. The addition of future star Vernon Davis in the draft and the expected returns of 2004 receiving leader TE Eric Johnson and second receiver Arnaz Battle immediately make this offense look better. Of course, it all depends early on the growth of Alex Smith over the off-season.

Many NFL fans would be hard-pressed to recall that Nolan was the defensive coordinator of the Ravens from 2002-2004. Fewer still would have expected him to be a QB coach, a role he served for Brian Billick in 2001. In any event, Nolan and his staff navigated through a spate of injuries that first year and the Ravens finished with the third-highest number of turnovers in the league. Nolan employed an aggressive scheme that allowed players to force the action and make plays. Though the personnel assembled in San Francisco doesn't have the pedigree of Ed Reed, Ray Lewis, and company, Nolan envisions building a defense in that vein. He'll begin that process without the two highest profile defenders on the roster last season. Both Julian Peterson and Andre Carter are making homes elsewhere in '06.

The 49ers allowed 114 yards per game on the ground last season and a respectable 3.8-yards-per-carry average. With the exception of veteran Bryant Young, the defensive line is very young and inexperienced. As such, they're still learning to read formations and blocking schemes. Nolan will be hands-on to help in the process as the 49ers work to effectively utilize the 3-4 scheme.

San Francisco ranked last in pass defense last season, allowing a monstrous 276.7 yards per game and 28 touchdowns in Nolan's first season at the helm. For a coach who experienced such success in Baltimore, it was certainly hard to swallow. To aid the secondary, San Francisco added CB Sammy Davis in a trade with San Diego and signed veteran CB Walt Harris. They should be able to add some stability in coverage and take some of the playmaking pressure off of linebacker Derek Smith.

Seattle Seahawks

Everything clicked last season for Mike Holmgren's Seattle Seahawks. Seattle generated a league-leading 28.3 points per game. The Seahawks rushed for an average of 153 yards per game, with Matt Hasselbeck throwing efficiently using a full complement of receivers. The offense returns intact with the exception of star lineman Steve Hutchinson, who made his way to Minnesota. The offensive line still ranks among the game's best, even without Hutchinson, and No. 37 Shaun Alexander still lines up in the backfield. Alexander has scored 16 or more touchdowns in five straight seasons entering 2006. The capable Maurice Morris remains Alexander's backup.

The Seattle passing game excelled last season, even though top receiver Darrell Jackson was slowed by injury and played in only six games. Seattle received tremendous production from Joe Jurevicius to the tune of 10 TD grabs, and Jerramy Stevens finally showed signs of becoming the player they envisioned he could be on draft day in 2001. The Seahawks will have Jackson at full strength for the new year, possession receiver Bobby Engram, and a new addition in former Minnesota star Nate Burleson. Burleson finished 2004 with over 1,000 yards receiving, but couldn't recapture the magic as early struggles and an injury stifled his follow-up effort. All the pieces are there for another huge season in Seattle.

After years of touts as a sleeper fantasy defense, the Seahawks delivered for fantasy owners in 2005. Seattle ranked seventh at 16.9 points allowed per game and limited opponents to just 94 rushing yards per game. All those hours of game planning certainly work both ways. In addition to their solid rushing defense, the Seahawks applied constant pressure to opposing quarterbacks, which generated a league-high 50 sacks. The Seahawks didn't rest on their laurels or Super Bowl appearance this season, as they added Julian Peterson from San Francisco to further bolster their linebacking corps.

The key to the stout run defense lies in the ability of Chartric Darby and Rocky Bernard to effectively plug the middle. Their efforts on the interior allow linebackers LeRoy Hill and second-year star Lofa Tatupu to rush up and finish plays. Tatupu registered 105 tackles, four sacks, and three interceptions as a rookie.

As I wrote earlier, the Seahawks piled up 50 sacks last season. Defensive ends Bryce Fisher and Grant Wistrom enjoyed tremendous success on the edges (13.5 sacks between them), and Bernard fought through the interior line for 8.5 of his own. Their efforts took some of the pressure off of Marcus Trufant and Kelly Herndon at cornerback and allowed safety Michael Boulware to take more chances and become a star in his own right.

The preceding information was written to offer perspective as you sit down during the preranking process. The information contained herein attempts to expose coaching successes of the past in order to predict fantasy dominance for your squad in 2006.

In the next chapter, I review another predraft strategy for creating separation among otherwise equally attractive draft options. Chapter 14 offers advice on schedule watching.

14 Schedule Watching

- ◆ Managing Bye Weeks
- ◆ Watching Playoff Weeks
- ◆ Weather Considerations

As fantasy football participants begin to contemplate their predraft rankings, they account for a wide variety of factors such as playing time, past injuries, the team's offensive personnel as a whole, coaching, and strength of schedule.

There are three other areas to consider with regard to scheduling, one of which is either ignored altogether or weighs too heavily on draft decisions. The acknowledgment of Bye weeks, reviewing a player's schedule for the fantasy football playoff weeks, and weather considerations are all variables that should carry weight on draft day.

MANAGING BYE WEEKS

To some degree, the concept of monitoring Bye weeks within fantasy drafts has been overblown. During the draft process, managers will often bypass the obvious player on the board if their Bye week coincides with their previous selection.

On some level, I can appreciate the logic of keeping one roster slot sound in every week of the year. However, that strategy actually serves to weaken the team for two weeks. I believe that managers should be cognizant of the Bye week situation, but that it shouldn't necessarily dictate the draft selection, particularly in the case of a second running back.

Obviously, once the manager returns to the running back position for the selection of a backup later in the draft, he or she will need to be sure to select a running back with a different Bye week so as to field a full roster. The only backup choice that should most definitely have a separate Bye week is the QB position. All league managers will carry at least two quarterbacks, which means that all viable options will disappear in the latter rounds of the draft. It is unwise to enter the season depending on an injury or position battle to solve a backup dilemma. While those situations will undoubtedly occur during the course of the season, there's no guarantee that they'll occur where or when you need them.

Table 14.1 displays the Bye weeks for each NFL team in the 2006 season. Note that Week 3 will see fantasy owners compete without the services of top fantasy choices Larry Johnson, LaDainian Tomlinson, Terrell Owens, LaMont Jordan, Randy Moss, and Tony Gonzalez, among others. Fantasy lineups will be most interesting to watch that week.

Table 14.1. NFL Bye weeks for 2006

Week 3	Week 4
Dallas Cowboys	Denver Broncos
Kansas City Chiefs	New York Giants
Oakland Raiders	Pittsburgh Steelers
San Diego Chargers	Tampa Bay Buccaneers
Week 5	**Week 6**
Atlanta Falcons	Cleveland Browns
Cincinnati Bengals	Green Bay Packers
Seattle Seahawks	Indianapolis Colts
Houston Texans	Minnesota Vikings
	New England Patriots
Week 7	**Week 8**
Chicago Bears	Buffalo Bills
Tennessee Titans	Detroit Lions
St. Louis Rams	Miami Dolphins
New Orleans Saints	Washington Redskins
San Francisco 49ers	
Baltimore Ravens	
Week 9	
New York Jets	
Philadelphia Eagles	
Arizona Cardinals	
Carolina Panthers	

WATCHING PLAYOFF WEEKS

Another issue to consider when creating predraft rankings is how a player stacks up in the all-important fantasy playoff weeks at the end of the season. While it may be somewhat cocky to look out that far ahead, nobody plays fantasy football with the expectation of losing.

Tables 14.2 and 14.3 display the "Ease of Schedule" calculations for teams based on last season's total defense rankings. The value was determined by averaging the opponents' ranks for the specified weeks. Based on this straightforward method, Pittsburgh has the most difficult schedule during the typical fantasy football playoff weeks, and Washington has the easiest.

This data can be used to break the tie in the ranking process between two closely valued players. Of course, you can certainly change the method by which the teams are ranked, either by evaluating how you'd rank defenses top to bottom for the new year based on off-season acquisitions and draft choices or adjusting for returning players. For the purpose of this example, I kept it simple.

Remember, rivalry games during playoff weeks generally toss all accepted statistical data to the side. Take, for example, Mark Brunell's late-season performance against Dallas last year. Dallas was highly ranked in pass defense, but it didn't stop Brunell from racking up four TD passes. Big games bring out big performances, and oftentimes, unexpected results and fantastic finishes.

Managers should revisit this grid at some time in the season as they evaluate possible free agent pickups. The savvy fantasy football player knows that the game is always changing.

Table 14.2. Fantasy playoffs schedule for Weeks 14-16

Team	Week 14 Opp	Rank	Week 15 Opp	Rank	Week 16 Opp	Rank	EOS
Washington	Philadelphia	27	New Orleans	28	St. Louis	30	28.33
Dallas	New Orleans	28	Atlanta	18	Philadelphia	27	24.33
Green Bay	San Francisco	30	Detroit	21	Minnesota	19	23.33
New York Giants	Carolina	14	Philadelphia	27	New Orleans	28	23.00
Seattle	Arizona	26	San Francisco	30	San Diego	13	23.00
Oakland	Cincinnati	22	St. Louis	30	Kansas City	16	22.67
Buffalo	New York Jets	23	Miami Dolphins	15	Tennessee	29	22.33
Miami	New England	17	Buffalo Bills	24	New York Jets	23	21.33
Minnesota	Detroit	21	New York Jets	23	Green Bay	20	21.33
Tennessee	Houston	32	Jacksonville	6	Buffalo Bills	24	20.67
Denver	San Diego	13	Arizona	26	Cincinnati	22	20.33
Indianapolis	Jacksonville	6	Cincinnati	22	Houston	32	20.00
Chicago	St. Louis	30	Tampa Bay	8	Detroit	21	19.67
New York Jets	Buffalo	24	Minnesota	19	Miami	15	19.33
San Francisco	Green Bay	20	Seattle	7	Arizona	26	17.67
New England	Miami	15	Houston	32	Jacksonville	6	17.67
Houston	Tennessee	29	New England	17	Indianapolis	2	16.00
Jacksonville	Indianapolis	2	Tennessee	29	New England	17	16.00
Kansas City	Baltimore	10	San Diego	13	Oakland	24	15.67
Detroit	Minnesota	19	Green Bay	20	Chicago	1	13.33
Arizona	Seattle	7	Denver	3	San Francisco	30	13.33
New Orleans	Dallas	12	Washington	9	New York Giants	14	11.67
Philadelphia	Washington	9	New York Giants	14	Dallas	12	11.67
St. Louis	Chicago	1	Oakland	24	Washington	9	11.33
Baltimore	Kansas City	16	Cleveland	11	Pittsburgh	3	10.00
Tampa Bay	Atlanta	18	Chicago	1	Cleveland	11	10.00
Cincinnati	Oakland	24	Indianapolis	2	Denver	3	9.67
Cleveland	Pittsburgh	11	Baltimore	10	Tampa Bay	8	9.67
San Diego	Denver	3	Kansas City	16	Seattle	7	8.67
Carolina	New York Giants	5	Pittsburgh	3	Atlanta	18	8.67
Atlanta	Tampa Bay	8	Dallas	12	Carolina	5	8.33
Pittsburgh	Cleveland	3	Carolina	5	Baltimore	10	6.00

Table 14.3. Fantasy playoffs schedule for Weeks 14-17

Team	Week 14 Opp	Rank	Week 15 Opp	Rank	Week 16 Opp	Rank	Week 17 Opp	Rank	EOS
Washington	Philadelphia	27	New Orleans	28	St. Louis	30	NY Giants	14	24.75
Minnesota	Detroit	21	NY Jets	23	Green Bay	20	St. Louis	30	23.5
Dallas	New Orleans	28	Atlanta	18	Philadelphia	27	Detroit	21	23.5
Oakland	Cincinnati	22	St. Louis	30	Kansas City	16	NY Jets	23	22.75
Denver	San Diego	13	Arizona	26	Cincinnati	22	San Fran	30	22.75
New York Jets	Buffalo	24	Minnesota	19	Miami	15	Oakland	24	20.5
New England	Miami	15	Houston	32	Jacksonville	6	Tennessee	29	20.5
Tennessee	Houston	32	Jacksonville	6	Buffalo	24	New England	17	19.75
Chicago	St. Louis	30	Tampa Bay	8	Detroit	21	Green Bay	20	19.75
New York Giants	Carolina	14	Philadelphia	27	New Orleans	28	Washington	9	19.5
Seattle	Arizona	26	San Fran	30	San Diego	13	Tampa Bay	8	19.25
Buffalo	NY Jets	23	Miami	15	Tennessee	29	Baltimore	10	19.25
Indianapolis	Jacksonville	6	Cincinnati	22	Houston	32	Miami	15	18.75
Green Bay	San Fran	30	Detroit	21	Minnesota	19	Chicago	1	17.75
Miami	New England	17	Buffalo Bills	24	NY Jets	23	Indianapolis	2	16.5
Jacksonville	Indianapolis	2	Tennessee	29	New England	17	Kansas City	16	16
Cleveland	Pittsburgh	11	Baltimore	10	Tampa Bay	8	Houston	32	15.25
Houston	Tennessee	29	New England	17	Indianapolis	2	Cleveland	11	14.75
San Francisco	Green Bay	20	Seattle	7	Arizona	26	Denver	3	14
Carolina	NY Giants	5	Pittsburgh	3	Atlanta	18	New Orleans	28	13.5
Baltimore	Kansas City	16	Cleveland	11	Pittsburgh	3	Buffalo	24	13.5
St. Louis	Chicago	1	Oakland	24	Washington	9	Minnesota	19	13.25
Philadelphia	Washington	9	NY Giants	14	Dallas	12	Atlanta	18	13.25
Kansas City	Baltimore	10	San Diego	13	Oakland	24	Jacksonville	6	13.25
Arizona	Seattle	7	Denver	3	San Francisco	30	San Diego	13	13.25
San Diego	Denver	3	Kansas City	16	Seattle	7	Arizona	26	13
Detroit	Minnesota	19	Green Bay	20	Chicago	1	Dallas	12	13
Atlanta	Tampa Bay	8	Dallas	12	Carolina	5	Philadelphia	27	13
Pittsburgh	Cleveland	3	Carolina	5	Baltimore	10	Cincinnati	22	10
New Orleans	Dallas	12	Washington	9	NY Giants	14	Carolina	5	10
Tampa Bay	Atlanta	18	Chicago	1	Cleveland	11	Seattle	7	9.25
Cincinnati	Oakland	24	Indianapolis	2	Denver	3	Pittsburgh	3	8

WEATHER CONSIDERATIONS

As I consider the elements that will impact a player's fantasy contributions for the year, I'll admit that the weather factor does not play a huge role. After all, I'm sure we've all screamed at the television or cursed the local meteorologist for that shower that came on unexpectedly to decimate a day at the beach or a ballgame. However, a visit to one or more cold-weather cities during the final month of the season can serve to slow even the most prolific of passing offenses. Again, it's not a reason to pass over an individual player in and of itself, but if other questions remain regarding overall game strategy and offensive fluidity, it may be worth moving down a notch to the next option.

Managers typically only consider weather on game day for second and third receivers or if they've been relegated to lower-tier quarterbacks due to an injury to their starter.

The next chapter examines one of the true goldmines of the fantasy football world. The Denver Broncos have turned out running back stars year after year. Chapter 15 reviews this phenomenon and offers a look ahead to 2006.

15 The Denver Juggernaut: Fantasy Gold

- ♦ The System Works: A Decade of Brilliance
- ♦ The Names Change, But Performance Doesn't
- ♦ A Look Ahead

Ask any longtime fantasy football player what position is most important in the game, and you'll likely hear the words "running back" fly off the tongue. Occasionally, someone will make an argument for the quarterback or wide receiver, but running back is generally accepted as the king of the fantasy football universe.

Ask any longtime fantasy football player which backfield is the best in the game, and some may misinterpret the question and answer with the name of their favorite player. Tweaking the wording to say "most effective system" will bring a knowing smile and the name of the Denver Broncos.

THE SYSTEM WORKS:
A DECADE OF BRILLIANCE

The offensive system of the Denver Broncos ranks among the most advanced in the sport. Critics list the blocking schemes employed by Denver from chippy to dirty to everything in between. Regardless of their stance on the overall execution of the scheme, everyone from fans to opponents calls the system effective.

For fantasy football owners, there has been no more productive position over the past 11 years (Okay, QB for the Packers was productive until 2005). Mike Shanahan inherited a team that ranked 10th in scoring offense in 1994, but emphasized the arm of Hall of Fame QB John Elway. The team ranked 16th in rushing attempts, 23rd in rushing yardage, and called running plays only one-third of the time.

That all changed with the hiring of Shanahan. Since he assumed control of the whistle in Denver prior to the 1995 season, the primary ball carrier for the Broncos has amassed at least 1,000 rushing yards in every season but one. In 2005, they narrowly missed vaulting two players over that hallowed mark. Most amazing in this streak is that no player was selected higher than the second round of the NFL Draft.

As evidenced in Table 15.1, "A Decade of Brilliance a Mile High," Shanahan turned Denver's ground game into one of the most potent in the NFL. The team continues to score at a high rate (7.18 overall) with regular appearances in the top spots of both rushing attempts and yards. The key piece of evidence to the Denver dominance is the high percentage of rushing plays signaled in to the quarterback. The Broncos actually ran more rushing plays than passing plays in 2005.

Table 15.1. A Decade of Brilliance A Mile High

Year	Scoring Offense Rank	Rushing Attempts Rank	Rushing Yardage Rank	% of Rushing Plays
1995	9	16	5	36.06%
1996	4	2	1	45.96%
1997	1	6	4	47.38%
1998	2	2	2	48.31%
1999	18	9	12	42.46%
2000	2	4	2	44.59%
2001	10	6	10	44.27%
2002	7	11	5	41.85%
2003	10	2	2	49.74%
2004	9	2	4	46.84%
2005	7	2	2	50.97%
AVG RANK	7.18	5.64	4.45	45.31%

The Broncos consistently work to wear down their opponents through complicated blocking schemes and a steady dose of running plays. Sixty minutes of game action with offensive linemen tipping the scales over 290 pounds will wear opposing defensive players down. As such, the Denver running attack increases in efficiency as the game progresses, with running backs ripping off long runs.

THE NAMES CHANGE, BUT PERFORMANCE DOESN'T

The legend of the Denver backfield began in 1995 when sixth-round selection Terrell Davis joined Elway. He rumbled to over 1,100 yards in that rookie season with seven touchdowns, whetting the appetites of Broncos fans and fantasy owners for the three years that would follow. Davis increased his production in those next three seasons, peaking with a 2,000-yard, 21-touchdown campaign in 1998. Davis sustained an injury early in 1999 that limited him to just 67 carries. Not to worry, the Broncos had a fourth-round selection by the name of Olandis Gary ready to assume the reins.

Gary carried the ball 276 times for a respectable 4.2 yards-per-carry average and a total of 1,159 yards. His time as the feature back was short-lived, as an injury in Week 1 of the 2000 season sidelined him for the year. Rookie Mike Anderson, a sixth-round selection, took over for Gary and raced to 1,487 yards and 15 touchdowns to earn Offensive Rookie of the Year honors.

The 2001 season witnessed former fantasy hero Terrell Davis return to the starting role, but he was sidelined for half of the season after a 101-yard opener against the Giants. His injury promoted Anderson to the role of primary ball carrier with a handful of carries going to Gary. This split situation between Anderson, Gary, and Davis (when healthy) caused 2001 to be the lone year of the Shanahan era during which the Broncos did not field a 1,000-yard rusher. Anderson ran for 678 yards and Davis another 701.

The constant threat of injury and lack of cohesion in the Broncos offense prompted Denver brass to select former University of Miami Hurricanes standout Clinton Portis in the second round of the 2002 draft. His selection pushed the Denver attack to the forefront of television coverage and cemented its place in the fantasy football realm. Portis ran for 3,099 yards in two seasons with Denver, averaging 5.5 yards per carry and scoring 29 touchdowns. He bolted to join the Washington Redskins after the 2003 season.

Several backs attempted to assert themselves for the top spot vacated by Portis in training camp in 2004. Former 1,500-yard rusher Mike Anderson was in the mix, but a fourth-round selection from 2003, the diminutive Quentin Griffin emerged from the pack. He rushed for 156 yards and scored three touchdowns in a breakout performance before a nationwide television audience on Sunday night. Fantasy owners quickly rushed to the waiver wire to acquire his services. They were disappointed for several weeks by his play before a knee injury sidelined him for the year. A longtime fullback named Reuben Droughns got the opportunity to assume first chair. He raced to six 100-yard games in his first seven starts and finished the year with 1,240 rushing yards.

In the final weeks of 2004, Shanahan began to give carries to second-round selection Tatum Bell from Oklahoma State. He rushed for over 90 yards on two occasions and scored three touchdowns, whetting the appetite of fantasy owners for his eventual ascent to the feature role. However, former tailback-turned-fullback-turned-running back again Mike Anderson was still on the squad. Anderson won the top tailback spot in 2005, beating out Bell, Griffin and former Heisman winner Ron Dayne. Mike Shanahan drafted the much-maligned former Ohio State star Maurice Clarett in the third round of the 2005 draft in an attempt to prove his genius and power of the system. Clarett never posed a serious threat to those running backs already on the roster. The experiment failed, and Clarett was cut before training camp ended.

Anderson topped the 1,000-yard mark with a strong 4.24 yards-per-carry average. That didn't mean that Bell didn't receive his share of work. He totaled 173 carries and made the most of them, rushing for 921 yards and putting the exclamation mark on leagues in place of Anderson with a three-touchdown day in Week 17. Ron Dayne also got a chance to shine, rumbling for 98 yards on Thanksgiving Day. It was a banner year for the Denver system, as this trio of backs combined with minimal contributions from two others to go over 2,200 rushing yards for the season.

A LOOK AHEAD

Tatum Bell enters training camp as the lead back with the departure of Mike Anderson to Baltimore through free agency. Bell possesses a 5.3 yards-per-carry average with 11 career touchdowns. Ron Dayne was re-signed to play backup to Bell and offer aid in short yardage and goal-line situations. In early May mini-camps, Dayne received nearly an equal split of carries, so it is possible that Mike Shanahan runs some semblance of a workload shift as he did with Anderson and Bell in 2005. Cedric Cobbs (22 career carries), a former fourth-round selection in the 2004 draft, will also receive an extended look in camp.

Notice that in the yearly breakdown after Terrell Davis missed time starting in 1999, that more than one back has assumed the role to great success. That means committing a second draft pick to a Denver running back, perhaps even a third if your league allows for a larger roster. Play the system. The system works.

Knowing Shanahan, there will be some shifts in personnel to add depth to this position ahead of your fantasy draft. Be prepared to secure Ron Dayne as the handcuff to Bell at least two to three rounds earlier than you might otherwise. The proof is in the yardage and scoring records. The Broncos produce, plain and simple.

16 Over the Hill at 30?

- ♦ Walking Away
- ♦ Check the Mileage
- ♦ Over 30 in 2006

One of the most generally accepted rules of thumb on draft day is to avoid those running backs whose odometers have flipped and whose birthdays occurred more than 30 years and a day before the fantasy draft. While a player may turn in a highly productive year in a historically potent offense, longtime participants contend that the productivity of running backs drops off the proverbial cliff as soon as the candles on the 30th birthday cake are blown out.

Unlike their baseball counterparts who can reduce some of the wear and tear on their bodies by assuming the role of designated hitter, thereby extending their careers, running backs must still face opposing defenders on each play. The theory stands up on the surface just by applying a simple equation to the workload undertaken by running backs through their careers. Add the hundreds of carries taken during each high school and college season before they even set foot on an NFL field. The average starting tailback then carries the ball 230 to 260 times per season in the NFL, barring injury. If the player comes in as a starter from day one of his NFL career, you're figuring on a player who has absorbed upwards of 3,000 hits when carrying the ball. That figure doesn't include blocking assignments on passing plays, practices, or exhibition contests. Improvements in conditioning and treatment certainly help somewhat, but it's no wonder that a significant drop-off occurs.

WALKING AWAY

Several prominent running backs walked away from the game at the peak of their respective careers, and ahead of the age of 30, citing either the wear and tear of the games on their bodies, the loss of enthusiasm for the game, or conflict with team management as reasons. Two of these players have been enshrined in the Pro Football Hall of Fame, one considered medical school, and the fourth later returned to the field.

Former Cleveland Browns star Jim Brown often appears at the top of experts' lists as the greatest running back of all time. He left the game after an incredible season in the fall of 1965 at the age of 29 to pursue a more lucrative career in film. In his final season, Brown gained over 1,800 yards from scrimmage and scored 21 total touchdowns.

Barry Sanders won a Heisman Trophy at Oklahoma State before joining the Detroit Lions for what turned out to be a Hall of Fame career in 1989. He shocked the football world when he followed Brown's example and walked away from the Lions after the 1998 season. Sanders recently revealed in his autobiography that the pressure he felt about approaching Walter Payton's all-time rushing record during Payton's battle with a life-threatening illness and the constant turmoil over contracts and a mountain of losses in Detroit led to his early retirement. Sanders averaged over 300 carries per season for the Lions and topped 1,100 rushing yards in every season he played.

Robert Smith rushed to four consecutive 1,000-yard seasons to close out his eight years with the Minnesota Vikings. He was voted to his second Pro Bowl appearance after piling up over 1,800 combined rushing and receiving yards with 10 total touchdowns. Smith has been very forthcoming about the physical demands and the toll that absorbing so much punishment had taken on his body. He had four knee surgeries prior to his retirement.

The fourth player in the "early departure" category has had an interesting path the last three years. Ricky Williams returned to the Miami Dolphins for the 2005 season after walking away from the team on the eve of training camp before the 2004 season. He stated that his passion for the game had dissipated after years of being the featured back in the NFL and his record-setting NCAA career at the University of Texas.

Whether he truly regained a passion for the game or was simply trying to pay off a large signing bonus payment made before he walked away (estimated at $8 million), Williams took to the field for new coach Nick Saban. He served a four-game suspension caused by a previously failed drug test before he was able to hit the field. Williams rushed for 743 yards and six touchdowns in a split backfield with rookie running back Ronnie Brown. The 29-year-old Williams recently lost an appeal on a suspension over yet another substance violation, and he will be unable to play in 2006. Only time will tell whether this second one-year absence from the game serves to extend or cripple his playing career.

CHECK THE MILEAGE

Many of the game's great running backs witnessed their careers wind down in the conventional fashion, either through the acquisition of the heir apparent via the draft or simply not being able to take the field for a full year after another 250 carries. One very large consideration that doesn't show up on the stats sheets, and therefore gets overlooked, is the salary of older, accomplished running backs. Though NFL contracts are not guaranteed, signing bonuses, deferred compensation, and other considerations complicate the cost structure of building a roster. As a result, older free agent running backs need to accept a backup role to extend their careers as teams search for the "next great thing."

One example of recent years was how NFL rushing king Emmitt Smith ended his career. First, the Dallas Cowboys brought in young Troy Hambrick to assume the starting job and watched him fail in the role before he was ultimately released. Smith signed with the Arizona Cardinals, who were high on Marcel Shipp to be the top back. Shipp failed to stay healthy, and Smith found himself in the feature role in 2004. At the age of 35, Smith narrowly missed the 1,000-yard mark and finished 11th among running backs with nine touchdowns.

Smith joins Marcus Allen, Ottis Anderson, Tony Dorsett, and Walter Payton to form a select class of retired backs who made significant contributions in their 30s. A quick review of several of the NFL's top rushing performers demonstrates how quickly this drop in performance typically occurs.

Earl Campbell made a career out of running over tacklers instead of around them. Campbell compared very favorably with fellow Texas alum Ricky Williams in that he carried the ball a ridiculous number of times in college. At the age of 30, Campbell rushed for 643 yards and a touchdown as a member of the New Orleans Saints in 1985. Most football fans familiar with the era would recognize Campbell only in his college uniform or as a member of the Houston Oilers. Even the most vociferous supporters of the NFL would be hard-pressed to recall Campbell's appearance in a Saints uniform.

Eric Dickerson played for three different teams in his final three seasons in the NFL. He piled up 2,450 carries ahead of the age of 30, reaching 400 carries in one season and approaching that mark in three others. In three partial seasons after he turned 30, Dickerson gained only 15 percent of his career yardage total and 10 percent of his career touchdowns.

If you mention the name Franco Harris, the image of the "Immaculate Reception" fills the minds of most football fans. If the play doesn't come immediately to mind, then the connection of Harris to the Pittsburgh Steelers certainly does. Harris saw his durability and yards per carry drop after the age of 30. Though he gained nearly 30 percent of his total yardage after the age of 30, his touchdown production dropped from the double-digit norm of his prime. He battled to 1,000 yards in his final season in Pittsburgh before appearing in eight games for the Seattle Seahawks in 1984. He gained only 170 yards.

Former Buffalo Bills standout Thurman Thomas helped the Bills to four Super Bowl appearances. Thomas averaged 285 carries and 46 catches per season through his first eight seasons. He topped 1,000 rushing yards with eight touchdowns at the age of 30, but watched his production drop markedly thereafter. From 1997-2000, Thomas battled injuries to amass only 1,312 yards and six total touchdowns. He had topped those marks in three consecutive single seasons in his prime.

The list of players can be expanded by reviewing the careers of players such as O.J. Simpson and Terrell Davis and countless others, but you get the picture. The combination of hits, schemes, and the ever-present pressure to win conspire to push forward the next generation of backs.

OVER 30 IN 2006

In 2006, there are several top draft options who have reached the proverbial fourth quarter of their respective careers. Their teams will be auditioning potential replacements or looking to shift the bulk of the workload to younger backs while relying on the experience of the veterans in big situations. Here is a quick peek at the backs over 30 on the board heading into 2006.

Corey Dillon rushed for 733 yards and 12 touchdowns in 11 games at 31 years of age for the Patriots in 2005. The time lost due to injury, combined with his birth certificate, will have owners shying away on draft day despite the large

TD total. The Patriots drafted Laurence Maroney in the first round of the 2006 draft as insurance for Dillon. He'll compete for carries early in the season and will ultimately become the Patriots' feature back. The Patriots will likely bring in another back to battle for the second role, as backup Kevin Faulk has battled injury issues of his own.

Curtis Martin of the Jets won his first rushing title in 2004 at the age of 31. He staved off the competition from LaMont Jordan, who ultimately moved on to become the feature back in Oakland. Unfortunately for the Jets, problems on the offense line, at QB, and Martin's own health curtailed his success in 2005. He gained 735 yards with five touchdowns and missed four games in their entirety and portions of several others. The Jets signed Derrick Blaylock to back up Martin, but he sustained a season-ending injury of his own. Cedric Houston, a sixth-round draft pick in 2005, showed promise in sporadic playing time, but he was injured in a car accident in April. This backfield is one to watch as training camp unfolds.

After winning the Super Bowl, Jerome Bettis of the Steelers retired. Young Willie Parker is the feature back entering 2006, but Bettis's role of goal-line back may be filled by former starter Duce Staley. Staley appeared in only five games during 2005 due to a tear in his right knee. He racked up 830 rushing yards in 2004, only to score one TD while watching Bettis score 12.

New Rams coach Scott Linehan expects former fantasy hero Marshall Faulk to return to the team in 2006. Faulk will serve as the backup to third-year starter Steven Jackson, but he still possesses superior pass receiving skills. Faulk caught 44 passes for the Rams last season.

Tiki Barber of the Giants dismissed any notion of a 30-year-old jinx by turning in his finest professional season yet. He tallied 2,390 yards of offense with 11 touchdowns and appeared in all 16 games for the fourth consecutive season. Second-year player Brandon Jacobs may pilfer some third-down and goal-line carries, but Barber's overall workload and production are safe. His 357 carries in 2005 marked a career high.

Longtime fantasy star Priest Holmes of Kansas City started out with a bang, as always, scoring seven touchdowns in seven games before missing the remainder of the year with a neck injury. The Chiefs expect the 32-year-old Holmes back in 2006, but he will serve the backup role formerly occupied by Larry Johnson, who set the league aflame when he ascended to the top role. Holmes has played in 15 of 32 games in the last two seasons.

The man tagged with the nickname of "Fragile," Fred Taylor, joined this club in January of 2006. His string of three consecutive seasons of 1,200 or more rushing yards ended with an 11-game performance in 2005. Taylor ran for 787 yards and three touchdowns and battled ankle issues all season. The Jaguars will work in young backs Greg Jones and LaBrandon Toefield to reduce Taylor's workload and keep him on the field.

Don't merely look at the date of birth. Look deeper to review a player's workload, injury history, and the makeup of the team around him. If the player has been successful and injury-free in a functional system for years, there's no reason to assume that it will suddenly cease.

As you head into draft day, do not immediately pass over a more experienced back in favor of the next great thing. After all, the performances of most players fail to reach the advanced print. If you follow conventional draft logic, you'll acquire two or more starting running backs to protect your starters. However, make sure you protect your investment with the backup or another suitable option. If a veteran's team falters early, management may press to see immediate dividends from the high-priced rookie.

17 The Legend of the Third-Year Receiver

- ♦ The Foundation of the Theory
- ♦ Strict Versus Loose Interpretations
- ♦ Historical Instances 2001-2005
- ♦ Breakout Candidates for 2006

Fantasy football owners are always looking for that one piece of magical information or set of data that will unlock the secrets of the game and send them vaulting to the top of the standings. As such, some theories espoused by fantasy football writers are taken as gospel. One of the most prevalent theories relating to draft strategy in recent years is the notion that wide receivers reach maturity and a new level of performance as they enter their third year in the league.

THE FOUNDATION OF THE THEORY

The general feeling among coaches, scouts, and NFL observers is that it takes two full cycles of workouts, training camps, and games to become fully comfortable within a system. The playbooks and rules and responsibilities of the NFL, both on and off the field, are a much different world than the college experience. Players leave the comfort of college and the "big man on campus" effect for life among experienced professionals.

It takes time to establish a rapport with the team's quarterback and their fellow receivers. More significant is the adjustment to the variety of defensive coverages and schemes to which they will be exposed. This learning curve is accelerated for those players who ascend to a starting role upon hearing their names announced from the podium at the NFL Draft. But that isn't to say that it's necessarily a slam dunk, to mix sports for a moment, that receivers selected in the first round of drafts go on to NFL stardom. A number of factors, including injuries, competition on the team, work ethic, and the relationships forged with teammates and coaches are just several of the factors that can delay one's development.

STRICT VERSUS LOOSE INTERPRETATIONS

There are two schools of thought as to how to apply this theory. The strict interpretation considers players who are only in their third season removed from college. While this puts players on equal footing with regard to their "experience," it fails to account for a considerable number of variables as outlined previously.

The proliferation of free agent movement, coaching turnover, and the reliance on mistake-free football are two other factors that warrant consideration. Younger wide receivers are usually brought along slowly to learn the offensive system and to work toward running precise routes. The most important statistic toward determining wins and losses remains the turnover battle. The team that turns the ball over fewer times wins the game 81 percent of the time. With a number like that staring NFL coaches in the face, players do not see the field until they're really ready. Therefore, the third-year receiver theory needs to be broadened to incorporate a wider range of players.

Trying to set the bar as to what truly constitutes a "breakout" season is difficult when you consider the wide range of scoring and roster configuration options available to leagues. For instance, if a league uses the category of receptions, a player who assumes the role of possession receiver can rack up a large reception total without accruing a large receiving yard total or scoring touchdowns. If the receptions category is omitted from the scoring configuration, then a wide receiver must be more productive in terms of yards and a touchdown threat to warrant fantasy consideration.

One of the best leading indicators of a wide receiver's breakout potential is how he finished the prior season. If the player became an integral part of a team's offense in the latter half of the prior campaign, then he stands to retain at least that place in the pass distribution. Oftentimes, off-season activity by a team will be predicated on its expectations for that player to make the next step forward. Examples of players who fit this profile for 2006 are Reggie Brown of the Philadelphia Eagles and Samie Parker of the Chiefs. Both flourished in expanded roles as the season progressed and figure to be frequent targets of their quarterbacks this season.

To use an example of how off-season movement and decisions can impact one's fantasy stock, I turn to the situation that developed in May for the Jacksonville Jaguars. After months of deliberation, longtime fantasy star and Pro Bowl receiver Jimmy Smith decided to retire. As a result, a trio of young wide receivers will contend for the numerous passes that were thrown to Smith on a weekly basis in 2006. The training camp progress of Matt Jones, Ernest Wilford, and Reggie Williams should be monitored closely this summer, as one or more of these players will elevate their games.

Historical Instances: 2001-2005

The following table isolates performers from each of the past four seasons whose performance levels increased over their previous contributions to make them fantasy football standouts. In several instances, the statistics from the player's previous season were already somewhat impressive. Those players are included in this discussion because their roles evolved in the subsequent season. As such, their receptions, receiving yards, and touchdowns advanced in some combination. Ultimately, this advancement made them more dependable and consistent targets during the season, and automatic fantasy football starters.

Table 17.1. Third-year breakout performers 2001-2005

Third-Year Breakout Performers 2001-2005			
Year	Player	Previous Season Stats	Breakout Stats
2001	David Boston	71 Receptions, 1,156 Receiving Yards, 7 Touchdowns	98 Receptions, 1,598 Receiving Yards, 8 Touchdowns
2001	Peerless Price	52 Receptions, 762 Receiving Yards, 3 Touchdowns	55 Receptions, 895 Receiving Yards, 7 Touchdowns
2001	Marty Booker	47 Receptions, 490 Receiving Yards, 2 Touchdowns	100 Receptions, 1,071 Receiving Yards, 8 Touchdowns
2002	Laveranues Coles	59 Receptions, 868 Receiving Yards, 7 Touchdowns	89 Receptions, 1,264 Receiving Yards, 5 Touchdowns
2002	Jerry Porter	19 Receptions, 220 Receiving Yards, Zero Touchdowns	51 Receptions, 688 Receiving Yards, 9 Touchdowns
2002	Plaxico Burress	66 Receptions, 1,008 Receiving Yards, 6 Touchdowns	78 Receptions, 1,325 Receiving Yards, 7 Touchdowns
2003	Chad Johnson	69 Receptions, 1,166 Receiving Yards, 5 Touchdowns	90 Receptions, 1,355 Receiving Yards, 10 Touchdowns
2003	Santana Moss	30 Receptions, 433 Receiving Yards, 4 Touchdowns	74 Receptions, 1,105 Receiving Yards, 10 Touchdowns
2003	Chris Chambers	52 Receptions, 734 Receiving Yards, 3 Touchdowns	64 Receptions, 963 Receiving Yards, 11 Touchdowns
2004	Javon Walker	41 Receptions, 716 Receiving Yards, 9 Touchdowns	89 Receptions, 1,382 Receiving Yards, 12 Touchdowns
2004	Ashley Lelie	35 Receptions, 525 Receiving Yards, 2 Touchdowns	54 Receptions, 1,084 Receiving Yards, 7 Touchdowns
2004	Ronald Curry	5 Receptions, 31 Receiving Yards, Zero Touchdowns	50 Receptions, 679 Receiving Yards, 6 Touchdowns
2005	Donte' Stallworth	58 Receptions, 767 Receiving Yards, 5 Touchdowns	70 Receptions, 945 Receiving Yards, 7 Touchdowns
2005	Joe Jurevicius	27 Receptions, 333 Receiving Yards, 2 Touchdowns	55 Receptions, 694 Receiving Yards, 10 Touchdowns

BREAKOUT CANDIDATES FOR 2006

I would be remiss if I failed to look into the crystal ball for 2006 to project players who will serve as future examples in validation of the third year receiver theory. Each of the players represented in the table below has seen his fantasy

Table 17.2. Breakout candidates for 2006

	Breakout Candidates for 2006			
	Player	Years Pro	2005 Final Stats	Expected 2006 Role
1	Ernest Wilford	2	41 Receptions, 681 Receiving Yds, 7 TDs	Battle for #1 Receiver
2	Reggie Brown	1	43 Receptions, 571 Receiving Yds, 4 TDs	#1 Receiver
3	Eric Parker	4	57 Receptions, 725 Receiving Yds, 3 TDs	#2 Receiver
4	Mark Clayton	1	44 Receptions, 471 Receiving Yds, 2 TDs	#2 Receiver
5	Reggie Williams	2	35 Receptions, 445 Receiving Yds, 0 TDs	Battle for #2 Receiver
6	Brandon Lloyd	3	48 Receptions, 733 Receiving Yds, 5 TDs	#2 Receiver
7	Samie Parker	2	36 Receptions, 533 Receiving Yds, 3 TDs	#2 Receiver
8	Michael Jenkins	2	36 Receptions, 508 Receiving Yds, 3 TDs	#1 Receiver
9	Braylon Edwards	1	32 Receptions, 512 Receiving Yds, 3 TDs	#1 Receiver
10	Kevin Curtis	3	60 Receptions, 801 Receiving Yds, 6 TDs	Either #2 or #3 Receiver

fortunes improved by one or more factors this off-season. Reggie Brown welcomes back All-Pro QB Donovan McNabb under center. Eric Parker elevated his game in the second half and showed great presence in the red zone. Brandon Lloyd changed coasts to a more potent offensive scheme. And so on.

The key to determining a breakout star is finding that glorious point in time when talent and opportunity meet.

The next chapter examines one of the most prevalent draft strategies regarding running backs and quarterbacks within prolific offenses. The term handcuffing typically draws a snicker when first mentioned, but brings rejoicing when a fantasy football participant has properly prepared for the inevitable injuries and performance issues that conspire to thwart one's championship dreams.

18 Find a Buddy: The Need for Handcuffing

- ♦ Injury Histories
- ♦ Tenuous Holds
- ♦ Breaking the Cuffs

The mention of the term "handcuffing" likely draws a snicker or blank stare from a person examining fantasy football for the first time. It's not a reference to *Cops* where hilarity ensues each and every time that the arresting officer attempts to apprehend a suspect.

Rather, the act of handcuffing means to acquire a player and his most likely backup to ensure one's self against injury or a demotion. Typically, these selections require a participant to use a draft pick on a backup one or two rounds earlier than normal to prevent an opponent from breaking the link. These selections apply almost exclusively to the quarterback and running back positions.

This portion of draft strategy requires participants to consider three different scenarios by which the application of the handcuff or prevention of its application might be beneficial. The following sections examine the use of this process to prepare for injury, position battles, and to block the opposition with specific instances for 2006 fantasy drafts.

Injury Histories

As fantasy draft day approaches, there will undoubtedly be a number of players highlighted on local news reports and fantasy Web sites whose availability has been called into question due to a pulled muscle, twinge in the throwing shoulder, or tweaked ankle during training camp practices or exhibition games. There are others whose past injuries cloud the expectations for the coming year.

For instance, Fred Taylor of the Jacksonville Jaguars missed 23 games from 1999-2001 due to a variety of ailments, forever earning him the tag of "Fragile" Freddy. Even though Taylor played in all of Jacksonville's games in 2002 and 2003, he could not shake the moniker. Taylor has since missed seven games over two years and watched his TD scoring opportunities dwindle. In each of the last several seasons, Taylor has been among the last of the feature backs taken due to his propensity to become injured. He stands as one of the top backs for whom the handcuffing strategy is a must. Last season, Greg Jones rushed for 70 or more yards in four different contests in Taylor's absence.

The need to be mindful of handcuffing has been demonstrated most famously in the high-powered offenses in St. Louis and Kansas City.

- In 1999, a preseason injury to then-Rams QB Trent Green paved the way for Kurt Warner to get his shot and ultimately win the league MVP with 41 TD passes.

- Warner experienced the same issue in 2003. He was battered and bruised in two appearances before being knocked out of a game. Marc Bulger took the reins and never looked back.

- Priest Holmes owners who failed to secure the rights to Larry Johnson in 2005 watched him rip off 1,750 rushing yards and 20 touchdowns in one half of a season. When Holmes was injured at midseason and did not return, those owners who had secured Johnson certainly felt no ill effects.

Entering 2006, several running backs are making their returns from serious injuries. Their progress should be monitored through training camp, as slow starts may force the integration of new backfield options. Additionally, those running backs reaching their 30s (as discussed in Chapter 16) should also be considered for handcuffing, regardless of the expectations of their team's offense as a whole.

Curtis Martin of the Jets struggled through 12 games in 2005 before finally being shut down with an ankle injury. Martin averaged a mere 3.3 yards per carry while playing through injury. It's unlikely that Martin returns to his 2004 form during which he raced to the rushing title, but he's also a player who hadn't missed a game since 1998. With that said, owners who select Martin will need to look in the direction of Cedric Houston for their bench. Houston ran well for the Jets down the stretch in '05 with two games over 70 yards rushing in the final four.

After several years of sheer brilliance, Ahman Green failed to top 60 rushing yards in five games before being shut down for the year. Green had scored 28 touchdowns in the two seasons prior, and his loss, combined with that of Javon Walker, sent the Green Bay offense into a downward spiral. In addition to bringing Green back this off-season, the Packers also have Najeh Davenport and 2005 rookie sensation Samkon Gado at the ready. Owners will need to determine how many roster spots they're willing to commit to the Green Bay backfield.

Corey Dillon of the Patriots scored 13 touchdowns last season despite missing four games in their entirety and suiting up, but not playing, in a fifth. Dillon offers a more complex option based on the cloud of secrecy hanging over the New England injury report. They'll acknowledge an injury, but not the severity. As such, many owners were left holding the bag in Week 10 when Dillon suited up against Miami and then sat on the sidelines the whole game. That move cost many a fantasy owner a zero in a starting RB slot. In any event, the Patriots added rookie Laurence Maroney in the draft to set the position for the future.

As mentioned before, Priest Holmes owners in 2005 who didn't secure Larry Johnson in the draft kicked themselves all off-season. The situation is reversed this season if Holmes should return to the game after sustaining a severe neck injury last year. Johnson will be the incumbent and workhorse in Herman Edwards' system, with Holmes providing a change of pace.

Julius Jones has been electrifying at times for the Cowboys, but he's also been cause for concern so far as injuries are concerned. He's missed 11 games in their entirety and parts of several others with various ailments. Though Jones could be huge in the rebuilt Dallas offense, he may not be able to carry a heavy workload. That opens opportunities for second-year man Marion Barber III, who shone in his absence.

The Cardinals drafted Matt Leinart this year with the idea of grooming him behind Kurt Warner for a full season. However, Warner has missed at least a handful of games in each of the past few years. Though one normally benefits from pinning fantasy hopes on a rookie QB, the arsenal of offensive weapons assembled in Arizona may make Leinart a productive fantasy player immediately.

I've already mentioned Fred Taylor, who might be on the move as camps unfold. The Jaguars were pleased with the efforts of Greg Jones, but also added Maurice Drew from UCLA in this year's draft. Drew stands as the likely successor to Taylor, with Jones offering a bruising presence and goal-line threat.

TENUOUS HOLDS

The second use of the handcuffing strategy is to secure the backup for runners or QBs who enter training camp with a tenuous hold on the starting job through some combination of age, injury, and performance. These position battles are frustrating for fantasy owners, particularly those in leagues whose drafts occur before the dust settles.

Remember that running backs thrust into a starting position are more likely to produce numbers to rival the starters than their QB counterparts.

This summer, fantasy owners will need to monitor several running back and QB situations. The pressure in the NFL is to "win now," meaning that underachieving players at all positions are under the microscope.

Kevan Barlow and Frank Gore will begin camp in a competition for the starting job. Barlow has failed to take advantage of efforts to install him as the starter, watching his rushing average dip to 3.3 yards per carry. Gore ran well down the stretch in 2005, busting off several longer runs and demonstrating toughness between the tackles.

For the time being, Chris Brown and Travis Henry will both occupy the Tennessee backfield, with rookie LenDale White expected to challenge for playing time as well. Brown has shown good power and speed since entering the league, but his upright running style leaves him continually injured. Brown retains the top spot entering the year, but his propensity for getting injured leaves the door open for Henry to pilfer additional carries.

Thomas Jones of the Chicago Bears had the finest year of his career after the Bears drafted Cedric Benson to compete for the job. Benson failed to sign his contract in time to gain any extensive work on the practice field and didn't factor much into Chicago's 2005 season. However, the team plans to integrate Benson more prevalently in the offense this season.

The movement of Drew Brees to New Orleans opens the door for Philip Rivers to start in San Diego. He has great weapons in LaDainian Tomlinson and Antonio Gates and an emerging star in Eric Parker, but in the event that he struggles early, the Chargers added veteran A.J. Feeley. Rivers will be a starter only in those leagues using two active quarterbacks, but those owners using a pick on Rivers as a sleeper will need to secure the rights to Feeley as well.

Alex Smith struggled in the starting role as a rookie in San Francisco. He threw only one touchdown pass against 11 interceptions. The 49ers made significant upgrades to the offense in the draft and added Antonio Bryant (1,000 yards in 2005) to the receiving corps. In the event that Smith's progress is slower than expected, the 49ers made a deal to bring in former Super Bowl winner Trent Dilfer as his backup.

In one of the more intriguing training camp battles, the Lions brought in both Jon Kitna from Cincinnati and Josh McCown from Arizona to take the place of the underachieving Joey Harrington. Kitna was a bona fide star with the Bengals in 2003 (3,591 yards and 26 touchdowns) while Cincinnati waited for Carson Palmer to develop. Josh McCown also shone in moments for the Cardinals but wasn't consistent in the role. With the strength of the skill position players in Detroit, whoever is under center has the ability to become a fantasy star.

BREAKING THE CUFFS

Often you'll hear the quote "the best defense is a good offense." In this use of the handcuffing strategy, owners help themselves by defending against another owner's monopoly of a good offense. In the past, this strategy has been particularly effective when applied to the Denver backfield (see Chapter 15), the high-flying St. Louis offense as described earlier, and the big steal last season when owners found a draft-day bargain in Larry Johnson of the Kansas City Chiefs.

The use of the handcuffing strategy does carry some risk to it, as it forces participants to reach a little sooner for a player who will not immediately help their championship dreams. As a result, they'll need to forego depth short-term.

There are going to be times when that handcuffed player never sees the field. Perhaps the player for whom the handcuff was secured performs to his highest level and more importantly, avoids injury. However it plays out, the participant breathes easier with that handcuffed player on their bench for the duration of the year. It's a much easier situation than scrambling to the waiver wire after losing a back to injury and watching the natural handcuff dominate for another team.

In the next chapter, we'll examine one of the more frustrating scenarios in fantasy football: the dreaded platoon situation in NFL backfields.

19 The Problem with Platoons

- Multiple Backs on the Radar
- Uncertainty
- The Vulture Effect

Fantasy owners have enough to worry about with the fact that every hit on the field could result in a twisted ankle or worse. They don't need the coach playing games in the backfield to rob their starter of important goal-line opportunities.

In this chapter, I examine the current state of backfields employing two or more running backs as the 2006 season approaches. Fantasy owners can trust that LaDainian Tomlinson, Larry Johnson, Edgerrin James, and a handful of other running backs will shoulder a heavy workload and make major contributions to the fantasy bottom line. However, there are several teams where multiple backs figure to have more than one back in play, several others where the workload is yet to be determined, and others who employ specialists around the goal line.

MULTIPLE BACKS ON THE RADAR

The worst of all situations occurs when multiple backs are set to share time in the backfield with no clear-cut decision as to how backs will be used in the all-important goal-line situations.

Jeff Fisher had two strong running backs in Travis Henry and Chris Brown before the 2006 NFL Draft. He then added USC bulldozer LenDale White. On the surface, it would appear that Henry and Brown will continue to split time between the 20s and that White assumes the goal-line back duty, but he's also a strong runner between the tackles, so he'll likely make this a three-headed monster for fantasy owners to be wary of.

The Broncos have long been a fantasy juggernaut (see Chapter 15), and this year's team features young star Tatum Bell and the resurgent Ron Dayne. Mike Shanahan likes to employ a two-back system, and he was impressed by Dayne's rededication to the game last season. He'll take the inside runs once owned by Mike Anderson, with Bell remaining the slasher on the outside.

Frank Gore made the most of his audition for the top spot in San Francisco last year, but the continued presence of former 1,000-yard running back Kevan Barlow on the roster leads one to believe that a split workload is in the offing in 2006. There is a chance that Barlow is cut ahead of training camp due to his large contract and decreasing productivity (his rushing average dropped by one yard per carry from 2004). If he is released, then the 49ers will proceed with Gore and speedy Maurice Hicks, who averaged 5.2 yards per carry in 2005, as the primary ball carriers. Only time will tell.

Fantasy owners won't have to contend with the fickle nature of Mike Tice in assigning running back duties in Minnesota this year. However, there are still several strong backs on the roster. New addition Chester Taylor stands to be the workhorse, but Mewelde Moore and second-year back Ciatrick Fason (who excelled in short-yardage situations) remain on the roster.

Brian Westbrook rarely exceeds 20 touches in a game, meaning that backups Ryan Moats and Correll Buckhalter (if healthy) will factor into the game plan. Buckhalter displayed great power and agility in the past, and Moats set the fantasy world on fire with a number of scintillating long runs down the stretch.

The Baltimore Ravens re-signed Jamal Lewis and brought in Mike Anderson from the Broncos. Lewis was hampered by a sore ankle last year and ran tentatively ahead of his free agent period. Anderson runs hard between the tackles and would just as soon run over opposing defenders as run around them. I suspect that a workload split is in the offing to keep Lewis fresh down the stretch

Chicago's Thomas Jones took advantage of Cedric Benson's failure to get into camp on time and ran to a career year. However, as the season progressed, Benson improved dramatically in practice and showed great quickness and vision when given the opportunity to play late in the year. Lovie Smith wants to install a ball-control offense to keep his attacking defense fresh, and the utilization of both backs seems a sure-fire solution. One thing to watch is Jones' attitude during camp. He was clearly perturbed with all the trade rumors ahead of the NFL Draft and still considers the job his. There's an outside chance that he is actually moved prior to the year.

In addition to these situations where a workload split is almost a certainty, there are several teams that currently have two or more viable backs on the roster and whose roles are clouded.

UNCERTAINTY

Entering spring mini-camps, several teams face uncertainty as to the availability of past fantasy superstars and have added fresh talent through the draft. These selections suggest a change in workload for these longtime fantasy producers, if not an outright loss of their roles.

In Jacksonville, the much-maligned and oft-injured Fred Taylor appeared at mini-camp in shape and ready to take on a heavy workload. Longtime fantasy players have become accustomed to resurgences by Taylor on an annual basis. While he's still a highly productive back when healthy, the Jaguars have selected a running back early in the draft each of the last three years in anticipation of his departure of more severe injury. There's a chance that Taylor will be released this summer, which would force Greg Jones and rookie Maurice Drew into a battle for the starting job. Any selection of Fred Taylor should be backed up with a handcuff pick of Greg Jones later in the draft.

The Jets lost both Curtis Martin and Derrick Blaylock to season-ending injuries in 2005. Rookie Cedric Houston ran well in their absence, but it appears to be a three-back committee situation in 2006 for new coach Eric Mangini. The Jets don't want to expose the veteran Martin to the heavy workload he's experienced in the past, and Houston and

Blaylock offer solid power running game and receiving skills, respectively.

Carolina retained DeShaun Foster as their top back by re-signing him to a huge free agent deal. However, concerns about his health forced them to draft another running back this year in the form of speedy DeAngelo Williams. Lest we forget, the Panthers also drafted Eric Shelton last season. He lost his entire rookie year to a foot injury.

Finally, the free agent signing of Edgerrin James by Arizona opened the starting tailback job in Indianapolis. Dominic Rhodes is a past 1,000-yard rusher and has played in the system for years. However, Joseph Addai appears ready to make his case for playing time immediately. The expected battle through training camp will likely devalue both players on draft day. Use this to your advantage, as the winner will undoubtedly pile up numbers in this offense.

THE VULTURE EFFECT

A number of coaches have traditionally utilized a running back in the role commonly referred to as a "vulture." While the name isn't terribly flattering, it is appropriate. These players typically watch other running backs traverse up and down the field, only to enter the game to push the line in short yardage and goal-line situations.

Perhaps the most famous example of this situation occurred with former Pittsburgh Steelers great Jerome Bettis in Week 1 of 2004. Duce Staley helped move the Steelers offense down the field all day and watched Bettis turn in a stat line even he chuckled about when I had the opportunity to speak with him before the '05 campaign. Bettis carried the ball five times that day for one yard and three touchdowns. Managers who were beaten in this fashion on opening weekend were most definitely dejected.

There are several teams who employ this strategy, so be sure to factor these players into your strategy on draft day.

Though Bettis has exited the scene, Pittsburgh still figures to fill this role in 2006 with Duce Staley or Verron Haynes. Willie Parker will be the workhorse back, but will be spared the goal-line pounding in favor of one of these backs.

Warrick Dunn continues to log the majority of carries in Atlanta, but gives way in close to bruising tailback T.J. Duckett. Duckett also sees action in between the 20s, but excels in short-yardage situations. There was some speculation that Duckett would be dealt ahead of training camp. Keep an eye on this situation as camp opens in late-July. If Duckett were to depart, it would potentially open goal line opportunities for rookie Jarious Norwood, fullback Justin Griffith or for Dunn to finish his own dirty work.

Jon Gruden no longer gives Mike Alstott a heavy workload in Tampa Bay, but he does offer prime glory chances. Alstott scored six rushing touchdowns in only 34 carries last year.

The Jacksonville situation was profiled above as one where multiple backs stand to see playing time and touches. If veteran Fred Taylor stays in Jacksonville, it is likely that any goal line carries will be handled by the powerful Greg Jones.

LaMont Jordan was afforded the opportunity to finish drives last season, but he started to break down toward the end of the year after a heavy workload all year. Therefore, look for new coach Art Shell to get Zack Crockett more involved this year to keep Jordan fresh. Crockett has scored once every 13 touches during his career.

The Giants used rookie Brandon Jacobs as a battering ram near the goal line and in short-yardage situations to great success last year. He scored seven touchdowns in only 38 carries and only fumbled once despite operating in such close quarters. Look for much the same role as the Giants seek to keep Tiki Barber healthy and fresh for a run deep into the playoffs.

Perhaps the best stat total of the entire football season belonged to Washington Redskins fullback Mike Sellers. Sellers touched the ball only 14 times last year and scored eight touchdowns (seven receiving). His presence, as well as that of TE/RB Chris Cooley, serves to devalue skill players Santana Moss and Clinton Portis to some degree.

The need to win now forces coaches to rotate lineups and make play-calling decisions that serve to frustrate and annoy not only fantasy owners but also the hometown faithful. Be sure to secure the rights to at least one back who is sure to handle a heavy workload.

In Chapter 20, I don the thinking caps of all 12 teams to produce the always-entertaining one-man mock draft.

20 This Man's Mock Draft

Over the past several years, I've engaged in a somewhat unorthodox way of preparing myself for the approaching fantasy football drafts against friends, family, and colleagues. I pull back from the hours of research, writings, and ramblings to take a snapshot of the fantasy football landscape at a given point in time to create a one-man mock draft.

One of the first reasons to perform this exercise is to familiarize yourself with those players deep at the running back and wide receiver positions that become draft-day gold in the later rounds. Doing this type of analysis early in the preseason (in the first mini-camp in my case) is to take note of the early rises and falls on depth charts.

The second purpose of the exercise is to get acquainted with the areas of the draft during which the historical runs and drop-off points at each position will occur. Based on my early analysis for 2006, the early string of running backs lasts into the second round before a mix of wide receivers and Peyton Manning came onto the board.

As you complete this exercise, remember that once you hit the point of committee situations or uncertainty of which player on a team will shoulder the load, it's time to consider an alternate position where performance is somewhat more assured.

Another reason to complete this exercise is that it allows you to get into the mind-set of selecting at each position on the draft board without participating in a dozen drafts. At each position, you have to pause and take stock of those players selected previously and take stock of team and position needs.

I offer this sheet, which begins on the next page, as an example of the approach and an early look at the draft board as I see it playing out. It's intended to be a reference guide as you work through your cheatsheets and further evaluate player values.

This board will be updated as training camp swings into full gear in late-July on our Web site at:

http://savvyfantasysports.com.

Round	Team 1			Team 2		
1	Shaun Alexander	RB	SEA	Larry Johnson	RB	KAN
2	Warrick Dunn	RB	ATL	Peyton Manning	QB	IND
3	DeShaun Foster	RB	CAR	Antonio Gates	TE	SD
4	Terry Glenn	WR	DAL	Andre Johnson	WR	HOU
5	Jeremy Shockey	TE	NYG	Joseph Addai	RB	IND
6	Drew Bledsoe	QB	DAL	Lee Evans	WR	BUF
7	Keyshawn Johnson	WR	CAR	Isaac Bruce	WR	STL
8	T.J. Duckett	RB	ATL	Chris Brown	RB	TEN
9	Jason Witten	TE	DAL	Cedric Benson	RB	CHI
10	Brett Favre	QB	GB	Braylon Edwards	WR	CLE
11	Mark Clayton	WR	BAL	Chicago Bears	DEF	CHI
12	Pittsburgh Steelers	DEF	PIT	Chris Simms	QB	TB
13	Brandon Jacobs	RB	NYG	Neil Rackers	K	ARI
14	Troy Williamson	WR	MIN	Ryan Moats	RB	PHI
15	Josh Brown	K	SEA	Reche Caldwell	WR	NE
16	Brandon Stokley	WR	IND	Jeb Putzier	TE	HOU
Round	**Team 3**			**Team 4**		
1	LaDainian Tomlinson	RB	SD	Tiki Barber	RB	NYG
2	Chester Taylor	RB	MIN	Torry Holt	WR	STL
3	Larry Fitzgerald	WR	ARI	Marvin Harrison	WR	IND
4	Roy Williams	WR	DET	Fred Taylor	RB	JAC
5	Tony Gonzalez	TE	KAN	Deuce McAllister	RB	NO
6	Dominic Rhodes	RB	IND	Matt Hasselbeck	QB	SEA
7	Kevin Curtis	WR	STL	Alge Crumpler	TE	ATL
8	Reggie Brown	WR	PHI	Laveranues Coles	WR	NYJ
9	DeAngelo Williams	RB	CAR	Frank Gore	RB	SF
10	Ben Roethlisberger	QB	PIT	Jake Plummer	QB	DEN
11	Byron Leftwich	QB	JAC	Michael Clayton	WR	TB
12	Jerramy Stevens	TE	SEA	Kevan Barlow	RB	SF
13	Michael Jenkins	WR	ATL	Ben Watson	TE	NE
14	Jason Elam	K	DEN	Cincinnati Bengals	DEF	CIN
15	Atlanta Falcons	DEF	ATL	Jay Feely	K	NYG
16	Mewelde Moore	RB	MIN	Jabar Gaffney	WR	PHI

Round	Team 5			Team 6		
1	Clinton Portis	RB	WAS	LaMont Jordan	RB	OAK
2	Reuben Droughns	RB	CLE	Steve Smith	WR	CAR
3	Willie Parker	RB	PIT	Anquan Boldin	WR	ARI
4	Joey Galloway	WR	TB	Jamal Lewis	RB	BAL
5	Kurt Warner	QB	ARI	Tom Brady	QB	NE
6	Donovan McNabb	QB	PHI	Randy McMichael	TE	MIA
7	Chris Cooley	TE	WAS	Samkon Gado	RB	GB
8	Keenan McCardell	WR	SD	Koren Robinson	WR	MIN
9	Antonio Bryant	WR	SF	LenDale White	RB	TEN
10	Michael Vick	QB	ATL	Kellen Winslow Jr.	TE	CLE
11	Indianapolis Colts	DEF	IND	Reggie Williams	WR	JAC
12	David Givens	WR	TEN	New York Giants	DEF	NYG
13	Mike Vanderjagt	K	DAL	Jon Kitna	QB	DET
14	Michael Pittman	RB	TB	Jeff Wilkins	K	STL
15	Marcedes Lewis	TE	JAC	Samie Parker	WR	KAN
16	Peerless Price	WR	BUF	Antowain Smith	RB	HOU
Round	Team 7			Team 8		
1	Steven Jackson	RB	STL	Edgerrin James	RB	ARI
2	Terrell Owens	WR	DAL	Chad Johnson	WR	CIN
3	Randy Moss	WR	OAK	Tatum Bell	RB	DEN
4	Reggie Bush	RB	NO	Thomas Jones	RB	CHI
5	Javon Walker	WR	DEN	Marc Bulger	QB	STL
6	Corey Dillon	RB	NE	Todd Heap	TE	BAL
7	Eli Manning	QB	NYG	Drew Bennett	WR	TEN
8	Matt Jones	WR	JAC	Muhsin Muhammad	WR	CHI
9	Marion Barber	RB	DAL	Ernest Wilford	WR	JAC
10	L.J. Smith	TE	PHI	Michael Bennett	RB	NO
11	Ashley Lelie	WR	DEN	Ben Troupe	TE	TEN
12	Cedric Houston	RB	NYJ	Mark Brunell	QB	WAS
13	Steve McNair	QB	TBD	Amani Toomer	WR	NYG
14	Dallas Clark	TE	IND	Sebastian Janikowski	K	OAK
15	Jacksonville Jaguars	DEF	JAC	Washington Redskins	DEF	WAS
16	Lawrence Tynes	K	KAN	Brian Calhoun	RB	DET

Round	Team 9			Team 10		
1	Rudi Johnson	RB	CIN	Domanick Davis	RB	HOU
2	Brian Westbrook	RB	PHI	Willis McGahee	RB	BUF
3	Hines Ward	WR	PIT	Chris Chambers	WR	MIA
4	Donald Driver	WR	GB	Santana Moss	WR	WAS
5	Ron Dayne	RB	DEN	Joe Horn	WR	NO
6	Rod Smith	WR	DEN	Deion Branch	WR	NE
7	Nate Burleson	WR	SEA	Eric Moulds	WR	HOU
8	Trent Green	QB	KAN	Aaron Brooks	QB	OAK
9	Heath Miller	TE	PIT	Roddy White	WR	ATL
10	Drew Brees	QB	NO	Maurice Drew	RB	JAC
11	Chris Perry	RB	CIN	David Carr	QB	HOU
12	Brandon Lloyd	WR	WAS	Jerious Norwood	RB	ATL
13	Adam Vinatieri	K	IND	Shayne Graham	K	CIN
14	Lee Suggs	RB	CLE	Leonard Pope	TE	ARI
15	Seattle Seahawks	DEF	SEA	Sinorice Moss	WR	NYG
16	Courtney Anderson	TE	OAK	Denver Broncos	DEF	DEN
Round	Team 11			Team 12		
1	Ronnie Brown	RB	MIA	Carnell Williams	RB	TB
2	Kevin Jones	RB	DET	Julius Jones	RB	DAL
3	Reggie Wayne	WR	IND	Darrell Jackson	WR	SEA
4	T.J. Houshmandzadeh	WR	CIN	Plaxico Burress	WR	NYG
5	Eddie Kennison	WR	KAN	Ahman Green	RB	GB
6	Curtis Martin	RB	NYJ	Derrick Mason	WR	BAL
7	Carson Palmer	QB	CIN	Jake Delhomme	QB	CAR
8	Donte' Stallworth	WR	NO	Laurence Maroney	RB	NE
9	Joe Jurevicius	WR	CLE	Jerry Porter	WR	OAK
10	Jermaine Wiggins	TE	MIN	Daunte Culpepper	QB	MIA
11	Priest Holmes	RB	KAN	Mike Anderson	RB	BAL
12	Greg Jones	RB	JAC	Carolina Panthers	DEF	CAR
13	Philip Rivers	QB	SD	Vernon Davis	TE	SF
14	Baltimore Ravens	DEF	BAL	Mike Williams	WR	DET
15	David Akers	K	PHI	Jeff Reed	K	PIT
16	Robert Ferguson	WR	GB	Chad Jackson	WR	NE

21 Round-by-Round Draft Strategy

- ◆ First Round
- ◆ Second Round
- ◆ Third Round
- ◆ Fourth Round
- ◆ Fifth Round
- ◆ Sixth Round
- ◆ Seventh Round
- ◆ Eighth Round
- ◆ Ninth Round
- ◆ 10th-12th Rounds
- ◆ Last Call

As draft day approaches, the majority of fantasy owners typically obsess over the selections to be made in rounds one and two. After all, the players selected in those rounds are destined to post the most eye-popping numbers and dominate the highlight films. In Chapter 9, "Draft-Day Preparation and Execution," I proposed several methods of assembling information and executing a successful draft. The following sections guide you through each round of the draft, offering an overview of what to expect and how to react to shifts in the draft to build a strong team from top to bottom.

FIRST ROUND

Unless your league is structured to greatly favor quarter-back production, the average first round of the fantasy draft will be dominated by running backs. In a 12-team league, as many as 10 running backs will be off the board before the first round ends. Peyton Manning and the first wide receiver (Terrell Owens, Chad Johnson, or Steve Smith most likely) break the flow of running backs.

This round typically flies, as virtually all owners script their first 20 players, much like a coach would script his first 15-20 offensive plays. The key to this round is to secure "a sure thing," or as close to one as you can expect in the NFL. That means that premier backs in prime situations, such as Larry Johnson behind a tremendous Kansas City line, perennial TD machine Shaun Alexander, and San Diego workhorse LaDainian Tomlinson, are no-brainer selections.

When considering other positions in the first round, make sure that the track history leaves you at ease with your expected returns.

Peyton Manning has never missed a start. Yes, fantasy owners cringed at the sight of Indianapolis clinching a first-round bye so early in 2005, but Manning still delivered stats to get teams into the fantasy playoffs. Perfect 14-0 starts to a season aren't commonplace, so that concern should be mitigated.

Among the wide receiver options, Chad Johnson awaits news on the health of his QB, Terrell Owens is returning from exile looking to regain his spot as the game's premier target, and Steve Smith missed all of 2004 with an injury. Remember, if the opportunity to procure a standout running back presents itself, take it. Receivers and quarterbacks will be there in subsequent rounds.

Second Round

If you opted away from a running back in the first round, you'll need to address that position in this round. It is unwise to wait until the third round to address this need, as you'll need to field at least two starting running backs in virtually all leagues. The existence of multiple backfield-by-committee situations shortens the field of upper-tier selections.

However, if you did make a selection of a running back in round one, check back to your cheatsheets to determine where the drop-offs occur at running back, wide receiver, and quarterback. If you believe that the talent drop before your next pick will be far more severe at wide receiver or quarterback than at running back, then make your choice. Players such as Torry Holt, Randy Moss, the Arizona duo of Larry Fitzgerald and Anquan Boldin and all quarterbacks not named Peyton will be available to you in this round. In most leagues in which I have participated, running backs are hoarded early, with owners shifting attention to the receiver and quarterback positions later in the draft.

THIRD ROUND

This round serves as a proverbial "last call" for quality starting running backs. Those backs remaining on the board after this round are involved in committee situations (Chris Brown and Travis Henry in Tennessee) or play for teams whose offensive production is suspect (Frank Gore of the 49ers, for example). Those owners in your league who deviated from hoarding running backs in the first two rounds will undoubtedly turn back to the position to round out their starting backfields here.

If you have secured two top-flight running backs, you've reached the first critical decision point of the draft. You can select a third running back to fill a Flex (RB/WR) position if applicable, or you can provide yourself security with a bench running back. In doing so, you also force your opposition to potentially take a back beneath your next drop-off point.

Better still, you can leave the running back position behind for the time being and take the next top option at QB, WR, or even TE Antonio Gates of the Chargers. This move will help you to establish a strong core on which to build out in subsequent rounds.

FOURTH ROUND

With three roster positions filled, you should have a fairly clear vision of your most pressing need. In virtually all instances, the two starting RB positions will be filled, meaning that the next best QB or WR will be the player targeted for selection. At this stage of the draft, many top options at both of these positions will remain on the board.

FIFTH ROUND

This is the first round where the "need" factor comes into play and the pre-draft process of creating your cheetsheets truly pays off. At this juncture, you're most likely sitting on two running backs, a wide receiver, and either a quarterback or premier tight end. If you've already addressed your quarterback, then your decision point is between wide receiver and tight end.

Wide receivers such as Detroit's Roy Williams, Buffalo's Lee Evans, and Houston's Andre Johnson are likely among those available for selection. The most prominent tight ends at this stage of the draft are Baltimore's Todd Heap, Washington's Chris Cooley, and Atlanta's top target, Alge Crumpler.

Sixth Round

The sixth round offers a mixed bag of options for owners. Some owners opt to assure themselves of their elite running back's backup ("handcuffing" presented in Chapter 18), while others debate the merits of filling out the starting roster or returning to the best remaining running back. Still others will refer to their cheatsheet and opt for the "best available player" regardless of position.

As presented in Chapter 9, remember to chart the roster positions filled by your opponents. This exercise will be particularly important in later rounds, but also comes into play early when deciding between the selection of a second or third WR and a QB.

Round six also begins the process whereby owners nab so-called "sleeper" picks (see Chapter 25) and build a bench full of players for possible trade options. Though executing a trade proves difficult in most leagues, it's always better to have a breakout player corralled on your roster than beating you.

SEVENTH ROUND

The seventh round witnesses a run on the remaining backs in contention for a starting or goal-line job. Players such as T.J. Duckett, Duce Staley, and Brandon Jacobs help to solidify running back positions as part-time ball carriers and bye week plug-ins due to their proficiency around the goal line.

Those who have yet to draft a starting QB and have instead stockpiled running backs and upper-tier wide receivers will generally grab their signal caller here. Emerging star Eli Manning, new Raiders QB Aaron Brooks, and new Saints QB Drew Brees will be in the mix in this round.

Virtually all attention centers on the three main offensive positions in this round, with perhaps one owner looking to snag a starting TE. This becomes another round by which to consult the drop-offs on your cheatsheet and the list of players taken by each team. Since most owners will not opt for a second TE at any juncture, there's no need to address that position if almost all other owners already have one. You're better served finding another receiver or running back.

Though the temptation to snag a kicker or team defense may arise in this round, resist it. There will be ample quality options in later rounds. The drop-off at the other three skill positions will be much steeper.

EIGHTH ROUND

This round usually serves as the midpoint of the draft, with most starting slots filled and perhaps a reserve running back or receiver stashed away. Most owners will fill out the last of their QB, RB, or WR slots in this round. If they have already done so, then they'll move to the TE position and players such as Randy McMichael, L.J. Smith, and Ben Troupe. Again, the kicker and team defense positions will wait for another round.

It's also the point at which owners enter their strategy for building the perfect bench. For some, this means finding depth at wide receiver. Others nab the "next great thing" at RB. Still others use this opportunity to grab a backup QB. The thought process with regard to the QB position is that there will be a run of backups at some juncture, as all teams will carry two or three QBs on their roster. That means that as many as 36 players at the position will find their way off the draft board before it's over. With as many as 23 more picks ahead of their next selection, owners have to weigh the possibility of an extended QB run that leaves them exposed to injury.

Always work toward balance and depth. One twisted ankle should not be able to sabotage your championship dreams.

NINTH ROUND

Those owners who haven't drafted a backup QB at this juncture turn back to the position in this round. Otherwise, it's that round to reach for a WR or RB prospect to make sure another savvy owner doesn't take him from under your nose. For the most part, the obvious fantasy contributors will be off the board some 96 picks into the draft. However, some players on the road to recovery from injury may slip due to owners wary of a relapse. If you're encouraged by reports from training camp, this is the round to take a shot.

In the ninth round, you'll also see the first kickers and team defenses come off the board. Those owners who feel compelled to complete their starting lineup will make the move here. Adam Vinatieri, Shayne Graham, and the Chicago and Carolina defenses are the most likely foursome for consideration here.

10TH-12TH ROUNDS

At this stage, owners are in one of two camps. Either they've addressed their starting lineup as a whole (K and DEF included) and are just now addressing reserves, or they've almost filled out their bench with the K and DEF positions still open. The latter position is the more enviable, as they'll be assured of procuring a top-12 pick at both positions with most owners carrying only one of each. The former position isn't disastrous, but the owner will need to be most judicious about the value of his or her picks from that point forward.

These rounds present the opportunity to procure backups for starters and attend to Bye week replacements. However, it's unwise to bypass a much stronger player for the sake of a Bye week, particularly if the bye occurs later in the season. With the changes in personnel and rash of injuries certain to occur, there will be ample time to address those needs via the waiver wire.

LAST CALL

In most leagues, there are 14-16 roster positions including the bench. As such, there are just two to four opportunities to find those final gems.

Some owners will wait until their last two selections to choose a kicker and team defense. There are almost invariably two runs in the final rounds. The first consists of a string of kickers and the second a string of team defenses.

Mixed into the final rounds will be flier selections on long-shot WR and RB prospects. Others will make the selection of a second TE, K, or DEF, citing the Bye week as a reason. As referenced above, depending on the Bye week, a whole new set of players may have emerged at the position, or an injury or change in personnel will decimate the value of an individual kicker (see Joe Nedney in 2003 and 2004) or a team defense (Baltimore and New England in 2005). Therefore, you'll be able to draw on the achievements and trends of the new season on the waiver wire rather than tying up a second roster spot on a player or team defense that you plan to use only once.

Remember to keep your draft tracking system and drop-off sheets handy. You may just be able to find one last super sleeper to close the draft while other owners scramble to the magazines to find a name that has not yet been called.

With your final roster selection made, it's time to take a deep breath and relax for a moment. Relaxation time is over. It's time to get back to the list of available players to see if there's anything you missed.

In the next chapter, I examine a litany of top fantasy performers who will don a new uniform in 2006. This extensive list is chock full with moves that should not be overlooked on draft day.

22 Top Off-Season Movers

- ♦ Quarterback Movers
- ♦ Running Back Movers
- ♦ Wide Receiver Movers
- ♦ Tight End Movers
- ♦ Kicker Movers

It used to be that you could name an NFL player and immediately recognize that player's team. The concept of players switching teams via free agency or trade was unfamiliar, particularly for those at the high-profile skill positions. My, how things have changed!

This off-season witnessed one of the largest migrations of name players in recent memory, with top-tier players moving at every position except tight end. In a period filled with a litany of huge sporting events such as the NCAA Men's Tournament, the opening of the NASCAR season, the NBA and NHL playoffs, and the opening of the Major

League Baseball season, it's possible that one or more of these moves slipped under the radar. You can use the following information to update your scorecard as you begin the arduous task of preparing your fantasy draft cheatsheet.

QUARTERBACK (QB) MOVERS

Typically, off-season movement at the QB position is confined to perhaps one premier starter and a series of backups who exit a situation where a rookie has been selected as the heir apparent. That wasn't the case this off-season, as several perennial fantasy starters changed uniforms alongside some veterans in search of a starting opportunity.

- **Daunte Culpepper — Minnesota to Miami:** After a brilliant 2004 season in which his greatness was overshadowed by Peyton Manning, Culpepper rose into the first round of many fantasy drafts in 2005. Culpepper was positively dominant in 2004 with 39 TDs and only 11 INTs, but he struggled mightily to start 2005 before he tore three ligaments in his knee to end his season.

  He enters a great situation in Miami with a full complement of top-notch skill-position players and a coach who preaches discipline and execution. The Dolphins added Joey Harrington via trade in the event that Culpepper is unable to start the season under center.

- **Joey Harrington — Detroit to Miami:** Harrington's time in Detroit ends after four forgettable seasons of chaos and a palpable lack of chemistry. He enters a situation in Miami where he's not expected to be the star. The Dolphins have more than enough players willing to snag that moniker with Ronnie Brown, Daunte Culpepper, Jason Taylor, Zach Thomas, and Chris Chambers onboard. In Nick Saban's system, Harrington just needs to execute, and he'll have a fine instructor in coordinator Mike Mularkey.

• **Aaron Brooks — New Orleans to Oakland:** Brooks leaves New Orleans after having regressed to his turnover-prone self in 2005. His inconsistency has kept him from ascending to the status that his big arm should afford him. Brooks will certainly have weapons at his disposal this year in Randy Moss, Jerry Porter, and company. He will also need to utilize LaMont Jordan out of the backfield in order to keep his turnover total down and move the team into scoring position. Brooks opens draft season as a backup, but with the tools to deliver top fantasy numbers.

• **Drew Brees — San Diego to New Orleans:** The arrival of Brees to New Orleans immediately upgraded the value of his wide receivers, and the addition of Reggie Bush (early May hamstring issues notwithstanding) gives him that pass-receiving threat out of the backfield that turned him into a fantasy star in San Diego. Deuce McAllister will be healthy for opening day, and the Saints have a trio of stellar receivers in Joe Horn, Donte' Stallworth, and speedster Devery Henderson. I also like Zach Hilton with Brees under center. While Hilton is not the athlete that Antonio Gates was in San Diego, he's a big target with good hands.

- **Jon Kitna — Cincinnati to Detroit, and Josh McCown — Arizona to Detroit:** I'm coupling these two entries akin to a horse race. Whoever wins this job inherits a tremendous collection of skill-position players and Mike Martz's abilities to create superstars out of thin air. Both have shown the ability to lead in their former homes. It will come down to which quarterback can digest Martz's pile of plays sooner. I believe Kitna's experience gives him an early edge for the start of '06, but that McCown will be the QB of the future in Detroit alongside Mike Williams, Roy Williams, Charles Rogers, and Corey Bradford.

- **Patrick Ramsey — Washington to New York Jets:** Chad Pennington is eager to prove that his shoulder is ready to withstand the rigors of a full NFL season. That remains to be seen, but for the short term, Ramsey begins the year on the bench. He's made no secret that he sees himself as a starter in the league, and he just might be in that position again soon enough given Pennington's history. With that said, the additions of Nick Mangold and D'Brickashaw Ferguson on the offensive line will serve to keep Pennington upright. Now, it's just a question of whether his shoulder holds. Ramsey makes for a solid backup option, but he's flying off the fantasy radar for the moment.

- **Brian Griese — Tampa Bay to Chicago:** Griese was signed as insurance for the oft-injured Rex Grossman after the Bears' offensive struggles of the past two seasons. He was effective in Tampa Bay prior to an injury of his own that paved the way for his exit in free agency. Griese threw 20 touchdowns in 11 games during the 2004 season. Chicago coach Lovie Smith expects to open up the passing game with Bernard Berrian and Muhsin Muhammad this year. If Grossman struggles or ends up on the shelf again, Griese will get his opportunity to lead.

- **Gus Frerotte — Miami to St. Louis:** The Rams certainly have all the pieces to return to contender status in the NFC. The wide receivers return, the power back of the future is onboard in Steven Jackson, and Marshall Faulk and Tony Fisher offer great receiving targets out of the backfield. Marc Bulger is the undisputed top option here, but Frerotte could be a serviceable fantasy option if pressed into service.

- **A.J. Feeley to San Diego:** The loss of Drew Brees to New Orleans necessitated the acquisition of an experienced veteran QB to backup Philip Rivers. Feeley performed well on occasion for Miami, but most definitely knows how to prepare himself to enter a game (as he did in both Philadelphia and Miami). If Rivers falters, Feeley will be quite comfortable with targets Keenan McCardell, Eric Parker, Antonio Gates, and LaDainian Tomlinson.

- **Jeff Garcia — Cleveland to Philadelphia:** Veteran QB Jeff Garcia leaves Cleveland to serve as a backup in a more familiar offensive style under Andy Reid. Garcia excels in the short passing game that Philadelphia uses and will make a solid backup for Donovan McNabb.

- **Anthony Wright — Baltimore to Cincinnati:** Wright joins the Bengals to offer insurance in case Carson Palmer is unable to go to start the season. He was inconsistent at the helm for Baltimore, but did make enough good throws to get a look from Marvin Lewis. Wright possesses good arm strength and will fit it soundly with the full complement of offensive weapons in Cincinnati. He's not a fantasy starter, but if he were to be pressed into action, Cincinnati's stars remain viable options.

RUNNING BACK (RB) MOVERS

A number of free agent running backs opted to re-sign with their former teams this off-season. Shaun Alexander, Ahman Green, and Jamal Lewis are but three examples of longtime fantasy starters who shunned opportunities elsewhere to stay in their respective situations. One huge free agent signing occurred when Edgerrin James bolted from the juggernaut that is the Indianapolis Colts offense to a home in the desert with the Arizona Cardinals. James may be the biggest name on the list, but several other fantasy stars of the past have relocated in hopes of making some noise in 2006.

- **Edgerrin James — Indianapolis to Arizona:** James joins a potent passing offense in the desert and will look to be the workhorse that he was in Indianapolis. There are still holes on the O-Line to be addressed, which may limit his effectiveness early in games. However, the efficiency of the passing game will serve to open the field and give him room to excel as he's done for so many years.

- **Chester Taylor — Baltimore to Minnesota:** Taylor will get his chance to win the feature role among a bevy of other backs in Minnesota. He's a tough-nosed runner who can catch the ball out of the backfield. Look for Brad Childress to implement a running attack akin to that of his former home in Philadelphia, where the back serves double-duty as a receiver and rusher. I'm fearful of a goal-line vulture keeping his TD total down, but he should produce enough to warrant a No. 2 running back slot.

- **Mike Anderson — Denver to Baltimore:** The powerful Anderson leaves the dominant Denver running attack for life in the rough and tumble AFC North. The team re-signed Jamal Lewis shortly after inking Anderson to a deal, which clouded the picture somewhat. It would appear heading into camp that the players will split duties early on, with Brian Billick shifting duties as the season progresses.

- **Michael Bennett — Minnesota to New Orleans:** Bennett landed in New Orleans after injuries and a crowded backfield conspired to render him ineffective. Naturally, he's not terribly thrilled about the addition of Reggie Bush to the New Orleans mix, and there's a good chance that he'll end up elsewhere before the season begins. He's still got decent speed and hands and would make an effective backup elsewhere. In New Orleans, he's the odd man out.

- **Quentin Griffin — Denver to Kansas City:** Griffin rates a mention on this list based on his past effectiveness in the Denver attack and the fact that Kansas City's strong O-Line remains intact. The big question pertaining to his value is whether Priest Holmes returns to the fold.

- **Antowain Smith — New Orleans to Houston:** Smith played reasonably well for the Saints in '05, averaging 4 yards per carry in 166 attempts in relief of Deuce McAllister. The Texans passed on Reggie Bush and instead brought on the veteran Smith to back up Domanick Davis alongside Vernand Morency and Jonathan Wells.

WIDE RECEIVER (WR) MOVERS

With more starting jobs up for grabs at wide receiver than any other position, it's no surprise that more wide receivers shifted locales during the off-season. Additionally, with the exception of the top receiver on a given team, the workload of players down the depth chart varies greatly each week. As such, these players are likely to change teams more regularly with coaches looking for the appropriate fit to round out the receiving corps.

This season, a number of impact receivers switched locales, led by three outspoken and controversial big targets who also happen to catch their share of passes as well. The leader of this contingency looks to make some noise in his return to the field from a discipline-shortened 2005 season. He'll do so under a huge microscope for "America's Team."

- **Terrell Owens — Philadelphia to Dallas:** Owens has undoubtedly circled the dates of the two games against Philly this year. Fantasy owners missed his production for the second half of the year. He was on his way toward a phenomenal season when his words and actions sent him to the shelf. I look for

Owens to reclaim his place among the elite receivers in Dallas this year, and I do believe that he'll be on his best behavior in year one under Bill Parcells. I make no predictions for 2007.

- **Keyshawn Johnson — Dallas to Carolina:** The signing of Owens in Dallas made Johnson expendable, and he picked a great spot to land in Carolina alongside Steve Smith. Johnson enjoyed his most productive season in years in terms of TD production, and he should be in a good position to repeat his performance in a strong Carolina offense.

- **Antonio Bryant — Cleveland to San Francisco:** Bryant quietly topped 1,000 receiving yards for the Browns last year. He now goes to San Francisco where he'll be counted on to aid the development of Alex Smith. Bryant teams with Vernon Davis and Arnaz Battle to form a decent receiving corps for the second-year QB Smith. Bryant will slip an extra round or two due to the team designation, which makes him a solid sleeper play for 2006.

- **David Givens — New England to Tennessee:** It remains to be seen who will be under center in Tennessee to start the year. I suspect Billy Volek assumes the reins, but whoever is throwing the ball will appreciate Givens' presence. Though it's hard to believe Drew Bennett and the soon-to-be 26-year-old Givens are the veterans in the receiving corps. He caught 59 balls for 738 yards in the Patriots' system. I suspect he can crush those numbers with consistency at QB.

- **Nate Burleson — Minnesota to Seattle:** Burleson is one of those players who entered 2005 to great expectations, got injured, and was then just forgotten about. He caught 30 balls in 12 games while battling injury and caught just one TD pass after his huge 2004 campaign (1,006 yards, nine TDs). Burleson will fit in nicely in Mike Holmgren's season offense, where he'll battle Bobby Engram for the No. 2 slot opposite Darrell Jackson.

- **Eric Moulds — Buffalo to Houston:** After a long career in Buffalo, Moulds relocates to Houston to help Andre Johnson and David Carr in the passing game. Of course, neither Moulds nor Johnson plays on the offensive line, so they'll just have to get open quickly. I suspect Moulds' numbers take a hit based on the shift to a No. 2 role and the fact that Houston is still building an offensive line to protect David Carr. Moulds has caught 64 or more passes in eight straight seasons with 1,000-yard campaigns every other season. He had 816 yards last year. Does that mean another 1,000-yard season is in the offing?

- **Joe Jurevicius — Seattle to Cleveland:** Jurevicius will be hard-pressed to duplicate his TD prowess of 2005 in Seattle, but he will offer a big target for second-year QB Charlie Frye. The key to Jurevicius' production will be the health of Braylon Edwards and Kellen Winslow Jr. this season. If neither can perform up to expectations, it could be a long year for Jurevicius.

- **Brandon Lloyd — San Francisco to Washington:** Lloyd has become a highlight reel favorite with his body control and willingness to sacrifice to make a catch. He becomes the No. 2 option to Santana Moss in Washington, and will be used to stretch the field and also as possession receiver because of his great hands. The triple package of Moss, Lloyd, and Antwaan Randle El likely serves to keep all of their individual numbers suppressed to some degree, but the total offensive impact will be huge.

- **Antwaan Randle El — Pittsburgh to Washington:** Randle El parlayed his versatility and Super Bowl TD pass into a huge free agent contract. He and Brandon Lloyd will line up opposite Santana Moss and wreak havoc by turning short gains into big plays. With that said, don't expect his receptions to skyrocket, as Chris Cooley still looms large in the passing game.

- **Peerless Price — Atlanta to Buffalo:** After a couple lost years in Atlanta, Price returns to the scene of his greatest NFL accomplishments. However, he'll be doing so with question marks at QB and no Eric Moulds to draw double coverage. Lee Evans is still developing into a No. 1 role, but for now, he doesn't offer the protection to which he's become accustomed.

TIGHT END (TE) MOVERS

The list of impact free agent tight ends for the 2006 season stands at one. A number of starting tight ends chose to re-sign with their former clubs rather than change addresses. New Houston Texans coach and former Denver offensive coordinator Gary Kubiak brought former Broncos tight end Jeb Putzier to Houston.

- **Jeb Putzier — Denver to Houston:** New Houston coach Gary Kubiak brought Putzier over from the

Broncos to provide a safety valve for David Carr. Putzier offers a big frame and good hands. He's able to find space in coverage over the middle and sit down in the zone, which will be serve to extend possessions for the Houston offense. He's one of my fantasy sleeper selections for this year after being hand-picked by his former coach. That has to count for something.

KICKER (K) MOVERS

It's not often that kickers receive much more than a casual, "I guess I need to start one, so .". remark at the draft table. However, two kickers that traditionally exit the fantasy draft board well in advance of their colleagues changed teams this off-season. Super Bowl hero Adam Vinatieri signed a huge deal to join the Indianapolis Colts, while the Dallas Cowboys sought to upgrade their long-suffering kicking game with former Colts kicker Mike Vanderjagt. They are joined in this report by a perennial top-10 kicker and a former fantasy star on the comeback trail.

- **Adam Vinatieri — New England to Indianapolis:** Vinatieri leaves the Patriots to join the high-power Colts indoors. He leaves the elements of the AFC East and home games at Foxboro for the confines of the RCA Dome. The Colts wasted no time securing Vinatieri's services after former kicker Mike Vanderjagt missed a monumental kick in the playoff loss to Pittsburgh. The main question regarding his fantasy value concerns the efficiency of the offense and whether Edgerrin James' departure leads to more stalled drives and FG attempts.

- **Mike Vanderjagt — Indianapolis to Dallas:** Vanderjagt is the most accurate kicker in NFL history, but his big miss in the playoffs against Pittsburgh necessitated a parting between the two. Dallas jumped at the opportunity to sign Vanderjagt despite the hefty price tag after running through kickers with great regularity over the last several seasons. Cowboys kickers normally tally a large amount of FG attempts, as Bill Parcells plays percentages.

- **Ryan Longwell — Green Bay to Minnesota:** Longwell has been one of the most accurate kickers in the game for years while kicking outdoors on frozen Lambeau Field. He now makes the move indoors to division rival Minnesota, where his big leg will be put to the test with great regularity. I see the offense being able to move the ball under Brad Childress, but that a return to big TD totals is a year away. That means plenty of opportunity for Longwell to rack up points.

- **Martin Gramatica — Indianapolis to New England:** After struggling with the Buccaneers in 2004 and appearing in a handful of games for the Colts at the end of that season, Gramatica was out of football in 2005. He signed a deal with the Patriots in a bid to replace Adam Vinatieri. The Patriots drafted Stephen Gostkowski from Memphis for his big leg, and he'll get a chance to compete with Gramatica this summer.

The preceding list serves to update the pertinent trades and free agent relocations this off-season as they relate to players whose names will be called on draft day. Naturally, there were numerous other personnel moves that will impact your decision-making process such as coaching changes and shifts on the offensive line. Those moves will be reflected in the position-by-position and overall rankings presented in Chapters 27 through 32 and Appendix E in the back of the book. Chapter 13 explores the fantasy impact of coaching styles.

The following chapter examines the effectiveness of players inside the Red Zone, reviewing the standout performers to give you the edge in the scoring column.

23 Red Zone Performers

- ◆ Charting Teams
- ◆ Big Receivers
- ◆ Tight Ends
- ◆ Vulture Backs and Special Cases

The process of compiling an effective preranking list for the upcoming draft is a long and sometimes tedious one. After the initial players with the gaudy numbers are slotted, many of the players begin to look the same. Minimal yardage differences or an additional touchdown pass, reception, or run may not be enough to truly distinguish one player from another.

This chapter serves to offer several methods by which to create that separation, including a review of red zone efficiency statistics, breaking out the measuring tape, and player roles. In reviewing this data, I offer several standout players in each category.

CHARTING TEAMS

One of the first methods by which to create separation between players on your ranking list is to review the red zone efficiency of each team from the past season. While it is true that player personnel will change each season due to injuries, retirements, free agency, and trades, the core system remains in place. Of course, that handful of coaching jobs that change over from season to season can be looked at separately. Remember, the coach generally doesn't just walk away (Dick Vermeil and Herman Edwards are the exceptions for 2006). Generally, the firing of a coach is a symptom of larger issues, and in most cases, a lack of talent. As such, dismissing the previous year's data entirely would be shortsighted.

Table 23.1 displays the red zone efficiency for all 32 NFL teams from 2005, sorted by touchdown conversion percentage. It should come as no surprise that the league's highest scoring team, the Seattle Seahawks, tops this data set and that the Cleveland Browns rank last.

However, it is interesting to note that despite the huge numbers attained by the Arizona Cardinals' receiving duo of Anquan Boldin and Larry Fitzgerald, Arizona converted only 28.3 percent of its red zone appearances into touchdowns.

The data set also includes a straight count of red zone appearances. Again, Seattle ranks among the leaders with Indianapolis, New England, and the New York Giants.

Upon charting team efficiencies and finding the most intriguing scenarios, managers must then review team rosters to find the likely candidates for these scoring opportunities. The remainder of this chapter divides those per-

Table 23.1. NFL Red Zone Efficiency for 2005

Rank	Team	Possessions	Touchdowns	TD%	FG	FG%
1	SEA	60	43	71.7	11	18.3
2	SD	50	35	70	12	24
3	WAS	47	30	63.8	10	21.3
4	NE	58	37	63.8	15	25.9
5	PIT	56	34	60.7	21	37.5
6	IND	61	37	60.7	16	26.2
7	DEN	58	35	60.3	15	25.9
8	JAC	49	29	59.2	15	30.6
9	CAR	53	31	58.5	17	32.1
10	ATL	54	31	57.4	19	35.2
11	CIN	62	35	56.5	20	32.3
12	PHI	41	22	53.7	12	29.3
13	DAL	53	28	52.8	17	32.1
14	KC	54	28	51.9	20	37
15	TB	39	20	51.3	14	35.9
16	DET	36	18	50	12	33.3
17	TEN	46	22	47.8	14	30.4
18	GB	46	22	47.8	13	28.3
19	STL	51	24	47.1	19	37.3
20	OAK	45	21	46.7	16	35.6
21	CHI	43	20	46.5	16	37.2
22	NYG	59	27	45.8	22	37.3
23	MIN	51	23	45.1	17	33.3
24	NYJ	43	19	44.2	15	34.9
25	HOU	37	16	43.2	17	45.9
26	MIA	52	21	40.4	18	34.6
27	SF	28	11	39.3	16	57.1
28	BAL	42	16	38.1	16	38.1
29	NO	42	16	38.1	17	40.5
30	BUF	49	17	34.7	21	42.9
31	ARI	46	13	28.3	25	54.3
32	CLE	39	11	28.2	20	51.3

formers into three categories most prevalent among top scorers. The first category of player is the tall receiver who creates matchup problems and excels in jump-ball situations. The second category consists of pass-catching tight ends whose placement in a formation allows them to find space in the end zone. Finally, there are the legendary vulture backs who collect short-yardage touchdowns and sometimes very little yardage.

BIG RECEIVERS

Among big receivers in 2005, Joe Jurevicius of the efficient Seattle offense would rank first. Jurevicius caught 10 touchdown passes in 2005, most of which came in short range. He moves to Cleveland this season, so the Browns' efficiency should see an up-tick in 2006 while Seattle will need to find a suitable alternative. It would stand to logic that tight end Jerramy Stevens would be a candidate to assume this role.

The Lions saw the red zone only 36 times last season but converted 50 percent of those appearances into touchdowns. Roy Williams snagged eight touchdowns last season. In Mike Martz's newly installed offense, the number of red zone appearances should rise. As such, Williams (and fellow Detroit receiver Mike Williams) should be charted several slots higher.

Jacksonville made 49 red zone appearances and converted 59 percent of those opportunities into touchdowns. The Jaguars have two fine young receivers who can elevate over smaller defensive backs in Ernest Wilford and Matt Jones. Their respective roles in the offense are also elevated by the retirement of Jimmy Smith.

TIGHT ENDS

There are several obvious players that leap off the page among tight ends based on their gaudy touchdown totals from 2005. Antonio Gates and Chris Cooley were obviously a large component of their respective teams' offense in the red zone and will continue to be so.

The Steelers appeared in the red zone 56 times last season, and vulture back Jerome Bettis retired. As such, there's a strong possibility that tight end Heath Miller plays a larger role around the goal line as 2006 unfolds.

I mentioned Matt Jones and Ernest Wilford earlier when discussing the Jaguars' conversion rate. The team also drafted a 6-foot-6 tight end named Marcedes Lewis from UCLA who possesses tremendous leaping ability and excels in such jump-ball situations.

VULTURE BACKS AND SPECIAL CASES

There are several teams who employ goal-line specialists. Fantasy owners must analyze each week's matchup to determine the likelihood of that player receiving one or more opportunities to score. For instance, Mike Alstott rushed for six touchdowns in 2005, but only carried the ball 34 times.

T.J. Duckett scored eight touchdowns for the Falcons in 121 carries. He often relieved Warrick Dunn late in drives and finished the work. Duckett is currently in the proverbial doghouse with Atlanta's coaches, which may open the door for rookie Jerious Norwood to steal the goal-line job.

Mike Sellers of the Redskins provides perhaps the most interesting case of all, as he caught 12 passes and carried the ball once in 2005. He scored on eight of those 13 touches.

In summary, breaking apart the red zone opportunities for each team reveals patterns in play calling, personnel decisions, and can demonstrate which teams seize up under pressure. This review brings your inner coach into draft-day preparation.

The next chapter introduces the next generation of fantasy stars. The rookie review offers a glimpse into those players who may be called upon to contribute for their respective teams and your roster this season.

24 Rookie Review: 2006 Draft Impact Players

- ♦ Quarterbacks
- ♦ Running Backs
- ♦ Wide Receivers
- ♦ Tight Ends
- ♦ Kickers

The NFL Draft serves as a seminal moment in the lives of prospects and their families. For football fans and fantasy football players, it assumes a sort of holiday feel. Draft coverage overtakes all other sports stories of the day, regardless of the status of NBA or NHL playoff series.

I experienced day one of the 2006 Draft in person at Radio City Music Hall, polling fans for their instant reactions to the selections of their favorite teams and watching as the latest crop of NFL superstars was introduced. Virtually all those I spoke to at this event revealed their participation in one or more fantasy football leagues. Naturally, the conversations regarding each subsequent draft pick then turned to his fantasy impact.

This chapter serves as the introduction to the next wave of offensive fantasy prospects at each position with a nod toward their expected roles for the 2006 campaign. The expected immediate contributions vary greatly by position, with the quarterback learning curve typically being the longest.

QUARTERBACK

Vince Young, TEN

Analysis: Since the national title game against USC, Vince Young has been skewered in the media over his decision-making, test taking, and just overall preparedness for the next level. Floyd Reese looked back to the future with the selection of Young, seeing in him the same physical attributes and skills that led to the pick of Steve McNair in 1995. In fact, Reese drafted Young with the objection of the Tennessee coaching staff, who preferred Matt Leinart. Young can absorb hits with his big frame with the quickness to elude would-be tacklers. He can throw on the run and has the arm to make the big toss downfield and stretch defenses.

2006 Role: The Titans will enter the season with the first new starting quarterback since McNair assumed the reins in the mid-1990s. Young will challenge Billy Volek for the top spot during training camp, but it's unlikely that he'll start immediately. However, Tennessee remains in the rebuilding cycle with fresh talent at most skill positions. As such, I expect him to be in the starting lineup for the Titans by midseason after working with Norm Chow. He won't light up fantasy score sheets with great regularity, but Young may become worthy of a spot play down the stretch.

Matt Leinart, ARI

Analysis: Though you probably couldn't convince his accountants, Leinart's fall to Arizona is most advantageous for his long-term prospects in the NFL and his ability to secure a large second contract. Leinart gets to spend the 2006 season learning from Kurt Warner (although he's probably at least a bit miffed to see another No. 1 pick behind him) and will inherit three of the finest skill position players in the game when he finally takes the field. Forget about whether his arm is capable of the deep pass. It counts just the same when your top-flight receiver catches it 15-20 yards downfield and sprints another 40. Leinart possesses good touch and a head for the game and will surely benefit from the talented cast that has been assembled.

2006 Role: Leinart will start the year as Warner's backup, but all scouts and analysts agree that he is the rookie QB most ready to step in and play immediately if necessary. Given Warner's injury history, Leinart might just get a chance to prove them right.

Jay Cutler, DEN

Analysis: When the announcement of the trade by Denver to secure the 11th pick was completed, there was no question that the Broncos had successfully nabbed Jay Cutler. He's a tough leader who showed great heart and competitiveness at Vanderbilt, averaging 279 yards per game as a senior. Cutler has great arm strength and will be a big producer in the Denver attack with the acquisition of Javon Walker when his time comes.

2006 Role: Jake Plummer has been a durable quarterback over the course of his career, starting all 16 games in four of the last five seasons. As such, Cutler gets a year to learn Mike Shanahan's offense. This situation looks a lot like the 2004 San Diego Chargers when Philip Rivers was brought in behind Drew Brees. Fantasy owners can only hope it works out as well with their selection of Plummer this summer. I don't expect to see much of Cutler on the field this year.

Brodie Croyle, KAN

Analysis: Croyle slipped in the draft based on some concern about his ACL injury from 2004 (he had previously torn the other as well) and a slow finish to his senior season. He has the frame of the prototypical QB, standing 6-foot-3 and 205 pounds, and has demonstrated good arm strength at Alabama. Croyle completed 59.4 percent of his passes last year with 13 TDs and four INTs.

2006 Role: Croyle will hold the clipboard this season and work to learn the Kansas City system from incumbent Trent Green. Veteran Damon Huard remains on the roster as the backup should an injury befall Green. Don't expect to see Croyle on the field except for kneel-downs or mop-up duty in 2006.

Kellen Clemens, NYJ

Analysis: The Jets secured a strong QB prospect in the middle of the second round after addressing a need on the offensive line in Round 1. With the uncertainty at QB with Chad Pennington and the former first-round pick of the Redskins, Patrick Ramsey, the Jets certainly needed to address the QB position in the draft so that they could avoid calling Vinny Testaverde again. Clemens showed great arm strength and leadership ability at Oregon.

2006 Role: The selection of D'Brickashaw Ferguson should help to keep Chad Pennington upright and on the field. If not, the addition of Ramsey keeps Clemens on the sidelines for 2006. However, if things begin to look like 2005 revisited, there's always the chance that Eric Mangini will throw the rookie into the fire to test his mettle and assess long-term potential.

RUNNING BACK

Reggie Bush, NO

Analysis: The people of New Orleans are beside themselves with joy. I had expected to see Mario Williams in a Saints cap on draft day to shore up a suspect defense, but the Texans handed them the electrifying Heisman Trophy winner. Bush's TD runs at USC last year averaged more than 30 yards in length, making him a game-changer in a heartbeat.

2006 Role: Deuce McAllister will remain the workhorse in this offense, leaving coach Sean Payton and QB Drew Brees to find situations to break Bush free. Bush will likely be split as a receiver more this season than a straight tailback, looking to utilize his speed in mismatches against linebackers. Brees demonstrated an ability to find his running back out of the backfield when he completed 100 passes to LaDainian Tomlinson. He won't reach those heights, but with issues on the offensive line, that looks to be the best role for him this year.

Joseph Addai, IND

Analysis: The Colts addressed the loss of Edgerrin James early with the selection of the speedy tailback out of LSU. Addai can run inside the tackles and then kick his speed into another gear when he hits the second level. Does that sound familiar, Indy fans? There is some concern about past knee injuries, but he put those to rest with a 4.43 time in his 40-yard dash.

2006 Role: Dominic Rhodes is on the board as the top RB in Indy for now, but I anticipate that Addai will eclipse him ahead of the season opener. He brings too much talent to the table to sit behind Rhodes unless Addai fails to pick up the Indy offense. That would be my only concern. Addai also enters an enviable position here, as opposing defenses will scheme to slow Peyton Manning first and then turn their attention to Addai. I'm looking for him to be a solid sleeper pick this year, as rookies tend to be overlooked on draft day.

Laurence Maroney, NE

Analysis: Maroney showed great vision and quickness as a runner at Minnesota, rolling to three consecutive 1,000-yard seasons averaging 6 yards per carry as a senior. The big positive for Maroney is his durability. Though he slowed in the final two games, Maroney regularly topped 20 touches each week and twice got upward of 40. The only big knock on Maroney as he embarks on his NFL career is his inability to catch the ball out of the backfield. That means that Patrick Pass and/or Kevin Faulk fans should be happy.

2006 Role: Corey Dillon slowed a bit last season and has been battling injuries the last two seasons. Show your hand if you got caught in the switches with the injury reports on him last year. I expect Maroney to push for the top spot as a rookie, or at the very least, bid for a split backfield with Dillon. He's a necessary handcuff to any selection of Dillon.

DeAngelo Williams, CAR

Analysis: Williams shows good balance and speed and has the ability to fight off tackles. He's battled some injuries throughout his college career, so his selection by the Panthers seems like a perfect fit. Seriously, the Panthers needed to build depth in the backfield based on the loss of Stephen Davis and the histories of both DeShaun Foster and Eric Shelton. Williams was regarded by many as one of the best picks from Day 1 of the draft.

2006 Role: Williams begins the year at No. 3 on the depth chart with Shelton expected to fill the backup role to Foster. However, Shelton may find himself in the vulture role, with Williams serving as the primary ball carrier behind Foster. Foster has been a regular visitor to the injury report. As such, there's no doubt that Williams will get his chance to shine on a couple occasions this year

Maurice Drew, JAC

Analysis: Drew felt slighted ahead of the draft and that his accomplishments at UCLA warranted more attention than he received. In the end, he may be the RB equivalent of Matt Leinart, where he ends up thrilled with his destination. He runs a sub-4.40 40-yard dash and offers great strength, hands, and quickness at 5-foot-7. Drew averaged 5.2 yards per carry during his college career and dominated as a return man.

2006 Role: The recent return to his previous injury-plagued ways has Fred Taylor looking over his shoulder with this selection. Drew has been durable during his career (only missed one game at UCLA) and has the heart that Jack Del Rio loves. He likely opens the year as a change-of-pace back at 8-10 touches per game, but could surpass Taylor with a huge showing this summer.

LenDale White, TEN

Analysis: On my predraft board, I had put White's name in Sharpie next to the No. 32 pick for the Pittsburgh Steelers. His history screamed replacement for the retired Jerome Bettis. As we saw, the Steelers addressed needs at wide receiver and let White slip into the second round. Norm Chow finally got him off the board with the 45th selection, and the most prolific scorer in NCAA history had an NFL home.

2006 Role: Talk about motivation! Though White enters camp as the No. 3 back behind Chris Brown and Travis Henry, their injury histories and bouts with ineffectiveness leave the door open for White to rise up the charts in a hurry. I expect for that to occur before camp breaks and for White to claim 5-7 touches per game in the early part of the season before entering the feature role in the final weeks. If nothing else, look for him to assume the vulture role and rack up short TD runs.

WIDE RECEIVER

Santonio Holmes, PIT

Analysis: Holmes has proven to be a big playmaker at Ohio State both as a receiver and return man. Hmmm, this sounds familiar, no? The Steelers needed to shore up the receiving corps with the loss of Antwaan Randle El to the Redskins and did a nice job in securing a proven commodity from a top-notch program. Holmes immediately slides into the No. 2 slot on the depth chart with a shot of working past Cedrick Wilson this summer.

2006 Role: Holmes offers a big play threat with sure hands behind Hines Ward. He'll offer a speed threat to open up the field for Heath Miller and Ward. I expect Ken Whisenhunt and the Steelers to put the ball in Ben Roethlisberger's hands with more regularity this season, meaning that the rookie will get his share of opportunities immediately.

Chad Jackson, NE

Analysis: If you consider Maroney a steal in Round 1, then the selection of Jackson in Round 2 is a felony. Jackson was the top receiver on many draft boards and offers Tom Brady a sure-handed receiver with good speed. With the number of losses to the New England receiving corps this off-season, Jackson stands to make an immediate impact as a rookie.

2006 Role: Jackson opens the year at No. 2 opposite Deion Branch. He should be able to surpass Patriots favorite and sure-handed possession receiver Troy Brown for the role ahead of opening day. Though receivers often struggle to make an impact as a rookie, I believe Jackson contributes right away.

Sinorice Moss, NYG

Analysis: Moss slipped to the Giants with their second pick in April's NFL Draft, as Tom Coughlin looked to add depth to the receiving corps. Plaxico Burress tends to disappear if he isn't involved early. Amani Toomer, despite a strong showing last year, is on the downside of his career, and Tim Carter can't stay healthy.

2006 Role: Moss assumes the third receiver position as a rookie, offering a speed option for Eli Manning on the outside and a player with game-changing capability. Also, it evens the Moss count with the Redskins at one. Seriously, Moss could be a big play winner at the outset, but he's going to be hit and miss from a fantasy perspective.

Derek Hagan, MIA

Analysis: The leading receiver in Arizona State history falls into a good situation in the rebuilt Miami offense. He's a tall and physical receiver who isn't afraid to battle for balls. I expect him to make an impact as a rookie and compete for reps behind Marty Booker.

2006 Role: Hagan certainly has the physical tools to become a force immediately and to claim the No. 3 role behind Chris Chambers and Marty Booker.

Greg Jennings, GNB

Analysis: The deal that sent Javon Walker to Denver necessitated the selection of a wide receiver early in the draft. Jennings offers good speed and route-running skills. At 5-

foot-11, he may have some trouble creating separation against bigger corners. However, he goes after the ball with authority, and we've certainly seen other wide receivers dominate though several inches shorter.

2006 Role: Jennings will get into the rotation early, but it's unlikely that he makes a huge impact as a rookie so long as Robert Ferguson and Donald Driver stay healthy. Mike McCarthy and Brett Favre will look to use Jennings' speed to stretch the field and open things up for the running game.

Jason Avant, PHI

Analysis: Avant is a speedy receiver with great hands who makes catches in traffic. Avant runs precise routes and knows how to find pockets in coverage. He does carry a Hines Ward-like ability to block downfield, which will come in handy in a Philadelphia system that utilizes its running backs as receivers and relies heavily on the short to intermediate passing game.

2006 Role: Avant will make a bid for a third receiver role in the crowded Philadelphia receiving corps. Though the loss of Terrell Owens leaves Philadelphia with no established star, there are five other receivers on the roster vying for attention. This will be one of the training camp battles to watch. If Avant can secure reps and looks, he may be a valuable sleeper selection in deeper leagues.

TIGHT END

Vernon Davis, SF

Analysis: Davis won the crowd over at Radio City Music Hall when he wept during the call that informed him of his selection sixth overall. He'll also be quick to win fans and coaches over in San Francisco with his play. Davis is a good route runner who has the power to fend off would-be tacklers. Combine attendees marveled at his physique, labeling it statuesque. Once he gets in full stride, he's difficult to pull down. Scouts love his combination of size, speed, and athleticism.

2006 Role: Alex Smith will enjoy having a playmaking TE this season. I believe Smith would have been much more effective last year had Eric Johnson been healthy, so this addition has to have him positively giddy. Davis has the ability to reach the big catch number that Johnson had in 2004 (82) and to be a big factor in the red zone.

Marcedes Lewis, JAC

Analysis: The Jaguars addressed another big need with the addition of Lewis. No offense to George Wrighster, but the addition of Lewis expands the field for Byron Leftwich. He's got good hands and speed, and creates matchup problems with his 6-foot-6 frame.

2006 Role: Leftwich got the missing piece of the puzzle with a TE to eat up space over the middle. Lewis will cause matchup problems down the center of the field and will be a huge impact player in the red zone.

Leonard Pope, ARI

Analysis: Pope goes much later than expected due to the run on defensive players that extends much deeper than anticipated. He's a huge target who still runs a strong 4.65 40-yard dash. Pope is a good blocker who will help upgrade the line ahead of Edgerrin James.

2006 Role: The Cardinals added the last piece of the puzzle in Pope. They have two of the game's best receivers, an accurate passer in Warner, the heir apparent in Leinart, and the aforementioned James. Now, they have a massive pass-catching TE to cause matchup problems and dominate the red zone.

KICKER

Stephen Gostkowski, NE

Analysis: The Patriots lost Adam Vinatieri to the Colts this off-season and addressed the loss short-term by signing veteran Martin Gramatica. However, they turned to Gostkowski from Memphis to build for the future. He ranks 13th in NCAA history with 369 points and can boot the ball into the end zone with regularity on kickoffs. Gostkowski converted 22 of 25 field-goal attempts in 2005 and is virtually automatic inside 40 yards.

2006 Role: Gostkowski will win the job in camp due to his deep kickoffs and FG accuracy. If he does win the role, Gostkowski instantly becomes a candidate for a starting fantasy role, as the Patriots offense behind Tom Brady is efficient.

Kurt Smith, SD

Analysis: Nate Kaeding has been tremendously accurate for the Chargers in his two seasons. He will continue to be the regular kicker for San Diego going forward, but Smith was brought in to offer a strong leg for attempts over 50 yards and to take over kickoffs. Smith has a big leg and an ability to boot it into the end zone with great regularity.

2006 Role: Smith will be a kickoff specialist and attempt as many as five FGs from 50-plus yards. But, unless Kaeding gets hurt, he's not a fantasy option.

The next chapter evaluates "sleeper" potential heading into 2006. Whether felled by a lack of playing time, injury, or just plain underachieving, these are players whose situations have improved this off-season to make them viable fantasy performers in 2006. The "sleeper" tag indicates that the player is likely to come at a bit of a discount on draft day but has the ability to pay big dividends.

25 Sleepers

- ♦ Quarterback Candidates
- ♦ Running Back Candidates
- ♦ Wide Receiver Candidates
- ♦ Tight End Candidates
- ♦ Kicker Candidates

There's nothing more satisfying in terms of fantasy football than to choose a long-shot player in the later rounds of the draft and watch him grow into prominence as part of your squad. The term "sleeper" is traditionally reserved for players who have been active in the league but whose performance and opportunity have not necessarily reflected their talent.

In this chapter, I examine "sleeper" candidates at each of the offensive positions. Some of these players are past fantasy stars looking to rebound from an uncharacteristically bad season or where a change of uniform or offensive system will help them to shine on Sundays this fall.

QUARTERBACK CANDIDATES

- **Philip Rivers, SD:** With the loss of Drew Brees to the Saints, Rivers inherits the top spot in San Diego. He has attempted only 30 passes in two seasons and appeared in four games. However, I'm confident that he'll be able to find success in the AFC West. He'll be aided by his All-Pro TE Antonio Gates and will likely lean on LaDainian Tomlinson to resume a heavy pass-receiving workload. Remember, LT caught 100 balls in Brees' breakout year. Like all first-year starters, Rivers will experience some growing pains, but opening contests with Oakland and Tennessee will help him to get off on the right foot ahead of the early Bye week.

- **Aaron Brooks, OAK:** All the pieces are in place to allow Brooks to climb the ladder back toward the top of QB performers in Oakland. The Raiders possess tremendous depth at wideout and a bona fide star behind him in LaMont Jordan, who also catches more than his fair share of passes. If Brooks can cut down on early turnovers and resist the temptation to force the ball into Randy Moss, the Raiders will be able to score points. Brooks had topped 3,500 passing yards in four straight seasons with at least 21 TD passes ahead of last year's disaster. One positive to take from last season was that he cut his fumble total by 67 percent.

- **Mark Brunell, WAS:** It's difficult to qualify Brunell as a sleeper after he tossed 23 TD passes against 10 INTs last year. However, he'll definitely slip into the backup choices in the latter part of drafts. Brunell threw multiple TD passes in eight games, but also was shut out of the end zone in five others. I expect a more consistent effort from

Brunell this year with the upgrades in the receiving corps. He'll never pile up gaudy yardage totals (only seven games over 200 yards), but he'll be efficient.

The thing to watch this summer is the progress made by 2005 draft pick Jason Campbell. Washington brass is enamored with the second-year QB and projects him to be a long-time star in the league.

- **Jon Kitna/Josh McCown, DET:** This will be one of the big position battles entering training camp. Kitna has shown the ability to lead a team with his great 2004 season in Cincinnati and holds the experience card. Josh McCown showed great potential at times with Arizona, taking advantage of his big arm to hook up with his premier receivers. McCown is the long-term choice here, but they may put the veteran in to start the year with Mike Martz taking more time to get acclimated for a big run later on. Martz has made stars out of unknowns in Kurt Warner and Marc Bulger. With the complement of skilled receivers, a strong TE in Marcus Pollard, and a possible star in Kevin Jones (see the RB section), Martz certainly has the tools to make one of these quarterbacks a star.

- **David Carr, HOU:** Perhaps the Texans will figure out how to protect Carr this season. They certainly upgraded the offense with the addition of Eric Moulds to work opposite Andre Johnson, and the expected addition of Reggie Bush offers an explosive playmaker to run alongside Domanick Davis in the backfield. The switch to a former successful offensive coordinator in Gary Kubiak clearly won't hurt the efficiency of the attack. Carr is certainly worthy of a look-see for the backup role based on the changes in the attack and the presence of Kubiak on the sidelines.

- **Charlie Frye, CLE:** Frye looked good in spots last season as a rookie despite the constant shuttling of players in and out of the receiving corps due to injury. He's the favorite to win the starting role over Trent Dilfer and will be aided by the expected early return of speedster Braylon Edwards, the off-season acquisition of red-zone threat Joe Jurevicius, and the first extended look at former first-round pick Kellen Winslow Jr. Frye will be a waiver-wire player to open the season, but a full season of health from his receiving options could make him a serviceable second fantasy QB.

- **Joey Harrington, MIA:** Daunte Culpepper recently admitted that his repaired knee may not be available for the beginning of the year. As such, Harrington would take control of an offense consisting of wideouts Chris Chambers and Marty Booker and top tight end option Randy McMichael. His trials and tribulations in Detroit have been well documented, but I believe that a flawed offensive system and years of injured wide receivers hurt his progress as much as his own poor decisions. Therefore, in a new and more disciplined system under Nick Saban, Harrington still has the makeup to be a fantasy starter. I'm not ready to toss in the towel on the 27-year-old QB yet.

Running Back Candidates

- **Reuben Droughns, CLE:** Droughns did everything but get into the end zone for the Browns in 2005. He racked up 1,600 rushing and receiving yards combined, and played in every game. That's one aspect that works in his favor among oft-injured backfield mates Lee Suggs and William Green. Droughns has proven to be a durable option, carrying the ball 584 times over the past two seasons between Denver and Cleveland. The maturation of starter Charlie Frye and the return of top receiving targets Braylon Edwards and Kellen Winslow Jr. should allow better balance for the Browns and expanded red-zone opportunities for Droughns. He did score eight touchdowns with the Broncos in 2004.

- **Kevin Jones, DET:** Jones' appearance on this list is almost too easy, as he was widely considered the biggest bust of 2005. As such, owners will shy away from him on draft day this year, despite changes to the offense that will make it far more formidable. Jones struggled in a sputtering offense that was misdirected by Joey Harrington and Jeff Garcia under Steve Mariucci. Most troubling was Mariucci's abandonment of the run early within games. Jones topped 20 carries only three times last season, all wins by Detroit.

The introduction of Mike Martz immediately upgrades all aspects of the Detroit offense, as an opened-up passing attack will create space for Jones and allow him to get back to his success of 2004. The negativity associated with Jones' name from last season's performance will allow him to slip in the draft and create a potential bargain.

- **Ryan Moats, PHI:** As a rookie, Moats demonstrated game-breaking ability in late-season contests with two runs of 40 and 59 yards and three touchdowns. He also had at least one run of 10 or more yards in five straight games. This late audition will make him a viable option for Andy Reid in training camp to serve as the second back alongside Brian Westbrook. Westbrook is on track to be fully recovered from the foot injury that sidelined him for the second half of last year. However, his status for the opening weeks of the year won't be known until he goes full tilt in training camp. Moats stands as a solid midround selection to stash away in the event that Westbrook isn't ready to fully participate in the Donovan McNabb-led attack.

- **Correll Buckhalter, PHI:** Buckhalter also deserves mention in this space, as Andy Reid remains a huge fan of his toughness and running style. He missed two straight years with severe knee injuries, but will get a chance to compete for a roster spot this summer. When last we saw Buckhalter in 2003, he averaged 4.3 yards per carry and scored a total of nine touchdowns. If he's healthy and ready to contribute, he could factor in as a goal-line option for Philadelphia this season.

- **Frank Gore, SF:** Gore performed well in his audition for the starting tailback position in San Francisco with three nice efforts to close his rookie campaign. He ran for 255 yards over the final three weeks and added five catches for 70 yards in his attempt to wrest the top spot from Kevan Barlow. Barlow missed four of the final five games of the season with an injury, leaving Gore with a chance to make his case. He remains a capable runner, but his 3.3-yards-per-carry average allows Gore an opportunity to beat him out in camp.

Gore averaged 4.8 yards per carry on 127 attempts with six runs at 18 yards or longer. That breakaway speed will make him the top option for the 49ers in '06. He'll come at a bargain price as well, as the SF tag behind his name will cost him a few spots. Owners should be aware that the 49ers added Norv Turner as coordinate. Turner has been responsible for turning his pupils into perennial 1,000-yard backs with solid TD totals. Gore may be next.

- **Travis Henry, TEN:** Henry ran to consecutive 1,000-yard seasons with double-digit TDs in Buffalo and was one of the hottest young backs in the game before the Bills snagged the draft rights to Willis McGahee. He struggled through an ankle injury and the emergence of McGahee in 2004 to carry the ball only 94 times for 326 yards without a score. Henry moved to Tennessee and was limited to 10 games because of a four-game suspension. He carried the ball 88 times in a workload split with Chris Brown.

  Brown continues to get the nod as the first option out of the backfield, but he perennially battles injury concerns. That means that the selection of Brown needs to be accompanied by the selection of Henry several rounds later. Henry's past successes, combined with the fact that he's only 28 and has much less tread on the proverbial tires than most at that age, make him a solid sleeper option.

- **Cedric Benson, CHI:** The Bears will seek to get some return on their huge investment from 2005 this season. Thomas Jones shone brightly in 2005 after running unopposed for the top spot with Benson's failure to get into camp on time. Bears officials believe that Benson has the ability to carry the team, as evidenced by his performances when given the opportunity with Jones injured in Weeks 9 and 10. If Jones should revert to his struggles of the past or sustain an injury, Benson has the goods to dominate.

WIDE RECEIVER CANDIDATES

- **Drew Carter, CAR:** Carter appeared in only two games during the regular season last season, but showed big-play potential and earned a bigger role in the playoffs. Carter registered a catch of 29 or more yards in each of his four games played with two touchdowns. He's a huge 6-foot-3 target who can run the deep patterns opposite Steve Smith with Keyshawn Johnson owning the middle. Carter enters the season in a battle for the third position with Keary Colbert, but barring any issues with his health, he should win out.

- **Nate Burleson, SEA:** Burleson is another example of a player whose miserable 2005 season (performance and injury combination) lands him in the list of "sleeper" selections heading into draft day. Expectations were sky high after his 1,000-yard, nine-TD 2004 campaign, and he regularly flew off draft boards in the fifth round. Burleson failed to record more than three catches in a game until Week 16, topped 50 receiving yards just once, and scored a single TD in 11 games. He'll run opposite Darrell Jackson in the high-powered Seattle attack. With the other teams in the NFC West still addressing needs in their respective defensive backfields, opportunities will be there for Burleson to rise toward his 2004 numbers.

- **Samie Parker, KAN:** Injuries on the offensive line slowed the KC passing attack early in 2005, and late in the year, everyone witnessed the Larry Johnson show. Lost in the euphoria over the exploits of No. 27 was the stellar play of second-year speedster Parker. Parker averaged 14.8 yards per catch on 36 grabs in 2005. He had a five-game stretch toward the end of the season during which he caught at least four passes per game. Parker recorded a catch of 20 or more yards in four of those outings. He offers a big-play threat for Trent Green and will help stretch the field to get Johnson toward his coveted 2,000-yard mark.

- **Mike Williams, DET:** The Lions hired Mike Martz to run the offense after years of putting up pinball-like numbers in St. Louis. The thought of working within that scheme has been most enticing for the second-year receiver out of USC, watching highlight tapes and recognizing that the opportunity for stardom exists in Martz's system. Williams was a bit of a disappointment in 2005, as were most Detroit skill players. Williams caught 29 passes for 350 yards and a single TD in Week 1. In a spread attack, Williams will cause matchup issues with smaller cornerbacks. He's rededicated himself to the game and wants to prove the doubters and critics wrong.

- **Jabar Gaffney, PHI:** Gaffney quietly amassed 55 receptions in the Houston offense last year. In fact, he caught five or more passes in seven games. Though Gaffney averaged only 8.9 yards per catch, he demonstrated an ability to get open and make plays. He was used primarily as a possession receiver, as evidenced by the low 2.3-yards-per-catch average. Gaffney is a good route runner who will compete for a starting role in Philadelphia opposite Reggie Brown.

- **Mark Clayton, BAL:** Clayton turned in a solid rookie season as part of the retooled offense in Baltimore. The addition of veteran Derrick Mason helped to make the passing game more diversified and freed up TE Todd Heap. Clayton was a big part of Kyle Boller's strong finish — 24 balls over the final five games for 316 yards and two scores. The only question now is whether Boller can continue his growth from the end of the year or whether exiled Titans star Steve McNair joins the fold.

- **Isaac Bruce, STL:** Longtime fantasy star Isaac Bruce will slide down draft lists on account of his injury-riddled 2005 season and the fact that he'll turn 34 during the season. Bruce put up solid numbers after his return to the field in Week 10, even though St. Louis had already lost Marc Bulger for the year. Bruce caught four or more passes in five of his final seven games with two touchdowns and finished with 525 receiving yards and 36 receptions. Remember, he'd caught at least 64 passes with 981 passing yards for six straight seasons ahead of last year's injury-shortened year. Scott Linehan's system will feature RB Steven Jackson more, but that will only serve to make the passing game more efficient.

- **Bernard Berrian, CHI:** The Bears have a deep ball threat in the speedy Berrian. They just need a quarterback under center to get him the ball. Rex Grossman and off-season acquisition Brian Griese will battle for the starting job in training camp. Both players will be given significantly more opportunities to make plays downfield than rookie Kyle Orton received last season. Berrian offered a new wrinkle to the offense once utilized down the stretch. He caught passes of 34, 43, and 54 yards in three of four late-season contests.

- **Tyrone Calico, TEN:** Calico is a perennial sleeper pick due to his 6-foot-4 frame and leaping ability. Unfortunately, Calico has been unable to remain healthy the past two seasons after a strong rookie campaign. He caught 18 passes in 2003, four of which went for touchdowns. Last year, Calico appeared sporadically throughout the year, catching 22 passes for 191 yards. The Titans have loaded the receiving corps via free agency and the draft the last two seasons (David Givens, Brandon Jones, and Roydell Williams join 2004 breakout star Drew Bennett). However, Calico's athleticism and size make him one to watch in training camp, particularly with the prospect of big-armed rookie Vince Young lining up under center.

- **Eric Parker, SD:** Parker shone in Week 1 while Antonio Gates served a team-imposed one-game suspension (5 catches, 75 yards), but fell off of Drew Brees' radar until midseason. Parker caught at least three passes in 12 of the 15 games in which he appeared and topped 60 receiving yards on seven occasions. He scored two of his three touchdowns after the Week 10 Bye and finished the year with 85 looks (5.67 per game). The departure of Drew Brees will likely weigh on fantasy owners minds on draft day, allowing for a potential bargain to be had in the speedy Parker.

- **Roddy White, ATL:** White has reportedly put on noticeable muscle mass this off-season and has shown great speed in his workouts with Michael Vick. The Falcons knew they had something with this first-round pick from UAB, as he averaged 15.4 yards per catch on 29 receptions a year ago, but his off-season work has him looming large in their 2006 plans. White recorded a catch of at least 19 yards in 11 straight games to conclude the season, including two 54-yard bombs.

- **Ernest Wilford, JAC:** Wilford broke past former first-round selection Reggie Williams to become a strong possession receiver and red-zone threat in 2005. He teamed with rookie Matt Jones to form a formidable duo behind longtime Jaguars star Jimmy Smith. He quietly recorded a catch of at least 10 yards in every 2006 game, including touchdown receptions in seven different contests. With Jones only in his second year as a receiver, Jack Del Rio will lean on Wilford to become a larger contributor on a weekly basis. I suspect that his TD total stays at approximately the same level, but that his reception and yardage totals escalate.

Tight End Candidates

- **Zachary Hilton, NO:** Hilton recently re-signed with the Saints for one year. He became a popular waiver-wire pickup down the stretch, regularly targeted upward of seven times per game from Week 11 through the end of the year. He caught three or more passes in six of the final seven games of the year. I won't compare him directly with Antonio Gates, but Drew Brees didn't become a star in the league until he learned to utilize his TE. At 6-foot-8, Hilton offers a large target with good hands who will create matchup problems downfield. The addition of Reggie Bush and his likely involvement in the passing game will open the middle of the field for Hilton.

- **Jeb Putzier, HOU:** Former Broncos coordinator and new Texans coach Gary Kubiak brought his TE to Houston. Putzier stands 6-foot-4 and can make plays downfield. He averages 14.1 yards per catch on his career with two-thirds of his catches going for first downs. The Texans have been lacking a true threat at TE, and Putzier's addition (not to mention that of wide receiver Eric Moulds, of course) should help to push David Carr forward.

- **Kellen Winslow Jr., CLE:** After two lost seasons, Winslow Jr. is reportedly in shape and ready to contribute in 2006. A healthy tight end of his stature (remember, he was projected to ascend to the top of the TE list as a rookie in 2004) should help the development of Charlie Frye and get the Cleveland offense in motion. He's a bit of a stretch for a starting TE slot in Week 1, but is definitely one to watch on the waiver wire.

KICKER CANDIDATES

- **Jason Hanson, DET:** The addition of Mike Martz should jumpstart this long-sputtering offense. Though he can't kick for distance with the same accuracy that he did in his prime, he's still money from 40 yards in. Hanson is past the injury that slowed him in 2005, and the new spread attack should provide for increased FG and PAT opportunities. He attempted only 24 FGs in 2005.

- **Sebastian Janikowski, OAK:** Janikowski was one of many disappointments for Raiders fans last season, converting on a career-low 67 percent of his field-goal attempts. The normally reliable powerhouse from long range was just 7-for-15 on attempts of 40 or more yards. In 2003 and 2004, he converted 47 of 53 attempts (88.6 percent), including 20 of 25 attempts from 40 yards or further out (80 percent). A new coaching regime and a full season of health from skill position players should put Janikowski in position to reclaim his place as a fantasy starter.

- **John Hall, WAS:** Hall carries an injury risk for fantasy owners, as he's missed 14 games over the last two seasons. He converted five of six attempts from 40-plus upon his return to the team last year. The Redskins significantly upgraded their receiving corps with the additions of Brandon Lloyd and Antwaan Randle El, and this should put Hall in a position to return to his 100-point days achieved with the Jets (and first year with Washington).

In the next chapter, I examine the other side of the equation. I review a number of players for whom expectations might exceed their actual value on draft day and lead to fantasy headaches. At least one member of the list is sure to surprise.

26 Bust Candidates

- Quarterback Candidates
- Running Back Candidates
- Wide Receiver Candidates
- Tight End Candidates
- Kicker Candidates

The excitement of producing player projections and looking forward to the new season naturally brings positive feelings and hopes that teams who have struggled in the past will reemerge and that past favorites will continue to perform at a high level. Unfortunately, a number of circumstances often conspire to tear away at those lofty expectations. The player may himself get hurt or see his numbers dragged down by the injury of another player on the offense. Additionally, there's always the possibility that a player's performance goes into a tailspin and opens the door for a replacement to steal playing time.

This chapter examines players at each offensive skill position whose situations have changed or past performances have been so great that they are candidates to disappoint this season.

QUARTERBACK CANDIDATES

- **Brett Favre, GNB:** The Packers welcome their future Hall of Fame QB back to the field for 2006. Favre, Packers fans, and fantasy owners all suffered through the poor performances and injuries of 2005. The Packers lost their top receiver in the first game (Javon Walker) and lost their top two running backs (Ahman Green and Najeh Davenport) shortly thereafter. While it is true that the Packers return a healthy complement of running backs and star wide receiver Donald Driver, the ability to draft "Brett Favre" might force his selection several rounds too early. Favre still has the arm strength to deliver the ball, but I expect last season's problems on the offensive line to continue. Regardless of the injuries at skill positions, the biggest change for the Packers occurred on the offensive line where two longtime starters had been lost. A third member of that unit left this off-season. Favre may improve on his touchdown-to-interception ratio (20 TD and 27 INT in 2005), but a slow start to 2006 might force him to throw into double and triple coverage in a desperate attempt to make plays once again.

- **Jake Plummer, DEN:** Plummer was uncharacteristically careful with the football in 2005 and received numerous feature stories on the strength of an eight-game streak without an interception. Though Plummer accounted for multiple touchdowns in only five games, he was shut out in only three starts. Owners may be tempted to push Plummer up their draft charts based on his recent performances. Plummer controlled his turnover rate in two of the last three seasons, tossed 27 TD passes in 2004, and saw his receiving corps bolstered with the addition of Javon Walker. However, faced with pressure in the playoffs, Plummer reverted to his erratic form. The addition of first-round selection Jay Cutler will also weigh heavily on him. As such, while Plummer will make his share of plays, he'll try to force the issue and raise his turnover total.

- **Brad Johnson, MIN:** Johnson was hit or miss after assuming the reins for the Vikings last year. He tossed 12 touchdowns in 10 games with five multi-TD games. That also means that he was shut out on four occasions. Johnson threw for fewer than 200 yards on six occasions. Johnson is unable to scramble and buy time, which leads me to question how well he'll hold up over the course of the season. An interesting fact out of his stats from last season is that Johnson completed a pass of at least 21 yards in every start.

- **Matt Hasselbeck, SEA:** Can the Seahawks possibly be as efficient this year as they were in 2005? Hasselbeck tossed TD passes in all but one game that he finished and accounted for multiple TDs in eight games. He saved his best performances for the playoff weeks, accounting for nine touchdowns during Weeks 14-16. I'm slightly concerned that the loss of Steve Hutchinson changes the dynamics on the offensive line and leaves him exposed to hits, and that the loss of Joe Jurevicius will take away some of those matchup advantages in the red zone. A healthy Darrell Jackson and the addition of Nate Burleson will no doubt allow them to move the ball, but I'm expecting several more of these drives to end with Josh Brown's leg.

- **Trent Green, KAN:** Green has thrown for over 4,000 yards in three straight seasons. It marked the fifth time in seven NFL seasons that Green threw over 500 passes. However, Green threw for his lowest TD total (17) since his first year in Kansas City. Injuries on the offensive line limited production in several contests and forced Tony Gonzalez to serve more as a blocker. I'm intrigued by the possibility of Samie Parker offering a deep threat for the Chiefs and Gonzalez getting back to route running, but I'm more concerned about him losing TD tosses to the legs of Larry Johnson and Priest Holmes (assuming he returns).

RUNNING BACK CANDIDATES

- **Jamal Lewis, BAL:** The Ravens re-signed Lewis shortly after acquiring former Broncos star Mike Anderson. He certainly didn't run like a player in search of a big new contract in 2005. Granted, Lewis was limited early in the year as a result of off-season surgery, but he finished with 61 or fewer yards on nine occasions. He still managed to finish over 900 yards, further proof that 1,000-yard seasons for full-time backs are primarily due to health. Lewis finished with four total touchdowns.

Assuming that the deal with Steve McNair finally goes through, I expect the offense to continue its progress from the final weeks of 2005. Derrick Mason, Mark Clayton, and a healthy Todd Heap provide tremendous receiving targets and will create running room for the tandem of Lewis and Anderson. I expect Anderson to share carries with Lewis this season. Though Lewis may see the bulk of the action between the 20s, I suspect that the rugged Anderson gets the call around the goal line. As a result, Lewis moves a couple notches down my board. He's still a fantasy starter, but those who draft him must handcuff Anderson to the selection.

- **Larry Johnson, KAN:** The inclusion of Larry Johnson in this list certainly raised eyebrows, I'm sure. I know that I have Johnson ranked as the top overall player, and I stand by it. I put him on the list for two reasons. First, the expectations are sky high as a result of his huge accomplishments after Priest Holmes went down with a season-ending injury. Anything less than the equal of his 1,750 yards and 20 touchdowns will be considered a disappointment by many. The second issue to consider is the possibility that Priest Holmes may return to the field. If he is ultimately cleared for duty and chooses to return, Johnson will lose 8-10 touches per game and thereby moves his yardage down each week and possibly eats away at bonus point opportunities.

- **Carnell Williams, TAM:** Williams makes the list for one specific reason. I fear that he'll be overused as Jon Gruden works to keep the heat off of Chris Simms. Williams tallied an amazing 290 carries last year as a rookie. What makes that number even more staggering is that Williams missed two games in their entirety and carried the ball 14 or fewer times in five other contests. He'll provide a few big games, just as he did last year, but I'm fearful of the overall workload and vulture carries for Mike Alstott.

- **Julius Jones, DAL:** Jones is always going to be good for at least one monster game (see his 194-yard, 2-TD game in Week 16 vs. Carolina), and the addition of Terrell Owens will most certainly open up the Dallas attack. However, Owens' presence doesn't necessarily translate into TDs on the ground, nor does it preclude Jones from getting hurt. Jones was held scoreless in 10 of 13 games in which he played, despite the fact that Dallas averaged 20 points per game. His Week 16 effort was also his only 100-yard rushing game of the year for those eyeballing bonus point possibilities. I expect an up-tick over his disappointing 2005 campaign, but the enticement of the upgraded passing game will force him off the boards too early.

- **Thomas Jones, CHI:** Jones had a career year in Chicago after Cedric Benson, who had been expected to challenge him for the start, failed to participate in much of training camp. Chicago lost starting QB Rex Grossman to injury, and then relied on Jones extensively with rookie Kyle Orton under center. Jones skipped voluntary workouts in April and early May, prompting many to believe that there's discontent in the Chicago backfield. He was the subject of numerous trade rumors ahead of April's College Entry Draft, and it's believed that Benson will cut into his workload this year, if not eclipse him altogether.

WIDE RECEIVER CANDIDATES

- **Joe Jurevicius, CLE:** Jurevicius' role and expected contribution for Seattle in 2005 prompted a bit of a battle with a noted national journalist last season. I argued that he would factor heavily in the Seahawks' red zone attack and that he would make for a great sleeper pick given the strength of Seattle's offense. He disagreed and asserted that I needed to step away from the game for a spell. Needless to say, I won the argument on Jurevicius with his 10 TD receptions last year. Unfortunately, Jurevicius' brilliance last season makes him a target for overbidding or reaching this draft season. Jurevicius loses out in the move to Cleveland based on the level of QB play and the potency of the Cleveland attack. Charlie Frye will make for a good pro, but I'm not so sure it happens this quickly. Jurevicius' role will most definitely be expanded, as he assumes a starting role for the entire year without consideration for injuries as he had in Seattle. I'm confident that he improves on his catch total of 55 from last season and that his yardage count rises as well. However, he'll be hard pressed to run up on the 10 touchdowns scored last year in Seattle.

- **Keenan McCardell, SD:** Like Jurevicius, McCardell's totals are expected to slip based on a change at QB. Philip Rivers takes over for the departed Drew Brees, and that likely indicates good things for the workloads of LaDainian Tomlinson and Antonio Gates. However, I suspect that the wide receivers will suffer somewhat as Rivers adapts to game speed after being relegated to two years on the practice field. McCardell turned 36 in January, which typically marks the time of declining skills of receivers. Though his 70 catches for 917 yards and nine scores in 2005 demonstrate that he still has game, I suspect that McCardell's role slides as fellow wideout Eric Parker emerges. I believe McCardell still posts solid reception and yardage totals, but that his TD contribution will fall by half.

- **Ashley Lelie, DEN:** The acquisition of Javon Walker by the Broncos relegates Lelie to a third receiver role. Unfortunately for him, the Broncos rarely use three-receiver formations due to the need for multiple tight ends to assist the brilliant Denver running game. Lelie disappeared last season after a strong 2004 campaign in which he topped 1,000 receiving yards with seven touchdowns. Lelie was an infrequent contributor for the Broncos, reducing his reception total by nearly one per game and producing only one TD. If he plays in Denver, he has a reduced role. He's suggested that he may hold out, which isn't good for anyone. The third scenario has Lelie being released or traded. I don't expect the Broncos to surrender to his demands, particularly with Rod Smith being in his mid-30s and Javon Walker's return from injury.

- **Lee Evans, BUF:** Evans certainly has tremendous big-play ability downfield. There's no question that when utilized effectively, he can electrify a crowd and ranks among the best receivers in the game. Unfortunately, there's been no consistency to the workload, nor is there consistency at QB. The numbers at the end of the year don't look too shabby at first glance. He finished 2005 with 743 yards and seven touchdowns, but caught three or fewer passes in 11 games. Five of those touchdowns came in two games, so it's feast or famine. The loss of Eric Moulds to Houston will make him a more frequent target for Holcomb, Nall, or Losman, but I'd look to a more consistent performer early in the draft (third-year receiver theory notwithstanding).

TIGHT END CANDIDATES

- **Jerramy Stevens, SEA:** Stevens elevated his game in 2005 as Seattle awaited the return of Darrell Jackson from his knee injury. He caught 14 more passes than he did in 2004 despite missing two games and offered a bonus to fantasy owners by scoring a touchdown in each of the fantasy playoff weeks (Weeks 14-16). For all his successes in putting a troubled past behind him (including scoring in the NFC Championship Game and Super Bowl), Stevens is perhaps best remembered for a series of dropped balls in big moments. His inconsistency in being able to secure the ball may relegate him to a secondary role in the receiving corps this year, even with the loss of red-zone target Jurevicius. Additionally, Stevens continues to recover from off-season knee surgery that will likely limit his availability during camp. Those factors keep him on the edge of fantasy starters/reserves. He has the talent, but still needs to piece it all together.

- **Chris Cooley, WAS:** Cooley finished 2005 with 71 receptions to finish second to Santana Moss. He averaged 48 yards per game, finishing with fewer than 30 only three times from Week 4 to Week 16. However, with the exception of his huge Week 15 against Dallas, his overall numbers ranked him evenly with a number of other TEs. I expect his reception and yardage totals to drop this year with the additions of Antwaan Randle El and Brandon Lloyd. Mark Brunell will utilize his strong complement of receivers to pick up the short yardage and middle routes for which Cooley was used so prevalently in 2005.

KICKER CANDIDATES

- **Neil Rackers, ARI:** The Cardinals added a top-flight back in Edgerrin James, which will translate into more sustained drives and additional touchdown celebrations. Rackers was phenomenal last season, racking up multiple FG attempts in all 16 games (42 overall). I look for his FG attempts to decrease this season with the achievement of balance in the offense. Last season, Rackers kicked twice as many field goals as he did PATs. Look for that disparity to shrink this season.

- **Matt Stover, BAL:** Stover also booted an extraordinary amount of field goals in 2005, connecting on 30 of 34 attempts (tied for fourth). Stover tied Rackers for the most attempts from 40-49 yards with 14. The expected acquisition of Steve McNair combined with a potent 1-2 attack in the backfield with Jamal Lewis and Mike Anderson should sustain drives and turn a number of those four- and five-point FGs into lower-scoring attempts inside 30 yards and single-point PATs.

The next chapter begins a series of pieces designed to prepare you for your upcoming fantasy draft on a position-by-position basis. I offer my analysis of the top performers at each fantasy football position, beginning with the quarterbacks. Peyton Manning remains the leader of the pack, but the gap behind him is closing.

27 Quarterback (QB) Rankings

Fantasy owners flock to the running back position on draft day due to the frequency with which players are injured and the number of committee situations that thwart the fantasy upside of so many players. The first quarterback off the board is always Peyton Manning. It's just a question of when a manager gets bold and shifts away from the stream of running backs.

In this chapter, I offer detailed analysis of the top quarterbacks to consider on draft day. A complete ranking list for use in your draft preparation is available in Appendix F1.

Additional player profiles are available on our Web site at http://www.savvyfantasysports.com.

1. **Peyton Manning, Indianapolis Colts (Bye Week – 6):** Fantasy owners who banked on Manning to repeat his record-setting touchdown pace from 2004 were disappointed in 2005. Manning finished with 28 scores in an offense that featured running back Edgerrin

James and received tremendous support from its defense. Additionally, Manning barely took a snap in either of the final two games, as Indianapolis had clinched home field advantage in the playoffs. Manning threw multiple touchdown passes in 10 games last season, and it's unlikely that the Colts will be in the position of being able to sit him for the final two weeks again this year. The Colts will also be featuring a new starting tailback with James' departure for Arizona. Therefore, the possibility exists for Manning and the passing game to pile up touchdowns once again.

2. **Tom Brady, New England Patriots (Bye Week – 6):** Brady doesn't possess the classic QB arm, and the team has made its championship run with a complement of good, but not great, receivers. All the while, Brady has executed the system flawlessly and put the team in a position to win. He's also quietly put up excellent fantasy numbers for four straight seasons. Brady has averaged 3,797 yards and 26 touchdown passes per season since assuming the full-time starting job in 2002.

3. **Matt Hasselbeck, Seattle Seahawks (Bye Week – 5):** The 2005 Seattle offense ranks among the most prolific in NFL history. Quarterback Matt Hasselbeck took advantage of opposing defenses' preoccupation with Shaun Alexander to post his third consecutive season with at least 3,400 passing yards. Over the past three seasons, Hasselbeck has averaged 3,561 passing yards and 24 touchdown passes. The most impressive statistic in Hasselbeck's huge season was his ability to limit turnovers. He threw only nine interceptions and played turnover-free football in 10 of his starts.

4. **Donovan McNabb, Philadelphia Eagles (Bye Week – 9):** The Eagles' leader attempted to play through a

sports hernia injury before a host of other injuries to Philadelphia skill position players and the feud with Terrell Owens put him on the bench for good in Week 11. McNabb threw 16 touchdown passes in nine starts, including four multi-touchdown performances, and topped 250 passing yards in seven of his nine starts. Philadelphia opens the year without Owens. Although it limits the distractions, it forces another receiver to step up as the primary receiving option.

5. **Carson Palmer, Cincinnati Bengals (Bye Week – 5):** Palmer blossomed in his second year as a starting NFL quarterback and led the NFL in touchdown passes with 32. The Bengals have assembled a young and talented receiving corps to complement power running back Rudi Johnson. Palmer was shut out of the end in only one of 15 games that he completed, and he tossed multiple touchdown passes in 12 different outings. The Bengals return all of their offensive weapons this season, and only time will tell if the injury Palmer sustains keeps him out of the opener. All early reports indicate that Palmer will fully recover by opening day from the knee injury sustained in the playoffs.

6. **Eli Manning, New York Giants (Bye Week – 4):** Manning impressed fans and fantasy owners in his first year as a starter for the Giants. He threw for 3,762 yards and tied for fourth in the NFL with 24 touchdown passes. The main negative attribute in Manning's game at the moment is that he still forces throws into coverage, which results in a high turnover rate (17 interceptions). He continues to learn on the job, and with top receiving options Plaxico Burress and Jeremy Shockey to team with Amani Toomer and Tiki Barber out of the backfield, Manning is a favorite to challenge for the touchdown title in the NFC.

7. **Marc Bulger, St. Louis Rams (Bye Week – 7):** Bulger was on pace to post his best offensive totals ever in 2005, but an unfortunate injury sustained on an interception return against Indianapolis ultimately ended his season in Week 11. Bulger tossed at least one touchdown pass in each of his starts and averaged 287 passing yards per game. He'll return to run the offense for new coach Scott Linehan. Linehan had great success in Miami a season ago, and expectations remain high for another spectacular offensive run for the Rams.

8. **Jake Delhomme, Carolina Panthers (Bye Week – 9):** The Panthers welcomed back all-world wide receiver Steve Smith to the mix in 2005, which pushed Delhomme back into the game's elite. Delhomme completed a career-best 60.2 percent of his passes for 3,421 yards and 24 touchdowns. The Panthers added veteran wide receiver Keyshawn Johnson in free agency to run opposite Smith, and deep pass threat Drew Carter is ready to contribute for a full season. Delhomme has averaged 24 touchdown passes over the past three seasons and should reach that level once again in 2006.

9. **Trent Green, Kansas City Chiefs (Bye Week – 3):** The Chiefs remained a potent offense in 2005, relying chiefly on the strength of running back Larry Johnson. The brilliance of Johnson on a weekly basis allowed Green to pick his spots downfield, and he recorded his third consecutive season of at least 4,000 passing yards. However, his touchdown total dipped markedly from 27 to 17. The Chiefs expect the offensive line to be healthy, which will allow Tony Gonzalez to be a threat in the red zone once again instead of staying back in pass protection. The player to watch on this

squad is third-year receiver Samie Parker, who possesses game-changing speed and may vault Green back to the top of the fantasy charts.

10. **Kurt Warner, Arizona Cardinals (Bye Week – 9):** The pieces are in place for Warner to thrive for the Cardinals. Arizona has assembled a tremendous cast of offensive skill performers with receivers Anquan Boldin and Larry Fitzgerald leading the charge. The team added a premier tailback with the signing of Edgerrin James away from the Indianapolis Colts. Warner threw for 2,713 yards and 11 touchdowns in 10 games last season. The big question with Warner is how many games he'll be able to stand under center. He's missed over 20 games due to injury over the past three seasons. If Warner is able to stay upright and finds protection in the pocket, he is poised to rediscover some of the magic from his time in St. Louis. However, owners who turn to Warner on draft day would be well advised to draft his backup, who will be determined this summer.

11. **Drew Bledsoe, Dallas Cowboys (Bye Week – 3):** Part of Bill Parcells' winning formula is putting his offense in the hands of a veteran quarterback. The Cowboys added Drew Bledsoe to run the offense in 2005, and he responded with a tremendous year after two sub-par efforts in Buffalo. Bledsoe completed 60 percent of his passes for 3,639 yards and 23 touchdowns. The Cowboys added controversial wide receiver Terrell Owens this off-season after a tumultuous season in Philadelphia. Owens immediately upgrades the passing attack and makes Bledsoe a candidate to boost his numbers back to his 2002 highs (4,359 yards and 24 touchdowns).

12. **Daunte Culpepper, Miami Dolphins (Bye Week – 8):** Those disappointed by Peyton Manning's drop-off in production last season could at least find some comfort that they didn't wait to select Culpepper in last year's drafts. Culpepper struggled horribly in seven games (six touchdowns and 12 interceptions) before he tore three ligaments in his knee to end his season. This off-season, Culpepper was able to prompt a deal that sent him from Minnesota to Miami. He joins a Miami offense stocked with productive skill position players and a scheme that allowed Gus Frerotte to reach heights of 3,000 passing yards and 18 passing touchdowns. If healthy, Culpepper will return to form in Nick Saban's disciplined offense, and fantasy owners will find a potential bargain selection.

13. **Jake Plummer, Denver Broncos (Bye Week – 4):** Since his arrival in Denver, Jake Plummer has become a better all-around quarterback. He's been more decisive in his delivery and worked within the system, as opposed to his more frenetic style in Arizona. Plummer threw only seven interceptions for the second time in the last three years and topped 3,300 passing yards for the second straight season. He welcomes a new top-flight receiver in Javon Walker, who was acquired in a draft-day deal with Green Bay. The Denver offense relies heavily on the running game, but Plummer receives his share of opportunities to make plays with an average of 488 passing attempts the last two seasons.

14. **Ben Roethlisberger, Pittsburgh Steelers (Bye Week – 4):** The Pittsburgh offense has long relied on a strong running game. However, there were signs early last season that Roethlisberger and the passing game were destined to play a larger role in the team's fortunes.

He threw for multiple touchdown passes in five of Pittsburgh's first six games including four games over 200 yards passing. The passing game stepped back after he missed three games with a knee injury. With the exception of a shootout loss to Cincinnati in which he threw for 386 yards and three touchdowns, Roethlisberger attempted 20 or fewer passes in four of his final five games. The retirement of Jerome Bettis signals the dawn of a new era, and Bill Cowher will undoubtedly put more plays in Roethlisberger's hands in 2006.

15. **Drew Brees, New Orleans Saints (Bye Week – 7):** The Saints offered Brees a huge contract to take control of their offense after two strong years in San Diego. Brees made great use of his tight end and running back in rising to the upper echelon of quarterbacks. Those components await him in New Orleans, where emerging tight end Zach Hilton and No. 2 draft pick Reggie Bush will team up with the receiving duo of Joe Horn and Donte' Stallworth to provide a solid receiving corps. There still remains a question as to whether Brees' shoulder will be ready for opening weekend after a brutal injury sustained in the 2005 season finale. New Orleans failed to make another move in free agency and stood pat with the backups on the roster, leading everyone to believe that he'll be ready to contribute.

16. **Aaron Brooks, Oakland Raiders (Bye Week – 3):** Brooks left New Orleans after seeing his numbers regress in a difficult situation last season. He joins the Oakland Raiders as their signal caller and inherits a strong contingent of skill position players led by Randy Moss, Jerry Porter, and all-purpose running back LaMont Jordan. The main issue with Brooks has been

his decision-making later in games. If the team is struggling to advance the ball, he inevitably forces one too many throws and piles up turnovers. The Raiders will run their offense through Jordan and try to find Brooks a comfort zone

17. **Brett Favre, Green Bay Packers (Bye Week – 6):** The legendary Packers quarterback finally ended all the speculation and rejoined the team for another run. The Packers were decimated by injuries in 2005, losing three running backs and their No. 1 and No. 3 receivers for extended stretches. As such, Favre pushed the issue and made a number of questionable throws, which led to a disappointing 29 interceptions. His 20 touchdowns tied for 10th among NFL quarterbacks, but he threw just one touchdown pass in the Packers' final five games. The Packers re-signed running backs Ahman Green and Najeh Davenport with the hope of resurrecting a sound ground game, and receivers Donald Driver and Robert Ferguson offer experienced and familiar targets for Favre. . However, continued problems on the offensive line may make Favre's 2006 season as difficult as his 2005 season.

18. **Michael Vick, Atlanta Falcons (Bye Week – 5):** The Falcons and fantasy owners continue to await the elevation of Michael Vick's game. He remains a draft-day favorite due to his numerous highlight reel plays, but his performance has yet to match his high draft status. Vick threw only 15 touchdown passes last season, but added six rushing touchdowns to reach a reasonable level of performance. Unfortunately, it's difficult to depend on a quarterback's legs when setting a fantasy lineup, regardless of how effective such running plays have been in the past. Vick worked tire-

lessly with receivers Roddy White and Michael Jenkins this off-season with the hope of elevating the Atlanta passing game to achieve a semblance of balance with the NFL's leading rushing attack. From all reports, Vick has improved his delivery and decisiveness in early drills. We'll see how that carries over to the field come Week 1 at Carolina.

19. **Mark Brunell, Washington Redskins (Bye Week – 8):** Brunell enjoyed the finest season of his NFL career last year in his second year in Washington. He tossed a career-high 23 touchdowns against 10 interceptions and eclipsed the 3,000-yard mark for the first time since 2001. The team is installing a new offense under coordinator Al Saunders and upgraded the receiving corps with the additions of the athletic Brandon Lloyd and Antwaan Randle El. In the first year of a new system, Washington is likely to rely heavily on the legs of Clinton Portis which may limit Brunell's scoring opportunities.

20. **Byron Leftwich, Jacksonville Jaguars (Bye Week – 6):** The Jaguars received stellar play from Leftwich through 10 games with 15 passing touchdowns and over 2,100 yards passing. Unfortunately, Leftwich was lost for the year in the Week 12 game against Arizona after throwing only two passes. Leftwich and the Jaguars begin 2006 with the search to replace Jimmy Smith, who retired as the team's all-time receiving leader. The Jaguars have built a strong nucleus of young receivers in the last four drafts to prepare for this scenario. Reggie Williams, Matt Jones, Ernest Wilford, and Marcedes Lewis will offer Leftwich capable options, but his health remains a concern.

21. **Josh McCown, Detroit Lions (Bye Week – 8):** The Joey Harrington experiment ended in Detroit after four seasons. The Lions replaced him with the capable tandem of McCown and former Bengals QB Jon Kitna. Entering training camp, Kitna has a slight lead based on experience, but McCown has the arm Mike Martz wants under center. The winner in this battle will have ample receiving weapons (Roy Williams, Mike Williams, Charles Rogers, and Corey Bradford) to produce.

22. **David Carr, Houston Texans (Bye Week – 5):** The Texans have been unable to protect David Carr in his four years under center. He's been sacked an average of 52 times each season. This off-season, Houston upgraded the receiving game with the acquisition of longtime Buffalo Bills star Eric Moulds and former Denver tight end Jeb Putzier. Carr will be encouraged to roll out and buy time for receivers to find holes in coverage by new coach Gary Kubiak, who brings a strong pedigree from his potent offenses in Denver. There was much speculation this off-season that Carr and the Texans would part ways, as the Texans were in a position to draft hometown favorite Vince Young. Instead, the Texans gave Carr a huge vote of confidence by paying out a sizable roster bonus. Kubiak is convinced that Carr has the goods to be an NFL star, and he's tied his future to Carr's performance.

23. **Brad Johnson, Minnesota Vikings (Bye Week – 6):** Johnson was hit or miss after assuming the starting role in Minnesota. He threw multiple touchdown passes in five games and was shut out of the end zone in four others. Johnson also threw for fewer than 200 yards in six of 10 games to a receiving corps slowed by injuries. New coach Brad Childress utilizes his run-

ning backs as receivers out of the backfield, which indicates that new featured back Chester Taylor will be heavy involved on both sides of the game.

24. **Steve McNair, TBD (Bye Week – TBD):** The off-season saga involving Steve McNair is scheduled to end by July 1. After years of dutiful service, the Titans locked him out of team facilities as he attempted to train for the upcoming season. At issue is McNair's large salary cap figure for 2006, which the Titans would like to renegotiate. It has been widely speculated that McNair leaves the Titans at that time to join the Baltimore Ravens. The selection of Vince Young in this April's draft and the retention of Billy Volek indicate that his tenure in Tennessee is coming to a close. Coach Jeff Fisher would like to have his veteran quarterback on the roster in the fall, but it appears that a battle is brewing with upper management.

Should he join the Ravens, McNair would likely supplant Kyle Boller as the starter and inherit a strong running game and a solid group of wide receivers, including former teammate Derrick Mason and tight end Todd Heap. A change of scenery could put McNair back on the fantasy radar.

25. **Philip Rivers, San Diego Chargers (Bye Week – 3):** The Chargers allowed Drew Brees to exit for New Orleans in free agency, which means that 2004 No. 1 pick Philip Rivers ascends to the top spot. Rivers displayed all the physical tools to jump in and start immediately with Brees' struggles in 2003, but contract negotiations broke down and he missed much of training camp. As they say, the rest is history, as Brees responded with a breakout season in 2004. Rivers will follow much the same formula that made Brees a star

by throwing to tight end Antonio Gates and running back LaDainian Tomlinson with great frequency. With receivers Keenan McCardell and Eric Parker also in the mix, the growing pains will be fewer for Rivers in his first significant action.

The next chapter examines the top options available at the highly scrutinized running back position. The top three picks at the position are widely considered a notch above the rest of the field. The order in which they are drafted depends on the league's settings and faith in player history.

28 Running Back (RB) Rankings

The running back position is commonly referred to as the king of all roster positions. The first two rounds of the draft constitute a veritable feeding frenzy whereby every sure-fire starter is tucked away on a roster. Though quarterbacks score more on average, the separation between midlevel players isn't quite as stark as it is at the running back position. After all, coaches aren't switching out quarterbacks on a play-by-play basis due to down and distance charts.

This chapter offers analysis of the top running backs sure to be in the discussion as your team comes on the clock. A complete ranking list for use in your draft preparation is available in Appendix F2.

Additional player profiles are available on our Web site at http://www.savvyfantasysports.com.

1. **Larry Johnson, Kansas City Chiefs (Bye Week – 3):** Johnson took the fantasy world by storm when he ascended to the top spot in Kansas City following an

injury to Priest Holmes. He raced to 10 100-yard games and topped 130 yards in seven of them. Johnson tallied 21 total touchdowns on the year and displayed an ability to catch the ball out of the backfield with 33 receptions.

Herman Edwards has already declared him the starter, and we won't know about the status of Holmes until later this summer. Can he race to 2,000 yards? Johnson is still motivated from what he perceived as a lack of respect from former coach Dick Vermeil, and ran for 1,750 yards despite only one game with more than 20 carries before Week 9. I wouldn't count him out.

2. **Shaun Alexander, Seattle Seahawks (Bye Week – 5):** The Seahawks owned the league's highest scoring average at more than 28 points per game, and a large part of that production came from the legs of Alexander. He ran for a league-high 1,880 yards and scored an eye-popping 27 rushing touchdowns. It marked the fifth straight year that Alexander scored at least 16 total touchdowns.

Seattle lost guard Steve Hutchinson in free agency, so there is concern that the running game will be slowed somewhat. Even if that's the case, Alexander has some room to give before he'd play himself out of the elite level. Fantasy owners will be perfectly happy with another 1,500 yards and 20 touchdowns.

3. **LaDainian Tomlinson, San Diego Chargers (Bye Week – 3):** Tomlinson has been another automatic fantasy option since his arrival to the league in 2001. He's rushed for over 1,200 yards in each of his first five seasons and scored an average of 14 rushing touchdowns. Only Alexander can lay claim to a better streak.

The Chargers also effectively use Tomlinson as a receiver out of the backfield. He's averaged over 60 receptions per NFL season, and reached the remarkable total of 100 in 2004. The shift to a new quarterback will put the minds of all defensive coordinators to work to try and shut him down, but that's nothing new. He will achieve another all-world season in 2006 with an up-tick in his receiving totals from 2005.

4. **Tiki Barber, New York Giants (Bye Week – 4):** Tiki Barber carried the Giants on his back for a good portion of the 2005 season. The versatile tailback touched the ball an astounding 411 times last year and tallied 2,390 yards of total offense. Barber scored a total of 11 touchdowns (9 rushing, 2 passing) and reached double-digits for the third time in four seasons.

As Eli Manning gains experience and confidence, the Giants may pull back on his touches somewhat and perhaps work second-year running back Brandon Jacobs into the mix more frequently. With that said, coach Tom Coughlin is loyal to his veteran stars, and it would take a regression to Barber's fumble problems of 2002 and 2003 to affect much change. I fully expect Barber to touch the ball 20 or more times every game in 2006 and to approach double-digit touchdowns once again.

5. **Clinton Portis, Washington Redskins (Bye Week – 8):** Those who fail to consider offensive line play on draft day need only examine the contrast in performance for Portis between 2004 and 2005. The loss of Jon Jansen in the preseason of 2004 limited the offense's overall productivity. Though Portis ran for 1,315 yards that year, the offense never posed a consistent scoring threat.

In 2005, Portis returned to the level first attained in Denver. He rushed for 1,516 yards and reached double-digit touchdowns for the third time in four NFL seasons. The Washington offense has been upgraded in 2006 with two new wide receivers. The additions will serve to spread the field and create even more running room for Portis. If health smiles on Washington, Portis may enjoy a career year.

6. **Edgerrin James, Arizona Cardinals (Bye Week – 9):** James' move to the desert was one of the biggest news stories of the off-season. The Cardinals now have the power runner to go with the potent passing game, but still face major questions on the offensive line. James was effective in a similar system for years in Indianapolis, but the cohesion and technique on the offensive line were clearly superior. As a result, I suspect that his rushing yardage total will dip from its previous levels (four of seven years over 1,500 yards), but that he'll still reach double-digit touchdowns working with this potent passing game.

The threat of the downfield passing game will serve to prevent defenses from stacking eight defenders at the line of scrimmage. Therefore, James will find gaps to operate, and once he finds second gear, he's tough to bring down one-on-one.

7. **Rudi Johnson, Cincinnati Bengals (Bye Week – 5):** Johnson is in danger of suffering the same fate that Edgerrin James experienced in Indianapolis. You can dominate your part of the game each and every week, but a quarterback winging the ball to a receiver downfield will always take precedence on the highlight films. In the past two seasons, the workman-like Johnson has averaged 349 carries, 1,456 rushing yards,

and 12 touchdowns. With another year at this level of performance, Johnson must be put into the discussion of the game's elite backs.

The Bengals return all of their top receiving options this season, and eagerly await the return of Carson Palmer to the practice field. Should Palmer miss an extended period of time, look for Johnson's numbers to dip, as opposing defenses will stack the box against him. If Palmer is ready to go from day one, another season to match his performances of 2004 and 2005 is on tap.

8. **LaMont Jordan, Oakland Raiders (Bye Week – 3):** Jordan was one of the lone bright spots in a terribly disappointing season for Raider Nation. He excelled in his first NFL season as a feature back before succumbing to overuse down the stretch. Jordan averaged 24 touches per game in the 14 he played, racking up 70 receptions.

The Raiders had difficulty finding holes for him, and he finished with a rushing average of 3.8 yards per carry. Jordan finished the year with 1,578 total yards with one-third coming through the passing game. New coach Art Shell loves the power running game, but will be careful not to overwork his feature back and risk losing him down the stretch again.

9. **Ronnie Brown, Miami Dolphins (Bye Week – 8):** The Dolphins offense came alive during the second half of the season as Nick Saban worked his two-man backfield of Brown and Ricky Williams to perfection. Williams has been suspended for the 2006 season, leaving Brown to fend for himself. Saban will no doubt pair him with another back to keep him fresh and effective, but barring a trade, that option will not have

the impact of Williams. Brown finished his rookie season with 907 yards, but he did not carry the ball more than 15 times after Week 8.

Miami has assembled a potent passing game to complement Brown out of the backfield. The acquisition of Daunte Culpepper will help to push the vertical passing game and open the field for Brown.

10. **Steven Jackson, St. Louis Rams (Bye Week – 7):** Former Dolphins coordinator Scott Linehan worked the running game to make the tandem of Ronnie Brown and Ricky Williams extremely effective last year. This year, he'll apply the same formula to Steven Jackson as head coach of the Rams.

Fans and fantasy owners are accustomed to the potent passing game in St. Louis, but Linehan is excited about expanding Jackson's role. He reached the 1,000-yard mark last year and scored eight touchdowns in spite of the injuries and inconsistency that shaped the second half of the Rams' season. Additionally, Marshall Faulk retained a prominent role last season, particularly on traditional passing downs. With a healthy Marc Bulger under center and the role of Faulk expected to be limited, Jackson will find space to run in this offense.

11. **Domanick Davis, Houston Texans (Bye Week – 5):** Perhaps no player benefited more at this year's NFL Draft than Domanick Davis. The expected selection of Reggie Bush went by the wayside, leaving Davis unopposed for playing time and touches in the backfield. The lone downside to Davis for fantasy owners is his propensity for getting hurt. He missed five games last year, and carried an injury note and game-time anxiety for fantasy owners on virtually a weekly basis.

The Texans upgraded the wide receiving corps by bringing in Jeb Putzier and Eric Moulds. Their additions and a rolling pocket for David Carr should serve to reduce the number of negative plays that stalled drives. Davis likely increases his presence in the passing game this year to rival his 2004 totals. Kubiak wants motion in his offense and to get his running backs out in space to make plays. Given Kubiak's tremendous success in Denver, Davis has the opportunity to provide huge return for owners in 2006.

12. **Carnell Williams, Tampa Bay Buccaneers (Bye Week – 4):** Jon Gruden certainly got everything he could possibly extract from his rookie tailback in 2005. Williams carried the ball 290 times in 14 games played (20.7 per game) and left fantasy owners wondering when the breakdown would occur. Fortunately, Williams saved two of his best games for the fantasy playoffs (a total of 262 yards and three touchdowns in Weeks 14 and 16).

The Buccaneers figure to utilize Williams in much the same capacity this season. I don't expect he'll handle the ball 88 times in the first three weeks as he did last year, but Gruden follows the most fundamental coaching philosophy. "If we rush the ball more, we win." Look for him to shoulder another heavy load in 2006 and rush for another 1,100 or 1,200 yards.

13. **Willis McGahee, Buffalo Bills (Bye Week – 8):** Inconsistency at quarterback served as the most glaring issue for the Bills in 2005. McGahee did his part to aid the effort with eight games of 80 or more rushing yards, but save a four-game stretch early in the year, he failed to find opportunities near the goal line. He finished the season with a strong yardage total (1,247) but only five touchdowns.

The Bills have much the same issue facing them in 2006. J.P. Losman will contend with Kelly Holcomb and Craig Nall for the starting job, and longtime star Eric Moulds left for Houston. One thing is for certain, new coach Dick Jauron loves to play ball control with a heavy dose of rushing attempts and to allow his defense to finish games. That bodes well for a heavy workload for McGahee.

14. **Julius Jones, Dallas Cowboys (Bye Week – 3):** For the second straight year, Jones missed time due to injury. He sat out three games and missed time in several others but still finished with 993 rushing yards. Bill Parcells is enamored with the power running game, which means that his feature back will always pile up touches.

The addition of Terrell Owens will serve to open up opportunities for Jones. He has breakaway speed once he hits the second level of the defense, and the presence of Owens, Jason Witten, and Terry Glenn should spread the field to give him operating room. Health is always a concern for Jones, but if healthy, he is\ a top candidate for a breakthrough season.

15. **Tatum Bell, Denver Broncos (Bye Week – 4):** Bell becomes the latest candidate for the Denver Broncos running back Hall of Fame. As I discussed extensively in Chapter 15, the Denver tailback position is fantasy gold. Bell gets the opportunity to assume the role of primary ball carrier this season and will split the workload with Ron Dayne.

Despite a low number of carries (173), Bell used his quickness and power to bounce plays outside and turn 1-yard gains into a robust 5.3-yards-per-carry average. He also scored eight touchdowns and finished with 921 rushing yards. Mike Shanahan has another star in the making in his third-year tailback.

16. **Reuben Droughns, Cleveland Browns (Bye Week – 6):** Droughns did everything but score touchdowns last year. He anchored the offense at 19 carries per game and rolled up 1,232 rushing yards despite the decided lack of a consistent passing game. Droughns also showed an ability to catch the ball out of the backfield by hauling in 39 passes for 369 yards.

Romeo Crennel traded away veteran Trent Dilfer, so he must be convinced that second-year quarterback Charlie Frye is ready to lead. With off-season acquisition Joe Jurevicius now playing alongside Braylon Edwards and possibly even Kellen Winslow Jr., the passing game may be able to give Droughns more space and a few more red zone carries. His low touchdown total from 2005 (two) will deflate his value on draft day.

17. **Kevin Jones, Detroit Lions (Bye Week – 3):** The "other" Jones, Kevin was widely regarded as the bust of the year after his strong second half to the 2004 season. He missed extensive time down the stretch (three games in their entirety) to finish with 664 rushing yards and five touchdowns.

Detroit is possibly even more intriguing with Mike Martz at the controls. He's transformed unknown quarterbacks into stars in the past and obviously sent the fantasy numbers of players throughout the lineup into the stratosphere. The strong complement of wide receivers and a quarterback who can make all throws in Bulger makes Jones a very intriguing player to watch.

If he's sound physically and Martz's offense doesn't implode, he could become the running back steal of the draft.

18. **Thomas Jones, Chicago Bears (Bye Week – 7):** Jones produced a career year for the Bears after 2005 draft pick Cedric Benson failed to get into camp on time. The ineffectiveness of the quarterback position in Chicago led to a heavy workload for Jones on a weekly basis. He responded to the challenge by averaging 4.3 yards per carry (1,335 yards) with nine touchdowns.

    The Bears have been impressed with Benson's work ethic this off-season and he figures to begin to earn more of a look as the season progresses. The Bears' reported flirtation with the Colts about a trade on draft day did not sit well with Jones. However, a season of health from Rex Grossman or Brian Griese under center will do wonders for the psyche. The addition of a serviceable passing game will open the field for the running game and potentially make Jones and Benson a formidable 1-2 punch.

19. **Willie Parker, Pittsburgh Steelers (Bye Week – 4):** Parker electrified the crowd with his 75-yard scamper for a score in the Super Bowl. It capped a tremendous season in which he ran for 1,202 yards and four touchdowns. He enters 2006 as the main rushing option for the potent Steelers ground game, and will see another back handle the goal line carries again this season as he did with Jerome Bettis in 2005. Duce Staley and Verron Haynes will compete for the goal line roll. Parker will no doubt eclipse the 1,000-yard barrier if he stays healthy, but he'll need to break long runs to get into the end zone.

20. **Brian Westbrook, Philadelphia Eagles (Bye Week – 9):** The Eagles will always employ multiple backs in their offense, but all reports are that Westbrook's foot is healed and that he's ready to assume a bigger role this year. He's long been a big contributor in the passing game and will no doubt be counted on to do so again with the loss of Terrell Owens. Ryan Moats and Correll Buckhalter (assuming he's recovered from his injuries) will compete for touches behind Westbrook.

21. **Deuce McAllister, New Orleans Saints (Bye Week – 7):** The Saints lost McAllister for the year in Week 5 against Green Bay. He'd gotten off to a slow start with three games with fewer than 65 yards rushing and had already sent fantasy owners into a panic ahead of the injury. He is one of the more intriguing backs this season, as pundits and fantasy owners speculate as to how he and Reggie Bush will co-exist in the backfield. McAllister had rushed for over 1,300 yards per season in his previous three years prior to the injury.

    McAllister stands to be the every-down back once again, with Bush serving as a change-of-pace back and receiving target out of the backfield. The only limitation is Sean Payton's imagination.

22. **Jamal Lewis, Baltimore Ravens (Bye Week – 7):** The Ravens re-signed Lewis shortly after inking former Denver Broncos tailback Mike Anderson to a contract. Lewis played uninspired football in a contract year, failing to top the 100-yard rushing mark until Week 12 against Cincinnati.

    Lewis begins the season as the starting tailback, as Brian Billick is loyal to his veteran contributors. Early on, I suspect that Mike Anderson replaces Lewis every third series, akin to the Kansas City offense of the past several years. It serves to keep Lewis fresh, get the punishing Anderson some work, and win the field-position battle.

23. **Chester Taylor, Minnesota Vikings (Bye Week – 6):** After four years as Jamal Lewis' backup in Baltimore, Taylor earns the chance to be the featured back in Minnesota. Taylor is very similar to Oakland star LaMont Jordan, in that both men run with great power and serve as tremendous receiving options out of the backfield. Taylor's ability as a receiver will serve him well under Brad Childress, who favored versatile backs in his Philadelphia offensive scheme. Childress will no doubt work Mewelde Moore and Ciatrick Fason into the mix in some capacity, but all signs point to a heavy workload and great opportunities for Taylor. He qualifies as a prime sleeper pick in his new role as a starter.

24. **Warrick Dunn, Atlanta Falcons (Bye Week – 5):** Atlanta led the NFL in rushing on the strength of Dunn's huge 1,416-yard season. He averaged 5.1 yards per carry and 88.5 yards per game. Typically, those numbers are totally swayed by one or two huge outings. In Dunn's case, he rushed for 73 or more yards in 13 of his first 14 games played.

Unfortunately, the presence of T.J. Duckett and Michael Vick's footwork conspired to limit his rushing touchdown total to three. That seems likely to occur again in 2006, only rookie Jerious Norwood might be the man in the vulture role. Accept the huge yardage total gracefully and hope that one or two of the long runs he's apt to break go the distance.

25. DeShaun Foster, Carolina Panthers (Bye Week – 9): Foster is another player who constantly sends managers to the newswire on Sunday morning to confirm his eligibility for the day's game. He lost out early last season to departing tailback Stephen Davis, who turned in a crazy touchdown pace (12 total) before finishing the year on injured reserve. Foster made contributions in the passing game through the first several weeks, but didn't top double-digit carries until Week 8.

Two factors must be considered in the selection of Foster. First, he is seemingly injured for some stretch of every year. His 2002 and 2004 seasons ended prematurely, and he missed three complete games and parts of others in the other two seasons. Second, that injury risk and his frame necessitate a second back in the mix to keep him fresh and healthy to finish games. Stephen Davis served that role in the past, but he will not return in 2006. Second-year player Eric Shelton, rookie DeAngelo Williams (less likely), and Nick Goings are three candidates for carries alongside Foster.

26. Ahman Green, Green Bay Packers (Bye Week – 6): Changes on the offensive line made for a miserable start to 2005 for Ahman Green before an injury sent him to the bench for good in Week 7. He tallied 80 yards per game combined rushing and receiving in those outings, but failed to top 60 rushing yards in any of his five starts.

Green's overall game makes up for the lack of push by an offensive line in a rebuilding process. His ability to catch the ball out of the backfield will be a huge help to Brett Favre and serve to keep the game in control. Green has been written off in a lot places after one difficult stretch. It's hard to look past his five years of fantasy dominance and focus on the unfortunate run for the Packers that ended with mounds of injuries and a negative statistical return.

27. **Reggie Bush, New Orleans Saints (Bye Week – 7):** As mentioned in the Deuce McAllister section above, it remains to be seen how Sean Payton will utilize his two talented backs. He truly has nothing by which to compare them. Bush offers superior speed, instincts, and great hands out of the backfield, as evidenced by his tremendous numbers and Heisman Trophy win at USC. I expect him to begin the year as a change-of-pace back and part-time slot receiver and for Payton to slowly build his touches into an equitable split with Deuce McAllister by mid-season.

28. **Corey Dillon, New England Patriots (Bye Week – 6):** The selection of Laurence Maroney by New England has fantasy owners in early drafts turning a blind eye to the veteran Dillon. He missed five games due to injury in 2005 but still scored 12 touchdowns (13 total). At this juncture, there's no reason to believe that the injury will slow Dillon in the new year. However, it's possible that Bill Belichick works Maroney into the mix as a change of pace back and to keep Dillon ready for the playoff run. I would still expect Belichick to turn to his veteran tailback around the goal line.

29. **Joseph Addai, Indianapolis Colts (Bye Week – 6):** The Colts lost Edgerrin James to the Cardinals in free agency this off-season, and responded by selected a back in his image in LSU's Addai. He stands a stout 5-foot-11 and 215 pounds and demonstrates all of the qualities that Tony Dungy and the Colts staff envisions

for their feature back. In a May mini-camp, Addai also showed an ability to catch the ball out of the backfield that some had seen as less developed.

Heading into training camp, Addai will be competing for the starting job with veteran tailback Dominic Rhodes. Rhodes may have a slight edge based on his familiarity with the Colts' system, but I believe that Addai's athleticism and instincts will win him the job before long.

30. Chris Brown, Tennessee Titans (Bye Week – 7): The running back situation in Tennessee is murky to say the least as training camp approaches. In addition to Brown, the Titans are carrying Travis Henry and former USC bruiser LenDale White on the roster. Brown enters camp as the No. 1 option, but his hold on the role is tenuous after his rushing average dipped over a full yard from his 2004 total. Additionally, he's seemingly always checking out of games with injuries, and may therefore lose the short yardage and goal-line carries to White. Brown is fun to watch and a true fantasy force when he's healthy and going right, but those games seem too few and far between.

In the next chapter, I review the fantasy fortunes of the top options at the wide receiver position. Like the running backs of this chapter, there are several players for whom the argument could be made to place them atop the list

29 Wide Receiver (WR) Rankings

The wide receiver position is perhaps the most enigmatic for fantasy owners. After all, a player's value at this position can rise or fall faster than any other. If a team builds a big lead early, the running game takes over and grinds the clock. So, if your receiver didn't play a big role in the early explosion, then they were unlikely to contribute that week.

Conversely, if a team is being blown out early, the offense has no choice but to air it out. While nothing may become of it, all you can ask for is an opportunity to make plays.

In this chapter, I offer a detailed analysis of the top wide receivers in consideration for roster spots on draft day. A complete ranking list for use in your draft preparation is available in Appendix F3.

Additional player profiles are available on our Web site at http://www.savvyfantasysports.com.

1. **Terrell Owens, Dallas Cowboys (Bye Week – 3):** The impact of Terrell Owens cannot be denied. In just seven games, he racked up enough receiving yardage (763) to rank in the league's top 35 in the category. The receiver was ultimately left off the active roster for the final nine games of the year, decimating the championship dreams of those owners who had selected him in the third or early fourth round of their drafts.

   Owens stayed in the NFC East by signing a lucrative deal with the Cowboys. He gets to play in a big market with a storied franchise and finds himself at the center of heated debates on talk radio. The chief question for debate is whether he and coach Bill Parcells will be able to co-exist. For Parcells, it's about playing the game with pride and passion. For Owens, it's the latest stop on a career that alternates between brilliance on the field and comments that rip apart locker rooms off of it. For 2006, I rank Owens at the top of my receivers list because I believe he will be on his best behavior. I believe that he'll perform at a level off the charts and that he and Drew Bledsoe will be among the top tandems in the game. Of course, I would be remiss if I failed to acknowledge that all bets are off for 2007 and beyond.

2. **Steve Smith, Carolina Panthers (Bye Week – 9):** Smith returned with a vengeance after missing virtually all of 2004 with a broken leg. He led all receivers with 1,563 receiving yards and scored 12 touchdowns, proving that speed can triumph over size. He also tied for the league lead in receptions despite the fact that Carolina had no clear-cut No. 2 receiver opposite him in the lineup. That changes this season with the addition of Keyshawn Johnson from Dallas. Johnson is a

superb possession receiver who will command attention in the middle of the field, leaving Smith to work against cornerbacks one-on-one. In those matchups, Smith wins. In a side note, Panthers quarterback Jake Delhomme has averaged 24 touchdown passes per season over the last three years.

3. **Chad Johnson, Cincinnati Bengals (Bye Week – 5):** The outspoken Bengals wide receiver Chad Johnson made headlines with his checklist of opposing defensive backs who failed to contain him. Not 24 hours after the release of the 2006 team schedule, Johnson was holding court with the media about the "victims" on this year's list. Johnson was the prime beneficiary of Carson Palmer's coming-out party as an NFL star, catching 97 balls from his quarterback for 1,432 yards and nine scores. The strong receiving corps in Cincinnati and the presence of power running back Rudi Johnson forces defenses to play him straight up, and most of the time that means a big game is in store for him. He caught more than three passes in every game except one. In that contest against Chicago, Johnson caught three passes for 77 yards and scored two touchdowns.

The lone question facing him entering the season is the health of Carson Palmer, who was injured in the playoff loss to Pittsburgh. Early reports are that Palmer will be ready for Week 1, but keep an eye on this situation as the season approaches. Barring a move to bring in another veteran quarterback, the Bengals would start Anthony Wright. Though Wright has had experience in Baltimore, he is a markedly lower rated alternative to Palmer. His insertion as the starter for any length of time would drop Johnson's ranking.

4. **Marvin Harrison, Indianapolis Colts (Bye Week – 6):** The Indianapolis passing offense slid back toward Earth last season, but the venerable No. 1 receiver Harrison continued his Hall of Fame career unabated. Harrison remained at the forefront of quarterback Peyton Manning's mind, hauling in 82 passes for 1,146 yards and tying for the league lead with 12 touchdowns. The loss of Edgerrin James in free agency will put the passing game front and center once again this year. Of course, Harrison will be the leading target once again. Harrison retains his lofty ranking heading into training with the expectation that his elbow has sufficiency healed from his late-May surgery. He is expected to miss the team's voluntary workouts ahead of the late July reporting date for training camp. Keep an eye out for reports of his recovery heading into draft day.

5. **Torry Holt, St. Louis Rams (Bye Week – 7):** With the advent of the high-powered offenses in Indianapolis and Seattle, the continued success of the St. Louis Rams, and Torry Holt in particular, has become an afterthought. Holt turned in another fabulous season in 2005 despite the fact that starting quarterback Marc Bulger went down with an injury at midseason.

Holt still compiled a staggering 102 receptions, 1,331 receiving yards, and nine touchdowns. It marked the sixth straight season that he topped 1,300 receiving yards. The new St. Louis coaching staff presumes to feature third-year power back Steven Jackson more prominently this year and pull back on the reliance on a shoot-out each week. If this plan is executed correctly, it shouldn't impact the huge annual totals that have become commonplace for Holt, as defenses will need to respect the run again as they did in Marshall Faulk's prime.

6. **Randy Moss, Oakland Raiders (Bye Week – 3):** The last two seasons have been relatively unkind to Moss. Though he's still managed to put up strong statistics, Moss has battled injuries, coaching staffs, and ineffectiveness from his quarterback in that span. In 2004, he was severely limited by a hamstring injury, yet still managed to record 13 touchdown receptions. Last season, quarterback Kerry Collins struggled with his accuracy, but Moss returned to the 1,000-yard receiving club and hauled in eight touchdowns. Bothered by further leg and back issues, he managed to reach 1,000 yards in spite of seven games in which he logged fewer than 50 receiving yards.

The Raiders brought in former New Orleans quarterback Aaron Brooks to assume the starting role this season. Like former starter Collins, Brooks has also struggled with his accuracy and decision-making. He does possess a strong arm and will likely be excited to concentrate on football instead of the trying circumstances in New Orleans following Hurricane Katrina. Whether injured or in a broken system, Moss finds a way to perform.

7. **Anquan Boldin, Arizona Cardinals (Bye Week – 9):** The first half of the Arizona duo reached 100 receptions for the second time in three seasons and averaged 100 receiving yards per game played. Boldin is an excellent route runner with blazing speed who fits well with an accurate passer like the Cardinals' Kurt Warner. Boldin can catch the ball in stride to make a short pass into a game-changing long gain. He's set for the foreseeable future opposite Larry

Fitzgerald in the receiving corps, and he has another accurate quarterback in rookie Matt Leinart waiting for his opportunity.

8. **Larry Fitzgerald, Arizona Cardinals (Bye Week – 9):** Fitzgerald teamed with Boldin to record 205 receptions for a jaw-dropping 2,810 yards and 17 touchdowns last season. He has the speed and hands to catch balls in traffic, but he also has the size to elevate in the red zone. The key to Fitzgerald's game is his consistent approach and dedication to the craft. He caught three or more passes in every game he played including a nine-game stretch to end the season in which he caught at least four.

9. **Santana Moss, Washington Redskins (Bye Week – 8):** The Redskins received a career year from quarterback Mark Brunell in 2005, and his chief target returned to fantasy owners' good graces after a mediocre 2004 campaign with the Jets. Moss caught 84 passes for 1,483 yards and nine touchdowns including several huge multi-touchdown performances.

The Redskins' reliance on their tight ends and fullback is the lone drawback in his outlook for 2006. Chris Cooley and Mike Sellers combined for 14 touchdown receptions last season. Washington upgraded its receiving corps with the additions of Brandon Lloyd and Antwaan Randle El, who should serve to let Moss operate in one-on-one coverage more frequently. Cornerbacks will be calling for safety help with regularity.

10. **Hines Ward, Pittsburgh Steelers (Bye Week – 4):** Ward capped another tremendous season with Super Bowl MVP honors. His streak of four consecutive

1,000-yard seasons ended, as he finished just shy with 975. He did, however, reach double-digit touchdowns (11) for the third time in four seasons. Ward is the consummate pro, always exerting effort to do the little things to help the team win. The next time you cheer a long Willie Parker TD run, rewind the tape to watch No. 86 throwing a block downfield.

His value ticks up a notch with the retirement of Jerome Bettis. The Steelers will continue to stress the ground game, but Ben Roethlisberger will look to throw more often in short-yardage and red-zone situations. That bodes well for Ward's reception total (89 over the last four seasons) and his scoring opportunities.

11. **Chris Chambers, Miami Dolphins (Bye Week – 8):** Chambers enjoyed his finest season as a pro during 2005 in coordinator Scott Linehan's attack. Opponents' preoccupation with the running game of Ronnie Brown and Ricky Williams opened up opportunities downfield, and Chambers teamed with Gus Frerotte to capitalize on them. Chambers established new career highs with 82 receptions and 1,118 receiving yards (his first 1,000-yard season) and tied his career mark of 11 touchdown receptions.

For all the success experienced last year, the Dolphins figure to be even stronger in Nick Saban's second year. The Dolphins acquired quarterbacks Daunte Culpepper and Joey Harrington to lead the offense.

12. **Darrell Jackson, Seattle Seahawks (Bye Week – 5):** The Seahawks' incredible offensive efficiency in 2005 is made even more remarkable by the fact that their No. 1 receiver, Darrell Jackson, played in only six games. Jackson averaged 10 looks per game and racked

up 38 receptions for 482 yards with three touchdowns. The Seahwaks return most of the personnel from their top-ranked offense, but the team did lose All-Pro lineman Steve Hutchinson to free agency. It is possible that the running game bogs down slightly with his departure, which could force Matt Hasselbeck into more difficult passing situations. Ultimately, coach Mike Holmgren has the personnel and experience to work beyond the loss and keep Seattle among the league's top offenses. Barring any setbacks with his knee, Jackson will eclipse the 1,000-yard receiving mark for the fourth time in seven NFL seasons.

13. **Reggie Wayne, Indianapolis Colts (Bye Week – 6):** The second member of the high-scoring Colts receiving corps experienced a severe drop in his touchdown production despite an overall advancement of his role in the offense. Wayne caught six more passes in 2005 than he did in the record-breaking 2004 season, but his receiving yards fell by 10 yards per game and his touchdowns fell precipitously from 12 to five. Wayne's role is expected to expand yet again with the departure of Edgerrin James. The Colts will still rely on their running back (Dominic Rhodes or rookie Joseph Addai) to set the tone, but I expect for the passing game to be back on all gears this season.

14. **Plaxico Burress, New York Giants (Bye Week – 4):** The Giants are picked by many to challenge for a spot in the NFC Championship Game, and the combination of Eli Manning and Plaxico Burress is often cited as a chief reason why. Burress snagged 76 passes last season for 1,214 yards and seven touchdowns. Unfortunately for fantasy owners, Burress went ice cold down the stretch, failing to record a touchdown catch in eight

out of nine games after a strong start. Eli Manning figures to grow in his third NFL season and shake off some of the nerve issues that come with being a first-year starter. His passes sometimes sailed high, and while Burress may have the height to go up and snag some of them, fantasy owners and the Giants and their fans would just as soon he didn't. I expect tremendous advancement by this duo in 2006 and for Burress to record his first career double-digit touchdown season.

15. **Javon Walker, Denver Broncos (Bye Week – 4):** The Broncos executed a trade on draft day to bring disgruntled Packers receiver Javon Walker to Denver. Walker groused about his contract heading into 2005 after a phenomenal 2004 season (1,382 yards and 12 touchdowns). He then promptly tore up his knee in the first game of the season and was lost for the year. Instead of letting Walker make good on his threat to hold out and remain a distraction, Packers brass decided to deal him.

Walker is a tremendous leaper and big red-zone target who will offer Jake Plummer a consistent downfield option. The Broncos fully expect him to be ready to contribute in Week 1.

16. **Joey Galloway, Tampa Bay Buccaneers (Bye Week – 4):** Galloway enjoyed the best season of his career since 1998 with the Buccaneers. He established new career highs in receptions (83) and receiving yards (1,287) in his 11th NFL season. Galloway also hit double-digit touchdowns (10) for the first time since 1998. He remains the top option in the Buccaneers' attack for 2006 and will continue to see opportunities against man coverage with defenses geared up to slow down running back Carnell Williams. I suspect that

the Buccaneers will begin to trust Chris Simms to throw the ball downfield more as the year unfolds, making Galloway a threat to race off to another huge statistical year.

17. **Roy Williams, Detroit Lions (Bye Week – 8):** The Lions, and fantasy owners, are still waiting to see what Williams can do at full strength. For two straight seasons, Williams has been limited by leg injuries and the ineffectiveness of the overall Detroit offense, yet he still tallied 100 receptions, 1,504 receiving yards, and a solid 16 touchdowns. Unfortunately, fantasy owners had to wait anxiously at their computer's side each Sunday to find out whether this future star would be available to them. The Lions are installing a totally new offense from the mind of Mike Martz. His track history suggests that Williams could be poised for a monster year if he can stay on the field.

18. **Joe Horn, New Orleans Saints (Bye Week – 7):** In the "what have you done for me lately?" world of fantasy football, Joe Horn might take the biggest dip among wide receivers in this summer's drafts. The New Orleans offense struggled as a whole, but no single players dipped further than Horn's. He battled injury through almost the entire season and struggled to keep focus given the devastation of the Gulf Coast. Horn had caught 19 touchdown passes in the previous two seasons combined. He finished the 2005 season with one.

The Saints made a number of changes this off-season. First, there is a new coach in former Bill Parcells assistant, Sean Payton. There is a new quarterback with an accurate arm in Drew Brees. New Orleans finished a busy off-season by drafting Reggie Bush with the second overall pick in the draft. Bush's speed and receiving skills will serve to open the offense and get Horn matched up in one-on-one coverage.

19. **Andre Johnson, Houston Texans (Bye Week – 5):** Like Horn, Andre Johnson of the Texans also entered the 2005 season with high expectations. Unfortunately, the woeful state of the offensive line and constant losing teamed with an ankle injury to decimate his stats. Johnson finished with career-low marks across the board (63 receptions, 688 yards, and two touchdowns).

The new system of coach Gary Kubiak should boost the overall productivity of the Texans' offense for 2006. Johnson now has a star running opposite him in former Bills standout Eric Moulds, and the new scheme will focus on keeping the often-sacked quarterback David Carr on his feet. Johnson is another player whose draft will slip based on last year's failures. He may end up being the steal of draft day if Kubiak is able to achieve any fraction of the success experienced in Denver.

20. **Terry Glenn, Dallas Cowboys (Bye Week – 3):** How do you make a player who caught 62 balls for 1,136 yards and seven touchdowns a sleeper pick for the following season? That's the question being asked about Terry Glenn, who stands to be the biggest beneficiary of Terrell Owens' arrival in Dallas. Glenn returned from an injury-marred 2004 campaign to post his first 1,000-yard receiving season since 1999, and his seven touchdowns marked a new career high. The speedy Glenn will see one-on-one coverage due to Owens' presence, which will allow him to play catch with Drew Bledsoe for big gains. Glenn averaged a career-high 18.3 yards per reception last year. I expect him to reach that mark again.

21. **T.J. Houshmandzadeh, Cincinnati Bengals (Bye Week – 5):** Houshmandzadeh reminded fantasy owners and NFL fans about the power of the second receiver with a huge campaign opposite Chad Johnson in 2005. Houshmandzadeh caught 78 passes for 956 yards and seven touchdowns, and he missed two games during the first half of the season. He caught five or more passes in 12 different contests, and 52 of his 78 receptions resulted in first downs. Houshmandzadeh figures to put up numbers to rival those of Indianapolis' Reggie Wayne for a long time to come, so long as this unit remains intact. The health of Carson Palmer as training camp unfolds will dictate whether Houshmandzadeh needs to be knocked down a few pegs.

22. **Derrick Mason, Baltimore Ravens (Bye Week – 7):** Despite a passing game that was virtually nonexistent for the first 11 weeks of the season, veteran wideout Derrick Mason managed to reach the 1,000-yard mark for the fifth straight season. Kyle Boller showed great presence and maturity as the year went on, particularly once Mason, tight end Todd Heap, and rookie Mark Clayton were all on the field at the same time. Boller will likely take a step back in 2006 for Mason's former Titans teammate, Steve McNair. Mason averaged 81 receptions per season in his five full years as a starter alongside McNair.

23. **Eddie Kennison, Kansas City Chiefs (Bye Week – 3):** Veteran receiver Eddie Kennison of the Chiefs is another player often forgotten on draft day. Fantasy owners look to newer, shinier models out of the college assembly line and forget longtime stars. Kennison saw his career slow at the turn of the century before finding

new life in Kansas City. Though the running game and Tony Gonzalez get all the press, Kennison has been a valuable receiver for four years in Kansas City.

Kennison owns two consecutive 1,000-yard seasons and has averaged six touchdown receptions over the last three years. The Chiefs will rely heavily on running back Larry Johnson, but Kennison will still see his share of balls downfield. The key to the equation is the sustained health of the offensive line. A healthy line puts Tony Gonzalez back into pass patterns to garner heavy attention, leaving the crafty Kennison to find holes in the zone.

24. **Rod Smith, Denver Broncos (Bye Week – 4):** Rod Smith remains the lone underappreciated receiver with that surname after the sudden retirement of Jacksonville's Jimmy Smith. Rod Smith slips in drafts seemingly every year, yet always finishes with 1,000 receiving yards and at least a handful of touchdowns. He has topped 1,000 yards in eight of the last nine seasons.

The Broncos' offense remains focused on the ground game with Tatum Bell and Ron Dayne, but Mike Shanahan also allows his quarterbacks to throw. Jake Plummer has averaged over 3,600 passing yards in the last two seasons. As such, expect Smith to continue to excel, particularly now that he has a more consistent receiver opposite him in Javon Walker. Walker may win out in the glory plays for touchdowns, but Smith will likely rule the day in receptions, yardage, and overall opportunities.

25. **Keenan McCardell, San Diego Chargers (Bye Week – 3):** The loss of Drew Brees knocks the veteran McCardell down several places in the receiver

rankings. Of secondary concern is the fact that he turned 36 in January, but it's hard to argue that point too vehemently after he reached a new career high with nine touchdowns last season. With a new starter under center in Philip Rivers, Antonio Gates and LaDainian Tomlinson figure to see the lion's share of activity. However, McCardell is a capable route runner with good hands who will continue to pile up receptions. I would suspect that his touchdown total returns to the four to six range that he's seen for most of his career, but the sheer number of opportunities to make plays in this spread offense makes him a fantasy star.

In the next chapter, I turn my attention to the often-over-looked tight end position. The position was in a down time during the beginning of the fantasy football explosion with two viable options, but has since experienced a renaissance. Coaches and coordinators speak candidly and fondly of the mismatches and opportunities afforded by the presence of a big, playmaking tight end. This change in philosophy now requires fantasy owners to spend more time and attention distinguishing between the true stars in advantageous systems and the also-rans.

30 Tight End (TE) Rankings

The tight end position has experienced a resurgence in recent years. During the latter part of the 1990s, fantasy owners were forced to weigh the added value of superstar options Shannon Sharpe and Tony Gonzalez against a sea of mediocre fantasy options. Those owners who failed to procure the services of those elite options faced a season of minimal scoring output from the position. In 2006, each team in the league has the distinct possibility of securing a player who will be a contributor each and every Sunday.

In this chapter, I rank and review the top options at the tight end position. The top option slides back to the pack slightly with the loss of his quarterback to free agency. However, it was that need to aid a young quarterback that made him a star in the first place. The Chargers' Antonio Gates leads the pack.

1. **Antonio Gates, San Diego Chargers (Bye Week – 3):** Gates has become the standard bearer for the position with two brilliant seasons in San Diego. He led all tight ends in the three key metrics with 89 receptions, 1,101 receiving yards, and 10 touchdowns. Gates registered nine games with 60 or more receiving yards in 2005. New starting QB Philip Rivers will depend heavily on Gates' athleticism and ability to create separation from small defensive backs as he settles into the role.

2. **Jeremy Shockey, New York Giants (Bye Week – 4):** Shockey reached new career-high marks in receptions, receiving yards, and touchdowns (65, 891, and 7, respectively) despite playing much of the season with a sprained ankle. He creates matchup problems with his 6-foot-5 frame and can stretch the field by running deeper pass patterns. Quarterback Eli Manning continues to advance in his decision-making and reads, which will allow Shockey to exceed his 2005 production.

3. **Tony Gonzalez, Kansas City Chiefs (Bye Week – 3):** Gonzalez dips in the rankings slightly because of the new coaching style to be employed in Kansas City. He remains a top contributor at the position (78 catches, 905 yards, two touchdowns in 2005), but might see his opportunities diminished under Herman Edwards. The ground game and Larry Johnson will obviously rule the day, and the advanced ages on the offensive line may force Gonzalez to stay in as a blocker more frequently, as he did early in 2005. The other component of the game that will change is that Edwards likes to take more shots downfield. That strategy benefits speedster Samie Parker and takes looks away from Gonzalez.

4. **Todd Heap, Baltimore Ravens (Bye Week – 7):** Heap was having an ordinary year before the late-season blowup that elevated his numbers back toward draft-day expectations. He returned strong from an ankle injury that severely hampered his 2004 season to tally 75 receptions for 855 yards and seven touchdowns. Three of his scores came in the all-important fantasy football playoff weeks. Looking ahead to 2006, Heap will remain a huge part of the offense regardless of who lines up under center. His size and speed create problems for defensive backs and open the playing field for the Baltimore running game.

5. **Alge Crumpler, Atlanta Falcons (Bye Week – 5):** Crumpler slips a spot or two in the rankings based on the off-season development of the Falcons' young wide receivers. Michael Jenkins and Roddy White appear to be on track to contribute more consistently this season, which will effectively take looks away from Crumpler. Crumpler has been QB Michael Vick's most reliable target for the past three seasons, offering good route-running skills and pass-catching ability. If the passing offense clicks, Crumpler may see additional looks in the red zone, but that's still territory reserved almost exclusively for T.J. Duckett and the running game.

6. **Jason Witten, Dallas Cowboys (Bye Week – 3):** Witten saw his production dip markedly from his breakout 2004 season with a nearly 25 percent reduction in receptions. The addition of Terrell Owens should serve to make Witten a more potent weapon for the Cowboys in 2006. Opponents will double-team Owens, which will allow Witten to run free down the middle. However, Bill Parcells and the Cowboys brass drafted Anthony Fasano this April, and it appears that

the Cowboys will begin to implement two-tight end sets. With the addition of Fasano, it's unlikely that Witten reclaims his huge reception total of 2004, but he will receive more quality opportunities.

7. **Heath Miller, Pittsburgh Steelers (Bye Week – 4):** As a rookie in 2005, Miller became one of QB Ben Roethlisberger's favorite targets immediately, showing great field presence and athleticism. He scored all six of his touchdowns in the first half of the year before his production slipped due to injury. Miller finished with 39 catches for 459 yards and the aforementioned six TD grabs. The retirement of goal-line legend Jerome Bettis sends the Steelers back to the playbook to seek alternatives deep in opponents' territory.

8. **Chris Cooley, Washington Redskins (Bye Week – 8):** Cooley became an integral part of the Washington offense in 2005 with nearly double the number of receptions as he'd collected in 2004. Cooley caught 71 passes for 774 receiving yards with seven touchdowns. His reception total ranked fourth among tight ends, and had it not been for running back Mike Sellers (seven receiving touchdowns of his own), Cooley's touchdown total might have hit double digits. The Redskins upgraded their receiving corps this off-season, so it's possible that Cooley's reception total pulls back some. However, he will continue to be a huge factor in the red zone.

9. **Randy McMichael, Miami Dolphins (Bye Week – 8):** McMichael opened the 2005 season with a streak of four consecutive games with a touchdown reception. Unfortunately for fantasy owners who flocked to the waiver wire after his early season heroics, he would catch only one more the rest of the season. McMichael

did catch three or more passes in 12 of the 15 games in which he participated, so he was an involved member of the offensive system. The one knock that has dogged McMichael throughout his career is that he sometimes loses focus. In Nick Saban's locker room, that is something to be watched. Though he's an excellent playmaker, Saban is a stickler for attention to detail.

10. **Jermaine Wiggins, Minnesota Vikings (Bye Week – 6):** With injuries and off-the-field concerns afflicting the Vikings in 2005, Wiggins was one of the most reliable players on the squad. He caught 69 passes with 13 games of at least three receptions. Unfortunately for fantasy owners, he found the end zone only once. The hiring of Brad Childress speaks well for Wiggins as a fantasy option this season. Childress comes from the Philadelphia Eagles offense that made a Pro Bowl player out of Chad Lewis and L.J. Smith a valuable fantasy commodity. If Wiggins approaches his high reception of 2005 again, I suspect that his TD total surpasses his 2004 total (four).

11. **Jerramy Stevens, Seattle Seahawks (Bye Week – 5):** The Seahawks finally saw first-round production out of their 2001 draft pick. Stevens had battled problems off the field, and inconsistency on it, before claiming the starting role in 2005. He didn't pile up huge receptions or yardage in any particular week during the year, but he was constantly in the mix as the Seahawks drove downfield. Stevens saved his biggest games for those most commonly associated with the fantasy football playoffs, catching a touchdown pass in three consecutive weeks (14, 15, 16).

The one area of concern for Stevens is his propensity to drop passes. It happened several times in the playoffs and most noticeably in the Super Bowl. Those types of negative plays may lead coach Mike Holmgren to integrate another receiving option. Barring that occurrence, his outlook for 2006 is very bright. Top red zone target Joe Jurevicius signed with the Cleveland Browns this off-season. Therefore, if the Seahawks are even remotely as efficient as they were in 2005, Stevens stands to see a bounty of red zone looks and scoring opportunities.

12. **L.J. Smith, Philadelphia Eagles (Bye Week – 9):** In a season fraught with injuries and disharmony for the Eagles, Smith was the model of consistency. His development continued unabated, and he reached a new career-high of 61 receptions. Smith caught five or more passes on six occasions during the year. His low touchdown total can be attributed to the general state of discord. Quarterback Donovan McNabb will be back to lead the Eagles in 2006, and the loss of Terrell Owens in free agency means that roughly 13 more passes per game will be distributed among other receivers.

13. **Ben Troupe, Tennessee Titans (Bye Week – 7):** Troupe headed many experts' lists — mine included — as the sleeper tight end to watch in 2005. He responded with a strong campaign of 55 receptions and 530 receiving yards, but continued to split looks with fellow tight ends Erron Kinney and Bo Scaife and missed three complete games and parts of others due to injury. When healthy, Troupe is a game-changing tight end in the vein of Antonio Gates and Tony Gonzalez.

14. **Zachary Hilton, New Orleans Saints (Bye Week – 7):** The Saints began to look to Hilton frequently in the final seven weeks of the season, and he delivered tremendous results. Hilton caught four or more passes

in five of the team's final seven games. His role is expected to expand with the addition of Drew Brees, who found great success in San Diego by utilizing his tall, athletic tight end. Hilton causes problems in coverage with his 6-foot-8 frame and will become a factor in the red zone.

15. **Dallas Clark, Indianapolis Colts (Bye Week – 6):** Fantasy owners expected an encore performance from the Colts' high-powered offense in 2005. While the results were still strong, the pinball-like numbers did not appear. With Reggie Wayne and Marvin Harrison already top-line selections, attention turned to Clark as the potential breakout performer. Unfortunately, an ankle injury slow to heal and domination by the Colts on both offense and defense conspired to keep his numbers down. Clark still caught 37 passes for 488 yards and four touchdowns, but never became a weekly fantasy threat as expected. The loss of Edgerrin James to free agency may push the passing game front and center once again, which should help to improve his numbers. However, there are other tight ends on the roster, which will serve to limit his opportunities.

16. **Ben Watson, New England Patriots (Bye Week – 6):** Watson has great expectations placed upon him in 2005, but saw his opportunities limited by injuries and the presence of Daniel Graham. It also doesn't help that Bill Belichick enjoys using defensive players Mike Vrabel and Richard Seymour in goal-line situations. In any event, Watson caught 29 passes for 441 yards and four touchdowns. His athleticism and pass-catching ability suggest that he can reach much higher marks, but the spread-out attack of the Patriots and the aforementioned factors may limit his upside.

17. **Jeb Putzier, Houston Texans (Bye Week – 5):** Putzier never received the opportunity to make a big statement in Denver. First, Jake Plummer has never been particularly kind to his tight ends. Second, the running game generally ruled the day. Putzier still caught 37 passes for 481 yards. This off-season, new Texans coach Gary Kubiak brought him to Houston, where his 6-foot-4 frame will likely be more integral to the game plan. The Texans are seeking ways by which to keep quarterback David Carr from absorbing so many hits, and a pass-catching tight end is part of the solution.

18. **Vernon Davis, San Francisco 49ers (Bye Week – 7):** The 49ers selected Davis with the sixth pick in the 2006 draft, and he showed great emotion as he received the call in the green room. His excitement with the call leads me to believe that he'll enter camp on time and ready to contribute immediately. The 49ers already have Eric Johnson (who led them with 82 receptions in 2004) on the roster, so opportunities will be split early. Of course, the 49ers also ranked 32nd in the league in total offense last season, so there's plenty of room for improvement. New coordinator Norv Turner will utilize the tight end position frequently in an attempt to give second-year quarterback Alex Smith an opportunity to build confidence.

19. **Marcus Pollard, Detroit Lions (Bye Week – 8):** Pollard joined the Lions in 2005 after several productive years in Indianapolis. Though he did tally 46 receptions and 516 receiving yards on the season, he never became the fantasy factor one would have expected, given the talent assembled in Detroit. Then again, the Lions underachieved across the board last season. The new regime under Mike Martz will be more efficient

and will most definitely generate more points than last year's squad. Though an improvement over his 2005 numbers is anticipated, Martz has never featured the tight end prominently during his coaching career.

20. **Daniel Graham, New England Patriots (Bye Week – 6):** Injuries limited Graham to just 11 games and just 16 receptions in 2005. He still caught three touchdown passes, but never lived up to his past performance. Graham is a free agent after the season, and the Patriots already addressed the position with the selection of Ben Watson in 2004 and two new players in this year's draft. Graham has been an effective red zone performer during his career and will likely continue to see looks in those situations. However, the team will likely give the bulk of the opportunities to Watson.

21. **Kellen Winslow Jr., Cleveland Browns (Bye Week – 6):** A first-round draft selection in 2004, Winslow Jr. has never had the opportunity to showcase his talents on the field. A freak incident on a special teams play ended his rookie season as soon as it began, and a motorcycle accident claimed his sophomore campaign. According to reports, Winslow Jr. is running as well as he did at the scouting combine in early 2004 and projects to be a big weapon for Romeo Crennel this year. The receiving corps was upgraded this off-season, which should help quarterback Charlie Frye speed his development.

22. **Alex Smith, Tampa Bay Buccaneers (Bye Week – 4):** Smith leapt onto the fantasy radar immediately following a four-reception, two-touchdown performance in Week 1 against Minnesota. Unfortunately, he wouldn't see the painted grass again in 2005. Smith had nine more games with multiple receptions before

season's end, but topped 50 receiving yards only once. The Buccaneers tend to rely on their power running game in short yardage situations, so Smith's scoring opportunities will be limited.

23. **Erron Kinney, Tennessee Titans (Bye Week – 7):** Kinney serves as the reliable veteran to Ben Troupe's athletic downfield threat at tight end for Tennessee. The development of the young receiving corps and Troupe's ability to create matchup problems in coverage figures to cut Kinney's looks this year. With that said, an offensive coordinator always finds room for a sure-handed receiver.

24. **Marcedes Lewis, Jacksonville Jaguars (Bye Week – 6):** The Jaguars turned to two UCLA products with their first selections in the 2006 draft. Maurice Drew will compete for time at running back, and Marcedes Lewis becomes an immediate impact player with the sudden retirement of receiver Jimmy Smith. Lewis offers a lanky, athletic frame and will cause matchup nightmares for smaller defensive backs.

25. **Courtney Anderson, Oakland Raiders (Bye Week – 3):** Anderson made a splash in Week 1 with two touchdowns against the Patriots, but his performance and appearances on the field were limited thereafter. He missed six games due to injuries and caught two or fewer passes in seven of his final nine games. Anderson caught a total of 10 passes for 150 yards in his other two games.

26. **Leonard Pope, Arizona Cardinals (Bye Week – 9):** The Cardinals already had a strong receiving corps and added a top-tier running back in Edgerrin James. They found the final piece of the puzzle on draft day with tight end Leonard Pope. He offers a large target, good

hands, and can create separation from defenders. The presence of Anquan Boldin, Larry Fitzgerald, and Edgerrin James won't afford him the high number of looks as other tight ends, but he's likely to see some red zone opportunities if the Cardinals offense runs as effectively as expected.

27. **Stephen Alexander, Denver Broncos (Bye Week – 4):** The departure of Jeb Putzier moves Alexander into the top tight end slot in Denver. He caught 21 passes for 170 yards last season. Putzier's departure will result in more passes to Alexander, but as I mentioned earlier, Jake Plummer hasn't frequently targeted his tight end options in the past. In this offense, I suspect that he will reach levels in line with his 2004 totals (41 catches, 377 yards, one touchdown).

28. **Doug Jolley, New York Jets (Bye Week – 9):** The injury to teammate Chris Baker allowed Jolley to claim more opportunities down the stretch in 2005. He caught 29 passes for 324 yards and one score, including a strong nine-reception, 102-yard performance in Week 15 against Miami. Jolley and Baker will compete for looks in Eric Mangini's offense in 2006.

29. **Kris Mangum, Carolina Panthers (Bye Week – 9):** The Panthers utilized several tight ends throughout the 2005 season, making none of them a distinguished fantasy player. Mangum caught 23 passes for 202 yards and two touchdowns, a drop of nearly 33 percent in all three categories. He'll compete with Michael Gaines and Mike Seidman for looks this season.

30. **Bubba Franks, Green Bay Packers (Bye Week – 6):** The Packers were hit hard by injuries in 2005, and former red zone threat Franks was among them.

He returns to a crowded tight end competition, as David Martin and Donald Lee both flashed ability in his absence.

31. **Anthony Fasano, Dallas Cowboys (Bye Week – 3):** Fasano joins a team that should score points, but he'll have to contend for opportunities with one of the game's best in Jason Witten. Bill Parcells wants to install more plays utilizing two tight ends, so Fasano may be of some value in larger leagues. However, the coach also knows that he'll need to keep off-season acquisition Terrell Owens contented.

32. **Desmond Clark, Chicago Bears (Bye Week – 7):** Given the Bears' struggles in the passing game last season, it was surprising that Desmond Clark didn't assume a bigger role. The veteran tight end caught only 24 balls in the the 11 games in which he appeared and topped 40 receiving yards only twice. The return of Rex Grossman under center should allow the Bears to go vertical more often. Perhaps that will increase Clark's looks over the middle as the offense opens up.

33. **Eric Johnson, San Francisco 49ers (Bye Week – 7):** Johnson missed all of 2005 with a foot injury. He led the 49ers with 82 receptions in 2004 and figures to play a large role this season as Norv Turner works to acclimate Alex Smith to the pro game. Johnson's overall value will be held down with the selection of Vernon Davis, but he's still a viable fantasy option for leagues that reward receptions.

34. **Jerame Tuman, Pittsburgh Steelers (Bye Week – 4):** Tuman didn't play a large role in the passing game last year, contributing only three receptions for 57 yards. However, the retirement of Jerome Bettis will

have the Steelers looking for other options near the goal line. It's possible that a two-tight end set is among the solutions.

35. **Chris Baker, New York Jets (Bye Week – 9):** The Jets received a tremendous Week 1 performance from Baker with seven receptions for 124 yards and one touchdown. Unfortunately, the performance yielded his only touchdown of the season and nearly half of his reception and yardage totals. He missed the final eight games of the year with a broken foot. Baker will compete with Doug Jolley for the starting job this year.

36. **Matt Schobel, Philadelphia Eagles (Bye Week – 9):** Schobel showed promise with the Bengals in 2004 with 21 catches for 201 yards and four touchdowns. He failed to make a mark last season despite the huge increase in production from the offense overall. Schobel now joins a Philadelphia team that makes more frequent use of the tight end. He'll compete for looks behind L.J. Smith.

37. **Bryan Fletcher, Indianapolis Colts (Bye Week – 6):** Teammate Dallas Clark does well in the open field, but Fletcher owns the red zone with his 6-foot-5 frame. He caught 18 passes for 202 yards last year with three touchdowns. Fletcher won't see many passes in this offense, but the ones that he does will be high-impact chances.

38. **Steve Heiden, Cleveland Browns (Bye Week – 6):** Heiden slides into the backup role with the return of Kellen Winslow Jr. to the field. He offered a solid option for Browns quarterbacks in 2005, tallying 43 receptions, 401 yards, and three scores. Twenty of his 43 receptions resulted in first downs. That type of pos-

session receiver will always see chances, and coach Romeo Crennel certainly plays percentages.

39. Tony Scheffler, Denver Broncos (Bye Week – 4): The Broncos love the frame (6-foot-5) and playmaking ability of their second-round selection from Western Michigan. Scheffler offers the quickness and athleticism of a receiver in a tight end's body. He can create matchup issues downfield and run as a slot receiver. Early reports are that Mike Shanahan is enamored with the rookie. Stephan Alexander remains the every-down option, but Scheffler may work his way into the rotation early.

40. Robert Royal, Buffalo Bills (Bye Week – 8): Royal is known primarily as a superior blocking tight end, but he can also make noise in the red zone. He signed a large contract to join the Bills this off-season after three years in Washington. Royal was brought in primarily to provide more protection for J.P. Losman, or whoever lines up at quarterback, and to help seal the edge for Willis McGahee.

41. Kris Wilson, Kansas City Chiefs (Bye Week – 3): Wilson has the size and talent to be a productive tight end in the league. Unfortunately, he currently plays behind future Hall of Famer Tony Gonzalez. Wilson won't factor into the equation in Kansas City unless Gonzalez gets hurt.

42. David Martin, Green Bay Packers (Bye Week – 6): Martin caught 27 passes in 12 games for the Packers last season including three scores in the absence of Bubba Franks. He'll compete for the starting spot this summer, but figures to slide into the No. 2 role if Franks is physically ready.

43. **Christian Fauria, Washington Redskins (Bye Week – 8):** Fauria leaves the Patriots after four seasons. His opportunities declined each season, as Daniel Graham and Ben Watson were added to the mix. Fauria figures to serve primarily as a blocking tight end in Washington with the presence of Chris Cooley, but he'll also slide out into pass patterns on occasion. He only becomes a fantasy option if an injury befalls Cooley.

44. **Tony Stewart, Cincinnati Bengals (Bye Week - 5):** The Bengals utilize Stewart primarily as a blocker, but he occasionally slips into coverage. Given the depth at wide receiver and the tendency to let Rudi Johnson finish his own work around the goal line, Stewart has little fantasy upside.

45. **Visanthe Shiancoe, New York Giants (Bye Week – 4):** Shiancoe enters his fourth season with the Giants, and has seen little playing time since his arrival (23 catches for 172 yards and three touchdowns in three years). Jeremy Shockey plays through most injuries, so it would take something major to occur to earn Shiancoe heavy playing time.

46. **Justin Peelle, Miami Dolphins (Bye Week – 8):** Peelle received minimal looks in San Diego with the rise of Antonio Gates, but he's a steady receiver with good hands who will serve as the backup to Randy McMichael.

In the next chapter, I roll out the rankings of the oft-forgotten, but extremely important, kicker position. Former Patriots superhero Adam Vinatieri leads the charge with his move indoors.

31 Kicker (K) Rankings

With rare exceptions, the kicker position is among the final slots filled on fantasy rosters. Rarely can owners justify the selection of a kicker in advance of the final two or three rounds of the draft unless some component of the league settings makes him more valuable.

Those owners who fail to secure one of the top handful of kicking options sometimes begin to play the waiver wire on a weekly basis to find the most advantageous matchup. To that end, I offer a brief analysis of each team's kicking option.

1. **Adam Vinatieri, Indianapolis Colts (Bye Week – 6):** Super Bowl hero with the Patriots finds a new home in the RCA Dome. There is some potential downside in that the prodigious Colts offensive attack may limit him to a PAT machine. I suspect that Edgerrin James will prove a little more difficult to replace and that Vinatieri finds kicking indoors to his liking.

2. **Shayne Graham, Cincinnati Bengals (Bye Week – 5):** The Bengals offense was tremendously efficient in 2005 and provided Graham with 47 PAT attempts against 32 field-goal attempts. The injury to Carson Palmer may sideline him to start the season, which would put Anthony Wright under center. While he will undoubtedly lead this talented cast, I'm expecting additional field-goal attempts early in the season.

3. **Neil Rackers, Arizona Cardinals (Bye Week – 9):** Rackers performed like a rock star last year for the Cardinals, connecting on 40 of 42 field-goal attempts and 20 PATs. He kicked 21 of 21 from inside 40 yards and converted six attempts from outside 50 yards. Rackers' big leg affords owners a shot at frequent bonus points. He ranks third on my list because I believe that the addition of Edgerrin James will convert some of his FG attempts into sustained drives and ultimately PATs.

4. **Mike Vanderjagt, Dallas Cowboys (Bye Week – 3):** Vanderjagt made a loud exit from Indianapolis after his huge miss in the playoffs. He lands in Dallas alongside Terrell Owens. The Cowboys finally tired of bringing in kicker after kicker. This year, they brought in the most efficient field-goal kicker in the land, last year's season-ending miss notwithstanding. Vanderjagt converted 23 of 25 attempts in the regular season and 52 PATs. His acquisition serves to boost Dallas' chances in close games.

5. **John Kasay, Carolina Panthers (Bye Week – 9):** Kasay connected on only 76 percent of his attempts last year (26 of 34). To be fair, he was a perfect 17-for-17 inside 40 yards. Five of his misses came from outside of 50 yards (he also converted three kicks). The addition of Keyshawn Johnson offers Jake

Delhomme another premier receiving option who isn't afraid to give up his body to extend a drive. That will translate into additional opportunities for Kasay.

6. **Josh Brown, Seattle Seahawks (Bye Week – 5):** The Seahawks were frighteningly efficient in the red zone last season, putting Brown in position for 57 PAT attempts. He attempted only 25 field goals. It stands to reason that some of that efficiency will be lost this coming season and therefore translate into additional field-goal attempts for Brown.

7. **Lawrence Tynes, Kansas City Chiefs (Bye Week – 3):** The Chiefs annually rank among the top scoring offenses in the game. Last year, Tynes attempted 45 PATs and converted 27 of 33 field-goal attempts. He struggled from distances over 40 yards (6-for-11). This might be an area that Kansas City will seek to shore up this summer.

8. **Jay Feely, New York Giants (Bye Week – 4):** The brilliance of Tiki Barber worked the Giants into many scoring opportunities. In addition to his 42 field-goal attempts, Feely converted 43 PATs. The continued development and decision-making of Eli Manning should improve offensive efficiency and convert some percentage of the FG attempts to PATs.

9. **Ryan Longwell, Minnesota Vikings (Bye Week – 6):** After years of toiling in the harsh outside conditions of Green Bay, Longwell will enjoy kicking inside the dome for eight home games. Longwell has always been able to boot long field goals (7-for-10 from outside 40 yards last season), and the move inside will help to extend his range. Brad Johnson is typically efficient in leading the offense, which will lead to additional FG opportunities.

10. **Jeff Reed, Pittsburgh Steelers (Bye Week – 4):** Reed has been aided by the methodical approach to offense by Bill Cowher and coordinator Ken Whisenhunt. Ben Roethlisberger doesn't force passes and the power running game efficiently works downfield. Reed struggled from longer distances (6-for-11), but was a perfect 18-for-18 inside 40 yards.

11. **Jeff Wilkins, St. Louis Rams (Bye Week – 7):** Wilkins was once a top 2 or 3 kicker, but injuries on the offense sabotaged his once mighty production. Wilkins converted 27 of 31 attempts a year ago, with 13 of his 27 makes coming from outside 40 yards. Under new coach Scott Linehan, the Rams will utilize the power running game of Steven Jackson more frequently and work to create longer, sustained drives. This will lead to more opportunities for Wilkins as well as increased production from the Rams' skill players as they move away from the quick-strike attack of Mike Martz.

12. **Jason Elam, Denver Broncos (Bye Week – 4):** Elam's conversion percentage from 40-plus has been dropping, and the increased efficiency of the offense has led to an increase in PATs. He still possesses the ability to make longer field goals, but not with the certainty that he did several years ago. With an efficient ground game and the assumption that Jake Plummer takes care of the ball, Elam will again attempt in the neighborhood of 35 field goals. It just becomes a question of how well he converts.

13. **Matt Stover, Baltimore Ravens (Bye Week – 7):** The Ravens offense has been strong enough to put Stover in a position to kick field goals (30-for-34), but one has to wonder how the increased efficiency

of an offense under Steve McNair or a more mature Kyle Boller will impact his status. Stover has been a fantasy staple due to Baltimore's inefficiency inside the opponent's 30-yard line. If a shift occurs to make the Ravens more effective in the red zone, Stover owners will be trading three-point field goals for single-point PATs.

14. **Sebastian Janikowski, Oakland Raiders (Bye Week – 3):** Janikowski had the worst year of his professional life last year, converting on only 75 percent of his attempts (20-for-30). He was positively miserable from beyond 40 yards, which has been his strong suit through his career. Increased efficiency under Aaron Brooks would serve to convert some of those 15 attempts from 40-plus to more reasonable distances.

15. **David Akers, Philadelphia Eagles (Bye Week 9):** Akers was just one of many Eagles whose 2005 season was cut short due to injury. He converted 16 of 22 attempts (6-for-11 from 40-plus). The Eagles will welcome back a healthy Donovan McNabb and Brian Westbrook and reinforcements in the wide receiver corps to make up (at least somewhat) for the departure of Terrell Owens. Assuming the Eagles are not decimated by injuries once again, Akers could rise back into the ranks of fantasy starters.

16. **Olindo Mare, Miami Dolphins (Bye Week – 8):** Mare's point total is somewhat surprising given the disjointed nature of the passing game in Miami last season. However, the strong running tandem of Ronnie Brown and Ricky Williams served to put him in field-goal range. Mare converted 25 of 30 attempts and converted 33 PATs behind the combination of Frerotte, Feeley, and Rosenfels. Should the duo of Culpepper

and Brees be able to advance on those efforts at all, Mare would make for a great sleeper pick from the kicker position.

17. **Nate Kaeding, San Diego Chargers (Bye Week – 3):** The last two seasons have almost been too easy on Kaeding. The efficiency of Brees, Gates, and Tomlinson has led to a large number of PATs with fewer field-goal attempts than most kickers. That figures to change this year with Philip Rivers under center. I believe that the Chargers will still be able to move the ball with the collection of receivers at his disposal. However, I would not be surprised to see some early struggles near the red zone. This will mean more opportunities for Kaeding, and if a bigger leg is required, 2006 draft pick Kurt Smith may be called upon.

18. **Todd Peterson, Atlanta Falcons (Bye Week – 5):** As of mid-May, Peterson remained a free agent, but it was widely believed that he would return to the Falcons at a lower pay rate. Peterson was effective last season for Atlanta, converting 23 of 25 field goal attempts. One would have expected a larger number of attempts for Peterson last season given the dominance of the running game. The Falcons' skill-position players, led by Michael Vick, have been working diligently this off-season to increase their efficiency. If Vick and company are successful in doing so, then the Falcons will be able to sustain more drives and boost both his field-goal and PAT attempts.

19. **Rian Lindell, Buffalo Bills (Bye Week – 8):** The Buffalo offense was inconsistent to say the least in 2005, but that made Lindell a fantasy favorite. Lindell attempted 35 field goals in 2005 including 13 from beyond 40 yards (he converted 10). He has great

range, as evidenced by his perfect 3-for-3 in attempts beyond 50 yards. There are still questions about the Buffalo QB position heading into training camp, and the hiring of Dick Jauron as head coach signals a move to ball control and clock management. That type of offensive plan generally pays off on the stat sheet for kickers.

20. **John Hall, Washington Redskins (Bye Week – 8):** The veteran placekicker has long exhibited great accuracy and extended range. In his last full season (2003), he converted four field goals from beyond 50 yards. However, Hall has been limited to 18 appearances the last two years due to injuries. The Redskins offense figures to be efficient behind the running of Clinton Portis once again in 2006. If Hall can avoid the injuries that stalled his previous two seasons, he will have ample opportunity to contribute for fantasy owners this year.

21. **Jason Hanson, Detroit Lions (Bye Week – 8):** No player felt the frustration of the last several seasons in Detroit more completely than kicker Jason Hanson. He's attempted fewer than 30 field goals in four straight seasons and has topped 30 PATs only once in the last eight years. Hanson retains his extended range with the ability to convert from beyond 50 yards (two conversions in 2005). The addition of Mike Martz will not only aid the totals of the Lions' skill-position players, but could serve to boost Hanson toward fantasy starter status once again.

22. **Kris Brown, Houston Texans (Bye Week – 5):** The Texans failed to generate huge scoring totals overall, but they did create ample opportunities for Brown in 2005. He converted 26 of 34 attempts overall (76.5

percent), but curiously missed five attempts inside 40 yards. The Texans upgraded their receiving corps for 2006 with the additions of veteran Eric Moulds and TE Jeb Putzier. Those additions should help David Carr and the offense work into position for a high number of attempts this season.

23. **John Carney, New Orleans Saints (Bye Week – 7):** One look at Carney's stats for 2005 demonstrates the frustration experienced by the Saints in 2005. He attempted 13 field goals from inside 30 yards, meaning that the Saints offense sputtered frequently in the red zone. Those failures were further manifested in the 42 percent drop in PAT attempts from 2004. Curiously, Carney attempted only six field goals from 30-39 yards while doubling his attempts from 40-49 yards over his 2004 total.

24. **Phil Dawson, Cleveland Browns (Bye Week – 6):** Dawson quietly turned in a solid season for the Cleveland Browns last year, converting 27 of 29 attempts. He has lost some of his range in recent years, as demonstrated by his minimal chances outside of 40 yards (5-for-5). However, he makes the most of his opportunities afforded by the Browns offense overall with an 84 percent career conversion rate.

25. **Matt Bryant, Tampa Bay Buccaneers (Bye Week – 4):** After a lost 2004 season between Indianapolis and Miami, Bryant earned the kicking job for the Buccaneers in 2005 and made the most of his opportunity. He converted 21 of his 25 field-goal attempts including an impressive 10-for-11 from 40-49 yards away. As Chris Simms continues his development in the starting QB role for Tampa Bay this year, there's a good chance that Bryant's field-goal attempts will rise.

26. **Joe Nedney, San Francisco 49ers (Bye Week – 7):**
Veteran kicker Nedney has been an effective and efficient kicker when healthy. Nedney missed all but one
game due to injury in the 2003 and 2004 seasons. He
returned to the field in 2005 for the 49ers and regained
his form. Nedway converted 26 of 28 attempts in 2005
including a perfect 10-for-10 from 40-49 yards. He
also has the leg strength to attempt longer field goals,
as evidenced by his two conversions from beyond 50
yards.

27. **Josh Scobee, Jacksonville Jaguars (Bye Week – 6):**
Scobee enters his third season as kicker for the Jaguars. He's proven effective inside 40 yards (34-for-38),
but has struggled from longer distances. Scobee converted only five of 10 attempts from 40-49 yards in
2005, but he did provide bonus scoring opportunities
with two successful attempts from beyond 50 yards.

28. **Martin Gramatica, New England Patriots (Bye
Week – 6):** Gramatica returns to the NFL after sitting
out the 2005 season. He struggled in his final two seasons in Tampa Bay, converting only 60 percent of his
field-goal attempts (27-for-45). Gramatica had been
nicknamed "Automatica" early in his career because
of his accuracy from anywhere on the field. If he can
regain that form, New England's offense will offer
ample opportunities to let him shine. Gramatica will
compete with rookie Stephen Gostkowski in training
camp.

29. **Robbie Gould, Chicago Bears (Bye Week – 7):**
Gould assumed the starting placekicker role after the
Week 4 Bye and made his debut against Cleveland.
He went 1-for-2 on field-goal attempts from beyond
40 yards. That was the lone hiccup to Gould's other-

wise solid rookie season for the Bears. He was 18-of-19 from inside 40 yards, but only 3 of 8 from 40 yards or beyond. The availability of Rex Grossman or Brian Griese in the starting lineup should serve to balance the offensive equation and permit the Bears to traverse down the field more regularly into field-goal range.

30. **Mike Nugent, New York Jets (Bye Week – 9):** As a rookie with an injury-riddled Jets team in 2005, Nugent saw his opportunities limited by offensive inefficiency. He converted 22 of 28 attempts, with five of his misses coming from beyond 40 yards. The Jets expect to have injured stars Chad Pennington and Curtis Martin back in the fold, but they learned from last year's QB struggles by acquiring Patrick Ramsey. The additions of Ferguson and Mangold on the offensive line will serve to sustain drives and make Nugent a more regular contributor to the scoring column. He's some way from making the cut for fantasy purposes, but Jets fans will get to see why they drafted him this season.

31. **Rob Bironas, Tennessee Titans (Bye Week – 6):** Despite a number of issues pertaining to the offensive side of the ball in Tennessee, including a corps of young wide receivers, oft-injured running backs, and a quarterback playing hurt, Bironas had a solid year in 2005. He converted 23 of 29 attempts including two from 50-plus and 30 PATs. Bironas joined Phil Dawson as the only two regular kickers to miss two PATs.

32. **Billy Cundiff, Green Bay Packers (Bye Week – 6):** Former Cowboys kicker converted five of eight field-goal attempts in 2005 and 14 of 14 PATs. For his career, Cundiff possesses a mediocre 73 percent conversion rate that is punctuated by his 16-for-22 from 30-39 yards away.

33. **Stephen Gostkowski, New England Patriots (Bye Week – 6):** The Patriots lost Adam Vinatieri to the Colts this off-season and brought in former Tampa Bay Buccaneers kicker Martin Gramatica to assume the role. However, Gramatica struggled in his last year in the NFL and was out of the league last year. As such, the selection of Gostkowski in April's draft indicates that the team will at least have a friendly competition in camp this summer. If Gostkowski wins the job, the efficiency of the Patriots offense boosts his ranking by at least a dozen slots.

34. **Kurt Smith, San Diego Chargers (Bye Week – 3):** Smith was drafted by the Chargers this year to provide a charge on kickoffs and pin opponents deep in their own territory. Nate Kaeding has been an efficient kicker, but doesn't possess the leg strength to drive it deep consistently. Smith also figures to serve as placekicker on longer field-goal attempts to expand the Chargers' scoring range. While he won't assume regular kicking duties unless an injury befalls Kaeding, he does need to appear on the radar.

The next chapter examines the team defense position and presents my rankings from top to bottom.

32 Team Defense Rankings

In this chapter, I briefly review my preseason defensive rankings, noting the key elements that placed the teams in their respective slots. The amount of turnover in the defensive unit each year makes it difficult to project future achievements. The loss of a single cornerback or pass rusher could serve to place a team in a tailspin. Additionally, personnel changes on the offensive side of the ball may help or hinder a defense's performance. An offense that turns the ball over frequently can undermine a defensive unit's best efforts.

1. **Chicago Bears (Bye Week – 7):** The Bears return all 11 starters on a young defense that allowed only 12.6 points per game in 2005. The Steve Smith debacle in the playoffs is a distant memory. Save an off-season injury to Tank Johnson, the unit returns intact and ready to dominate in '06.

2. **Carolina Panthers (Bye Week – 9):** The Panthers ranked fifth in the league at 16.2 points allowed per game despite experiencing injuries that forced shuffling of personnel. Carolina boasts a strong defensive backfield and a good pass rush led by Julius Peppers.

3. **Pittsburgh Steelers (Bye Week – 4):** Pittsburgh works to stuff the run with nose tackle Casey Hampton (86 yards per game). With the run in check, linebackers and safeties are free to roam in coordinator Dick LeBeau's creative blitz schemes. Troy Polamalu is only getting better, and Joey Porter remains one of the best and most aggressive linebackers in the game.

4. **Indianapolis Colts (Bye Week – 6):** Tony Dungy finally has the talent on defense to match his high-flying offense. He can call an aggressive game with big hitters Bob Sanders and Mike Doss in the secondary, and the fact that they're constantly playing from the lead allows turnovers to pile up. The Colts ranked second in total defense last year at 15.4 points allowed per game.

5. **Washington Redskins (Bye Week – 8):** The Redskins brought in the athletic Andre Carter from San Francisco to fill the role vacated by LaVar Arrington. Washington employs an aggressive system, which leads to a high turnover rate and decent sack total. The big question going into camp is how Sean Taylor's situation off the field will impact his ability to participate.

6. **Jacksonville Jaguars (Bye Week – 6):** Jack Del Rio built his team on a strong defensive line (47 sacks), which creates opportunities for linebackers and defensive backs to make plays (34 turnovers and 2 TDs). Rashean Mathis is developing into a strong cover corner, and linebacker Mike Peterson regularly ranks among the league's tackle leaders.

7. **Seattle Seahawks (Bye Week – 5):** The Seahawks upgraded their defense last year and received tremendous production from rookie Lofa Tatupu. Now they've added another star in Julian Peterson, which should serve to strengthen their grip on the division. Seattle allowed only 94.4 rushing yards per game last season, forcing opponents into long passing downs and allowing them to accrue 50 sacks.

8. **Baltimore Ravens (Bye Week – 7):** The Ravens ranked 10th in total defense last season despite a mountain of injuries to key players such as Ray Lewis and Ed Reed. The selection of Haloti Ngata helps to occupy interior offensive linemen, which should allow Ray Lewis to return to past brilliance.

9. **Tampa Bay Buccaneers (Bye Week – 4):** The Buccaneers defense is aging, but it's not affecting productivity as of yet. The unit ranked ninth in total defense at 17.1 points per game and forced 33 turnovers.

10. **Miami Dolphins (Bye Week – 8):** Jason Taylor and Kevin Carter are regularly among the leaders in sacks, allowing linebackers such as tackle machine Zach Thomas to pursue ball carriers. Last season, Miami racked up 49 sacks and 32 turnovers. If Coach Saban can establish the ball-control offense he desires and build leads, those numbers could soar higher.

11. **New York Giants (Bye Week – 4):** The Giants have two of the best defensive ends in the game in Michael Strahan and Osi Umenyiora. They upgraded the defensive secondary with the addition of Sam Madison and will rely on health in the linebacking corps to prevent another late-season collapse. The addition of LaVar Arrington brings another top-tier talent into the

fold, and he's certainly motivated after being relegated to bench duty in 2005.

12. **Denver Broncos (Bye Week – 4):** The Broncos got the last laugh after importing much of an underachieving Cleveland Browns defensive line. Denver was tied for third in total defense at 16.1 points per game and tallied a strong 38 turnovers courtesy of John Lynch and Champ Bailey. The only issue was a low sack total (28), but the defensive line stood its ground to allow the linebackers to make plays.

13. **Philadelphia Eagles (Bye Week – 9):** The Eagles were positively decimated by injury in the 2005 season, dropping them from their usual perch at the top of team defenses. Jevon Kearse and Darren Howard will team to form a formidable duo up front. If they can pressure the quarterback, players such as Brian Dawkins and Sheldon Brown will be able to contain coverage and prevent long plays. The key for this defense's success in 2006 is simply to stay healthy.

14. **Dallas Cowboys (Bye Week – 3):** The Cowboys have a young and steadily improving defense. They have two potential stars in DeMarcus Ware and Marcus Spears who can help anchor the squad alongside safety Roy Williams for years to come. The Cowboys will get to be more creative on defense because of the field position and leads to be afforded by the improved offense.

15. **New England Patriots (Bye Week – 6):** New England battled through injuries throughout the whole year, from Tedy Bruschi's stroke in February 2005 to the rash of injuries in the secondary. Despite the adversity, the unit did not fall apart and rebounded to stuff the run and finish the year strong. Richard Seymour and Bruschi team with Mike Vrabel to supply a vet-

eran presence on this squad. Former Patriots star Ty Law is still not under contract for 2006, and New England's strict budgeting and sound cap management make it an instant contender for his services.

16. **Atlanta Falcons (Bye Week – 5):** The Falcons added two veteran stars this off-season in John Abraham and Lawyer Milloy. Abraham will team with Patrick Kerney to form one of the best defensive end tandems in the game and to mount a persistent pass rush. The youthful secondary will benefit immensely from the veteran presence of Milloy. He'll help to tutor emerging star DeAngelo Hall and rookie Jimmy Williams.

17. **San Diego Chargers (Bye Week – 3):** The Chargers received stellar play from rookie Luis Castillo and Shawne Merriman in 2005, both of whom are destined for stardom in this league. As a unit, San Diego recorded 46 sacks (tied for fifth) and topped all defenses by allowing only 84 yards rushing per game. The turnover count is likely to rise with such a strong presence on the line.

18. **Cincinnati Bengals (Bye Week – 5):** The Bengals capitalized on the opportunities afforded by their potent offense, which racked up 31 interceptions. The Achilles' heel for this defense was its poor results in stopping the run (115 yards per game). As a result, Cincinnati registered only 29 sacks.

19. **Minnesota Vikings (Bye Week – 6):** A sleeper defense for two seasons, the Vikings defense finally broke through in 2005. It registered 32 turnovers and 32 sacks last season while allowing 21.5 points per game. The Vikings have added two potential stars in Kenechi Udeze and Erasmus James. Their continued development will push this unit toward the positional elite.

20. **Cleveland Browns (Bye Week – 6):** Romeo Crennel had to be pleased with his team's overall defensive performance a year ago. The Browns ranked 11th in points allowed at 18.8 per game despite forcing only 26 turnovers and recording 23 sacks. Crennel has begun the process of building the Browns' defense in the image of his top-notch New England units, and he did so by bringing on former Patriots star Willie McGinest to mentor the younger players on the intricacies of the 3-4 defense. The AFC North figures to be a hotly contested division once again. Though Cleveland may not score a huge number of points, its defense will be able to contain opponents.

21. **Arizona Cardinals (Bye Week – 9):** The offense will put pressure on opponents to play catch-up, which should translate into turnover opportunities for the Cardinals defense. Arizona allowed 24 points per game last season and will need 2005 draft choice Antrel Rolle to play like a veteran on day one in order to improve its defensive presence. The Cardinals did allow a respectable 295 yards per game, but often surrendered the big play.

22. **Kansas City Chiefs (Bye Week – 3):** The Chiefs addressed their need for a pass rush with the selection of Tamba Hali in the first round of the draft. Kansas City allowed 20 points per game in 2005 with 35 turnovers, but accrued only 29 sacks. That total will need to improve in order to be competitive.

23. **New York Jets (Bye Week – 9):** The Jets added Kimo von Oelhoffen from Pittsburgh after trading John Abraham. New York allowed 22 points per game and registered 30 sacks and 36 turnovers. New coach Mangini comes from the Belichick family, so he knows

how to maximize effort and piece defensive backfields together. I'm just fearful that the offense continues to sputter and leaves the defense on the field.

24. **Green Bay Packers (Bye Week – 6):** With their selections of A.J. Hawk and Abdul Hodge, the Packers have solidified the core of their defense for the next 10 years. Kabeer Gbaja-Biamila and Aaron Kampman form a formidable duo up front. However, the unit combined for only 35 sacks and 23 turnovers.

25. **Buffalo Bills (Bye Week – 8):** The Bills gave up big plays with great regularity in 2005, which accounted for their 343 yards allowed average. Buffalo recorded 29 turnovers and a respectable 38 sacks. The Bills welcome back linebacker Takeo Spikes from injury. He'll serve to anchor the defense. Dick Jauron attended to defense with his first picks in the draft, looking to curb the proliferation of long passing plays that shifted field position against them.

26. **St. Louis Rams (Bye Week – 7):** New coach Scott Linehan will be able to keep the pressure on opposing defenses with his potent offense, but he'll need another year or two to turn this defense around. The Rams allowed 350 yards per game in 2005 and were tied for 30th in points allowed at 26.8 per game. They began the long road back by selecting five defensive players in the draft, but it will take more time to build a defense to contend with the offenses in Arizona and Seattle.

27. **Detroit Lions (Bye Week – 8):** Rod Marinelli will build on a strong 2005 by the Lions secondary. Detroit recorded 19 interceptions and 38 turnovers overall with 31 sacks. The Lions stayed in games on the

strength of five defensive touchdowns. You just can't bank on those from year to year. Look for a more disciplined squad this season.

28. **Houston Texans (Bye Week – 5):** Perhaps the selection of Mario Williams can help to get this unit off the field and provide better field position for the Texans offense. The Texans ranked last at 26.9 points allowed per game and surrendered 143.9 rushing yards per game. That signals a big loss in time of possession and a row of L's in the win/loss column.

29. **Oakland Raiders (Bye Week – 3):** Derrick Burgess provided the only excitement for the Raiders defense in '05 by leading the league in sacks. Otherwise, it was a poor effort from the league's 24th-ranked defense (23.9 points per game). Of chief concern was the lack of turnovers. The Raiders forced only 19 turnovers last year including five interceptions. Oakland addressed the departure of Charles Woodson with the selection of Michael Huff, but it will take more than one player to cure their ills in the AFC West.

30. **New Orleans Saints (Bye Week – 7):** Will Smith offers great production on the defensive line, but the porous run defense leaves the secondary exposed for big plays. The Saints allowed 24.9 points per game last season and forced only 19 turnovers.

31. **Tennessee Titans (Bye Week – 7):** The Titans defense has a strong presence in DE Kyle Vanden Bosch, but youth in the secondary remains an issue. The Titans allowed 28 or more points on nine occasions last year. It will take more time to build a contender.

32. **San Francisco 49ers (Bye Week – 7):** The 49ers lost Andre Carter and Julian Peterson while the offenses

within the division improved. The nonconference slate proves quite difficult as well, as the 49ers will face the potent offenses of the AFC West. The 49ers were tied for 30th in points allowed at 26.8 and forced only 24 turnovers.

In the next chapter, I take on the arduous task of ranking individual defensive players for those players looking to expand the league settings.

33 Individual Defensive Player (IDP) Rankings

In recent years, more fantasy football leagues are experimenting with the insertion of individual defensive players within the league settings. Part of the appeal clearly lays in the big hits, sacks, and exciting interception returns. For others, it's a way by which to make the game more "real" and to acknowledge the individual accomplishments that sometimes get lost in the box score.

In this chapter, I offer analysis concerning the top individual defensive players to consider on draft day. A complete ranking list for use in your draft preparation is available in Appendix F7.

Additional player profiles are available on our Web site at www.savvyfantasysports.com.

1. **Donnie Edwards, San Diego Chargers (Bye Week – 3):** This veteran linebacker is seemingly always around the ball at the end of the play. He's collected 103 or more tackles in nine consecutive seasons.

Edwards averaged 155 tackles over the last three seasons. The improved play of the San Diego run defense will allow him to roam a bit more in 2006 and raise his interception and sack totals.

2. **Jonathan Vilma, New York Jets (Bye Week – 9):** In only his second year in the league, Vilma has already established himself as one of the best linebackers in the game. He won Defensive Rookie of the Year honors in 2004 when he tallied 108 tackles, two sacks, and three interceptions. In what was otherwise a down year for the Jets, Vilma exploded for 173 tackles and forced four fumbles. He'll be called upon to assume a leadership role this season under new coach Eric Mangini.

3. **Brian Urlacher, Chicago Bears (Bye Week – 7):** Urlacher has become one of the most recognizable defensive players in recent memory. His penchant for making the big stop and his impeccable timing on blitz calls makes him a popular candidate for highlight film video. Of course, in the fantasy realm, it's time to step back and review the numbers. Urlacher averages 7.92 tackles per game and nearly 5.5 sacks per season.

4. **Dwight Freeney, Indianapolis Colts (Bye Week – 6):** The first-round selection by the Colts in 2002 has been an impact player from day one. Freeney owns four consecutive seasons with double-digit sacks (12.75 per year). Additionally, he's contributed 23 forced fumbles and was one of the building blocks to Indianapolis' recent defensive improvement.

5. **Keith Bulluck, Tennessee Titans (Bye Week – 7):** Bulluck has been among the leading tacklers for four straight seasons. He's averaged 138 stops per season

during that period and has recently begun to factor more prevalently in blitz packages. Bulluck recorded five sacks in each of the last two seasons.

6. **Julius Peppers, Carolina Panthers (Bye Week – 9):** A tremendous all-around athlete, Peppers played both basketball and football at the University of North Carolina. He came into the league in 2002 and immediately became one of the game's elite pass rushers with 12 sacks in 12 games. Peppers has recorded double-digit sacks in three of four NFL seasons and is a key component to the Panthers' defensive success.

7. **Zach Thomas, Miami Dolphins (Bye Week – 8):** Since entering the league in 1996, Zach Thomas could best be described as a tackling machine. Thomas covers as much or more ground than any linebacker in the league. He's recorded 129 or more tackles in nine of his 10 NFL seasons. The only time he failed to reach that mark he missed five games. The Dolphins rely on him as an emotional leader on and off the field.

8. **Mike Peterson, Jacksonville Jaguars (Bye Week – 6):** Peterson fits the mold of a Jack Del Rio player. He's a smart player who reads formations well and puts himself in position to make plays. Peterson has improved both his tackle and sack totals each season as he evolves into a full-fledged star. He piled up 132 tackles and recorded six sacks last season.

9. **Ed Reed, Baltimore Ravens (Bye Week – 7):** The former NFL Defensive Player of the Year missed six games in the middle of the 2005 season and never truly regained his typical dominant style. In fact, the Ravens' defense as a whole was beset by injuries. Therefore, to truly appreciate his impact on the game, one need

only look to his 2003 and 2004 totals (73 tackles, eight interceptions, and two forced fumbles per season). Reed has also developed a knack to exploiting weak special teams blocking schemes and recording multiple blocked field goals and punts per season.

10. **Jason Taylor, Miami Dolphins (Bye Week – 8):** Zach Thomas cleans up the action, but it's the pressure from Jason Taylor that set the Miami defense in motion. Taylor has averaged 10 sacks and 60 tackles per season during his nine-year career. He remains a huge presence in the locker room and a fantasy force.

11. **Charles Grant, New Orleans Saints (Bye Week – 7):** Grant's 2005 numbers may cause a double take in relation to his ranking. I consider 2005 a lost season for players on the New Orleans Saints. The consideration of the plight of family, friends, and neighbors in the wake of Hurricane Katrina certainly affected the team's play. I expect Grant to return to his pre-2005 dominance of double-digit sacks and a strong tackle total (average of 70 in two years prior).

12. **John Abraham, Atlanta Falcons (Bye Week – 5):** Both teams won in the trade that sent John Abraham to Atlanta. The Jets got rid of a locker-room headache, and the Falcons added their second premier pass rusher. Abraham recorded 20 sacks in his last two seasons with the Jets and averaged 53 tackles. He's energized by the move and will enjoy working opposite Patrick Kerney. Opposing line coaches will need to pick their poison, as they can't commit to double-teaming them both.

13. **Rodney Harrison, New England Patriots (Bye Week – 6):** The Patriots will welcome back All Pro Safety Rodney Harrison to the starting lineup after he missed

the final 13 games of the 2005 season due to an injury. In two previous seasons in New England, Harrison averaged 133 tackles and three sacks. When combined with his marks in San Diego, the 12-year veteran has eclipsed 100 tackles on seven occasions.

14. **Al Wilson, Denver Broncos (Bye Week – 4):** Wilson comes off of what would be considered a "down" year, as he recorded his lowest tackle total since 2000 (73). Each time his individual statistics have dipped, he's returned the following year with a vengeance, once raising his tackle total by 47 in one year.

15. **Takeo Spikes, Buffalo Bills (Bye Week – 8):** Spikes missed all but three games last season after sitting out only once in his seven previous NFL campaigns. He had registered at least 99 tackles in each of his seven full seasons with 19 career sacks. In Dick Jauron's defensive scheme, Spikes will see the opportunity to roam more, which may offer bonus sacks to go alongside his perennially robust tackle count.

16. **Michael Strahan, New York Giants (Bye Week – 4):** The charismatic leader of the Giants' defense enters his 14th season in the NFL with a defense that ranks among the game's best. In 2005, Strahan reached double-digit sacks for the sixth time in his career. He also registered the highest tackle total of his career (82). Teamed with Osi Umenyiora and backed by LaVar Arrington, Strahan figures to be among the league leaders in the sack category once again.

17. **Ray Lewis, Baltimore Ravens (Bye Week – 7):** The veteran leader of the Ravens and past Defensive Player of the Year returns after missing 10 games last year. He groused this off-season about the team's failure to

procure a big defensive tackle to clear space for him to make plays. The Ravens responded by trading for the draft rights to Haloti Ngata from Oregon. Ngata offers a sizable force upfront whose quickness will cause issues for opposing offensive linemen. The last time Lewis missed extensive time in a season (2002), he returned the following year to record 163 tackles and a career-high six interceptions.

18. Patrick Kerney, Atlanta Falcons (Bye Week – 5): Kerney has been a model of consistency at defensive end during his seven years with the Falcons. He's averaged 7.64 sacks and 49 tackles per year while forcing opposing quarterbacks into turnovers on account of a fierce pass rush. The Falcons got stronger this off-season with a deal that brought John Abraham over from the Jets. Atlanta figures to rack up sacks this season, as teams won't be able to double-team them both.

19. Nick Barnett, Green Bay Packers (Bye Week – 6): The Packers found a gem with their No. 1 pick from 2003. Barnett stepped into the starting lineup and began to make plays immediately. He's improved his ability to read formations each season and put himself in a better position to make stops. Barnett averaged 124 tackles per season through his first three years, and will now get additional help with rookies A.J. Hawk and Abdul Hodge onboard. The Packers' pass defense ranked among the best in the game last year, and with another year of film study from Barnett and the addition of former All-Pro cornerback Charles Woodson, it'll only get better this year.

20. Terrell Suggs, Baltimore Ravens (Bye Week – 7): The Ravens have watched Suggs evolve into one of the game's great defensive ends just three years into what promises to be a memorable career. He's averaged 10 sacks and 52 tackles per season and even snagged two interceptions last year. Baltimore returns virtually its entire starting unit and will look to reclaim its place among the elite defenses in the game, with Suggs providing the fuel through his pass rush.

21. **Roy Williams, Dallas Cowboys (Bye Week – 4):** Williams is widely regarded as one of the hardest hitters in the game and his quickness helps to cover up mistakes in the Dallas secondary. He's averaged 87 tackles and three interceptions per season through his first four NFL campaigns. The Cowboys figure to score points this season, which will put the pass defense and Williams front and center.

22. **Troy Polamalu, Pittsburgh Steelers (Bye Week – 4):** Polamalu became the face of the Steelers' improbable run through the AFC Playoffs. He was seemingly always around the ball and tallied 92 tackles from the safety position. Polamalu also recorded three sacks in coordinator Dick LeBeau's unique blitz packages.

23. **LaVar Arrington, New York Giants (Bye Week – 4):** After two years of insult and injury, former Pro Bowl linebacker LaVar Arrington is ready to shine again in Tom Coughlin's defense. Arrington topped 90 tackles for three straight seasons before he found himself in the coach's doghouse. He'll get an opportunity to roam more as he did during his breakout 2002 campaign (95 tackles and 11 sacks).

24. **Lofa Tatupu, Seattle Seahawks (Bye Week – 5):** The rookie linebacker from USC had his coming-out party in the playoffs, racking up 10 tackles in a thrilling 20-10 win over Washington. Tatupu contributed from day one as a rookie with five tackles against

Jacksonville and never looked back. For the season, Tatupu accrued 105 tackles and owned four of the league-leading 50 sacks.

25. Julian Peterson, Seattle Seahawks (Bye Week – 5): The Seahawks took an already dominating defense and added another key component by pilfering Julian Peterson from NFC West rival San Francisco. Peterson averaged 91 tackles and four sacks in his last three full seasons in San Francisco and will fit in well with Mike Holmgren's defensive game plan. His presence will allow teammate Tatupu (see above) to be more active in blitz packages.

In the next chapter, we switch gears and take a brief look at the Pro Pick'Em gaming style. For those who have yet to commit to knowing the players or who seek a quick way to enhance their enjoyment of Sunday's games, Pro Pick'Em offers participants a chance to test their wits with a minimal time investment.

34 Pro Pick'Em Review

- ◆ Game Style
- ◆ Configuration Options
- ◆ Strategy for Selection

Every week during the fall, co-workers compete in a battle of wits to determine who can most successfully predict the outcome of NFL games. With some combination of money and pride on the line, Pro Pick'Em contestants back up their alleged water cooler brilliance.

The beauty of the Pick'Em contest is that it can be run as easily through spreadsheet or pen and paper as it can through traditional fantasy sports Web sites. The administration of the offline game requires participants to provide a single list of choices (and whatever tiebreakers) to the group commissioner. Use of a fantasy sports Web site provides the immediacy of scoring updates so coveted by fantasy participants.

Most companies offer either a bulletin board or e-mail address for posting upcoming activities, clubs, or events. Create a flyer or craft an e-mail to invite members into the group.

Of course, I would be remiss if I failed to recognize the popularity of the Pro Pick'Em game as another excuse for the creation of office pools. Whether participants chip in to buy the winner lunch each week or agree to play for larger stakes, participation in Pro Pick'Em games gives further meaning to the list of scores scrolling across the bottom of the television each weekend. Additionally, given the quick and easy nature of the setup and selection process, it's hard to cite time constraints as an excuse for not participating. To this end, the Pick'Em game serves as a gateway to the fantasy world for the quasi fan who is unable or unwilling to commit to the larger time blocks required by full fantasy games.

GAME STYLES

The traditional Pick'Em game requires participants to make selections for each game on the NFL schedule each week. Over 17 weeks of the campaign, participants have 256 opportunities to demonstrate their brilliance. At most, participants make 16 selections in a given week plus any tiebreaker picks required by the group. Figure 34.1 dis-

Harmdog's Picks (ID# 4002)   Home · Rules · Help

PRO FOOTBALL PICK'EM

Group Home | My Picks | Group Picks | Group Settings | Commissioner Tools

Shoot It

Deadline: 5 minutes before each game
Week: 1 2 3 4 5 6 7 8 9 10 11 12 13 14 15 16 17

Tools: Expert Picks | Game Odds

Favorite	Mon	Tue	Wed	Final	Underdog	Pick Status	Game Details
KANSAS CITY	9.5	8.5	8.0	7.5	Houston	Incorrect	Hou 24, KC 21
ST. LOUIS	6.5	7.0	7.0	7.0	New Orleans	Correct	NO 28, StL 25
ATLANTA	9.5	10.0	10.0	10.0	Arizona	Correct	Atl 6, Ari 3
MINNESOTA	Off (0)	9.0	9.0	9.0	Chicago	Correct	Min 27, Chi 22
Baltimore	3.0	3.0	3.0	3.0	CINCINNATI	Correct	Bal 23, Cin 9
NEW YORK (NYG)	2.5	3.0	3.0	3.0	Cleveland	Correct	NYG 27, Cle 10
Philadelphia	Off (0)	4.0	4.5	4.5	DETROIT	Correct	Phi 30, Det 13
TENNESSEE	6.0	6.0	6.0	6.0	Jacksonville	Incorrect	Jac 15, Ten 12
DENVER	10.0	10.0	10.0	10.0	San Diego	Push	Den 23, SD 13
INDIANAPOLIS	6.0	6.0	6.0	6.0	Green Bay	Incorrect	Ind 45, GB 31
SEATTLE	11.0	11.0	11.0	11.0	San Francisco	Correct	Sea 34, SF 0
OAKLAND	3.0	3.0	3.0	3.0	Tampa Bay	Correct	Oak 30, TB 20
MIAMI	1.0	1.0	1.0	1.0	Pittsburgh	Correct	Pit 13, Mia 3
WASHINGTON	Off (0)	Off (0)	2.0	2.0	Dallas	Correct	Dal 21, Was 18
						Total Points 10/14	

Legend Details

Tiebreakers (Required)

Monday Night Score: Dallas vs. WASHINGTON

Sunday Night Score: Tampa Bay vs. OAKLAND

Who will score the MOST points this week?

Who will score the LEAST points this week?

Figure 34.1. Pro Football Pick'Em leader board

plays the end-of-season leader board from a recently completed competition.

The availability of scores through local newscasts, newspapers, Web sites, and even wireless devices keeps participants in touch with their selections. Group participants need commit only to an hour of a televised wrap-up show to review their achievements of the current week and to formulate an early opinion for the following week.

Scoring Styles

There are three basic types of scoring configurations to examine with regard to Pro Pick'Em contests. These scoring options are examined in the following sections.

Good: Straight Up

The simplest Pick'Em game format requires participants to merely select the winning team for each game. With the amount of exposure given to NFL highlights and standings in local and national media, most participants of a straight up Pick'Em contest have a clear distinction between good and bad teams as they sit to enter their picks. As a result, the process generally takes only several minutes each week.

For those seeking professional help of the Pick'Em variety, many sports Web sites prominently display the selections of their analysts and writers. The display of these selections serves two purposes. Reviewing the experts' picks offers reassurance to participants who are agonizing over a particular contest. It also gives participants the opportunity to match wits with these professionals and a forum to boast to friends and family on those occasions where they outpick the experts. Recently, the experts' selections and those of the general public in straight-up contests gravitated to a successful selection rate of 64 percent.

Examine the selections of the analysts for the major Web sites. If the consensus favors a particular team to win the game, then rely on their collective expertise and mirror the selection.

When compared with the 81 percent success rate of the College Pick'Em game, the straight-up Pro Pick'Em game makes for a compelling competition, but the more advanced configurations are a step better.

Expert Picks

Week 1 2 3 4 5 6 7 8 9 10 11 12 13 14 15 16 17   Sign up: Pro Football Pick'em

Week 17 Selections

	Cris Carter	Larry Bail	Brandon Funston	Mike Harmon	Yahoo! Users*	Consensus
Season Record	163 - 93	159 - 97	152 - 104	164 - 92	163 - 93	
Week 17 Record	8 - 8	9 - 9	9 - 7	8 - 8	7 - 9	
Green Bay at Chicago	GNB	GNB	GNB	GNB	GNB (89%)	GNB
Detroit at Tennessee	TEN	TEN	TEN	DET	DET (52%)	TEN
NY Jets at St. Louis	NYJ	NYJ	NYJ	NYJ	NYJ (68%)	NYJ
Cleveland at Houston	HOU	HOU	HOU	HOU	HOU (92%)	HOU
Pittsburgh at Buffalo	BUF	BUF	BUF	BUF	BUF (63%)	BUF
San Francisco at New England	NWE	NWE	NWE	NWE	NWE (97%)	NWE
Cincinnati at Philadelphia	CIN	PHI	PHI	PHI	PHI (60%)	PHI
Minnesota at Washington	MIN	MIN	MIN	WAS	MIN (80%)	MIN
New Orleans at Carolina	CAR	CAR	CAR	CAR	CAR (87%)	CAR
Miami at Baltimore	BAL	BAL	BAL	BAL	BAL (93%)	BAL
Atlanta at Seattle	ATL	SEA	SEA	SEA	SEA (69%)	SEA
Jacksonville at Oakland	OAK	OAK	JAC	JAC	JAC (51%)	JAC
Kansas City at San Diego	SDG	SDG	SDG	KAN	SDG (62%)	SDG
Tampa Bay at Arizona	TAM	ARI	TAM	ARI	TAM (57%)	TAM
Indianapolis at Denver	DEN	DEN	DEN	IND	IND (56%)	DEN
Dallas at NY Giants	NYG	DAL	NYG	NYG	NYG (55%)	NYG

Legend: Green = Correct, Red = Incorrect

* Figure following team represents the percentage of Yahoo! Sports users who picked that team. Includes only users in Pro Football Pick'em groups that do not use point spreads or confidence points.

Search: Yahoo Sports [v] for [   ]   [Search]

Figure 34.2. Yahoo! Sports Pro Pick'Em Experts Week 17 standings page

Better: Confidence Points

This system still requires participants to make straight-up selections for each game on the NFL schedule, but with an important strategic wrinkle: In these contests, participants must ascribe a numerical value to each of the week's games based on how confident they are of the outcome.

The values to be assigned depend on the number of games played in a given week. If there are 16 games scheduled, then participants must assign values from 1 through 16 to each game. Therefore, for a week in which all teams are playing (16 games), the maximum number of points to be assigned is 136 (16+15+14+etc.). Each value can be assigned only once, with a participant's proverbial lock of the week being assigned the maximum value and their most questionable the lowest the value of 1.

The addition of confidence points forces participants to be more scrutinizing in the selection process. The number of correct selections should not be impacted by the inclusion of confidence points. After all, the base of the game remains the selection of the winning team. However, the strategy and separation of team scores occurs in the assignment of these confidence points. Each participant will develop natural affinities or aversions to certain teams and shift points accordingly. Under the confidence points system, the rewards come to those who place large confidence point designations in predicting those defeats or go for broke in predicting the improbable upset.

Best: Point Spread

The most compelling competitions in Pick'Em-style games involve the use of the point spread. Point spreads are created by sportsbooks and organizations such as the Associated Press to create balance in the wagers placed on a specific contest. Without the spread, participants form quick decisions on each contest and quickly run through the games. Making a correct selection in games using the point spread requires a more thorough review of past performances, injury statuses, and trends.

 The thorough review of game logs and play-by-play accounts provides a better picture of the ebb and flow of the game than a simple glance at the box score. Putting forth a little extra effort will make it easier to make winning selections in the weeks ahead.

The point spread will fluctuate based on updated information (injuries, illness, weather, and so on) and will vary by source. For the purpose of fantasy games, the Associated Press typically furnishes the line.

 Reading and properly interpreting the point spread is sometimes confusing to first-time participants. Key terms are defined below, accompanied by an example.

- A minus (-) sign next to the team in the listing of games means the team is favored to win. In determining wins and losses with regard to the spread, the team must win by more than the listed number in order to "cover" the point spread and earn the participant a winning selection. If the team wins by less than that number or loses outright, then the participant receives credit for an incorrect selection.

- The term "push" is used to describe a situation in which the game is tied once the point spread is applied by adding or subtracting points.

- A plus (+) sign next to the team name indicates that the team is the underdog. In order for the participant to receive credit for a correct pick, the team needs to lose by fewer points than the number listed or win the game outright.

- A game marked as "OFF" indicates that no spread has been set for the game. This typically occurs when the availability of a star player is in question.

- The term "pick" is used for situations where the teams are indistinguishable and no line is set. This occurs in all but a handful of games each year.

Example

Detroit Lions (+4) at Chicago Bears

In this example, the Bears host the Lions and are favored by 4 points.

If the participant chooses the Bears, then they must defeat the Lions by 5 or more points.

If the participant chooses the Lions, they must win the game outright or lose by 3 or fewer points.

If the Bears defeat the Lions by 4 points, then the game is declared a "push" and no credit for a correct pick is awarded.

Shoot It

Deadline: 5 minutes before each game
Week: 1 2 3 4 5 6 7 8 9 10 11 12 13 14 15 16 17

Tools: Expert Picks | Game Odds

Favourite	Mon	Tue	Wed	Final	Underdog	Pick Status	Game Details
Cincinnati	Off (0)	Off (0)	3.0	3.0	● PHILADELPHIA	Incorrect	Cin 38, Phi 10
● BUFFALO	Off (0)	9.0	8.5	9.0	Pittsburgh	Incorrect	Pit 29, Buf 24
CHICAGO	3.0	3.0	3.0	3.0	● Green Bay	Correct	GB 31, Chi 14
Minnesota	Off (0)	4.5	4.0	4.0	● WASHINGTON	Correct	Was 21, Min 18
● Detroit	3.0	3.0	3.0	3.0	TENNESSEE	Incorrect	Ten 24, Det 19
● CAROLINA	7.5	7.5	7.5	7.5	New Orleans	Incorrect	NO 21, Car 18
BALTIMORE	9.5	10.0	11.0	11.0	● Miami	Correct	Bal 30, Mia 23
● New York (NYJ)	Off (0)	3.0	3.0	3.5	ST. LOUIS	Incorrect	StL 32, NYJ 29
● HOUSTON	10.5	10.5	10.5	10.5	Cleveland	Incorrect	Cle 22, Hou 14
● NEW ENGLAND	14.0	14.0	14.0	13.5	San Francisco	Correct	NE 21, SF 7
● ARIZONA	2.5	3.0	3.0	3.0	Tampa Bay	Correct	Ari 12, TB 7
● SEATTLE	Off (0)	5.5	5.5	5.5	Atlanta	Incorrect	Sea 28, Atl 26
● Kansas City	3.0	3.0	3.0	3.0	SAN DIEGO	Incorrect	SD 24, KC 17
DENVER	8.5	8.5	8.5	8.5	● Indianapolis	Incorrect	Den 33, Ind 14
OAKLAND	Off (0)	Off (0)	Off (0)	Off (0)	● Jacksonville	Correct	Jac 13, Oak 6
● NEW YORK (NYG)	3.0	3.0	2.5	2.5	Dallas	Correct	NYG 28, Dal 24
Total Points 7/16							

Figure 34.3. Pro Pick'Em week's selections and results

STRATEGY FOR MAKING SELECTIONS

Straight Up

Unlike the College Pick'Em game, where nary an upset occurs in any given week, the NFL prides itself on parity. Some pundits argue that the current state of the league is actually a parody of traditional NFL competition where mediocrity reigns. They cite rapid turnover of good teams to bad and vice versa as reasons to disparage the on-field play.

The adherence to the hard salary cap, the draft process, and active free agent market certainly serve to change the dynamics of the game from year to year.

Note the amount of rumors and speculation regarding coaching staffs and front office personnel each off-season. The more disharmonious the power structure, the more likely the team will struggle.

The early weeks of the season normally define the character and makeup of a team for that specific year. If the team underwent major changes, from coaching staffs to starting quarterbacks, it is typically primed to be selected against. Similarly, if a team turns to a rookie quarterback to man the ship, the team is likely in disarray and will take its lumps to start the season. Rarely will a quarterback enter a situation and achieve the remarkable success of Steelers rookie QB Ben Roethlisberger in 2004 (14 straight wins after assuming the starting job). To put this in proper perspective, Troy Aikman went 0-11 for the 1989 Dallas Cowboys as a rookie. Peyton Manning has become one of the most prolific passers in NFL history, but started his career with a 3-13 mark in 1998.

Review win/loss logs for the past several seasons. Mark the trends in head-to-head matchups and the streaks of teams at different points in the season.

Participants must be aware of the histories of certain franchises, such as Minnesota's blistering starts that cool as the weather does, or the tendency of New Orleans to play well in the final six weeks of each season.

Confidence Points

In reviewing games using confidence points, it is important for participants to trust their initial instincts, much as they would in a straight-up contest. This part of the contest plays out the same as the straight-up Pick'Em contest, running through the list of games, and selecting winning teams. In this initial run-through of the schedule, participants should begin to sort the games based on their gut instincts and base knowledge, remembering to note which games appeared particularly easy or difficult to select.

No doubt, there will always be a handful of games on the schedule that stand out as sure things. In the initial review of games, there are likely several games that fail to inspire a gut reaction and have the contestant flip-flopping as if they're seeking reelection. Participants should table those games for the moment and concentrate on the third batch, which consists of contests for which the participant has an initial leaning.

Separate each week's game slate into three batches: mortal locks, toss-ups, and brain-busters. Assign values to the two extremes and dedicate the bulk of time to the tossups.

Point Spread

The selection process with regard to the point spread requires much more attention to trend analysis and injury reports than the prior configurations. Remember, the point spread serves to equalize the activity on a particular contest. As a result, this type of contest narrows the gap between upper-tier and middle-of-the-road teams.

Evaluate the past performance of teams where turnover in skill positions and the coaching staff have been minimal. Consistency generally breeds success.

Just as in straight-up Pick'Em contests, participants rely on their gut instincts when picking games against the spread. Some participants will be unrealistic about the chances of their home team or their fiercest rivals. Others will tie their regular fantasy team selections to their Pick'Em choices. For instance, Brett Favre owners will place higher expectations on the Green Bay Packers in anticipation of a big offensive day.

Finally, use of the spread keeps participants fixed to their televisions or Internet connections until the final gun sounds. In many contests, the result is in doubt until the final minutes, making for a compelling and challenging contest. Longtime NFL fans, and certainly those betting on sports events, have seen their teams marching down the field for the tying or winning score, only to watch the QB throw an ill-advised screen pass or sideline route that gets returned for a touchdown by the defense. Suddenly, that sure winning selection turns into a loss. That's the glory and the agony of fantasy Pro Pick'Em contests in a nutshell.

The next chapter applies the game formats and configuration settings of this chapter to the realm of college football. For some, the College Football Pick'Em structure loses some of its appeal because not all schools will be represented in the selection options. Participants must track performance trends and team histories with the hope of predicting a huge upset. There may be no better feeling during any fantasy season (aside from being in first place after the final statistics have been tabulated, of course) than correctly choosing against a college football powerhouse.

35 College Pick'Em

- ♦ Game Styles
- ♦ Configuration Options
- ♦ Strategies for Making Selections

As fantasy football participation began to flourish in the latter part of the 1990s, it only made sense that game providers would seek to celebrate the passion and enthusiasm associated with the college game. The Saturday ritual in the fall for millions of Americans is to load up the school gear, tailgate among friends and fellow revelers in the parking lot, and then take to the stands to cheer themselves hoarse from the opening kickoff to the final gun.

Unfortunately, as video game players know, there are restrictions on the use of individual player names in merchandising NCAA products. NCAA rules prohibit the identification of individual players in all efforts while they remain on scholarship. For instance, while Reggie Bush was dominating the competition en route to the Heisman Trophy with USC in 2004, any video game issued before or during the season was required to identify him as "RB #5." It was only after he'd left USC that he appeared on game packaging.

Fantasy game providers experience these same restrictions when attempting to conjure up games that capture the excitement of college football while maintaining the interest of longtime fantasy participants. Without the ability to include individual players, the options are limited.

GAME STYLES

The most prevalent gaming option for college football competitions involves the classic Pick'Em style. The excitement and success of fantasy football has spawned salary cap games that have been well received. Occasionally, groups of friends and family will organize their own full fantasy college football games. CBS SportsLine offered a college fantasy football game utilizing individual players in 2005. As of this writing, there was no mention of the game on its Web site. For the purpose of this discussion, I will limit the review to Pick'Em contests.

Standard

The bulk of fantasy games available to college football enthusiasts involve some variation of the Pick'Em style. The game providers will offer an overall leader board to recognize top participants, as seen in Figure 35.1. For most contests, participants need only make selections from a lim-

Figure 35.1. College
Football Pick'Em
leader board

ited number of options. That is to say, the game providers
limit the number of college football games for which a
participant must choose a winner. For college football
games, that generally means that participants make selections only for games involving Top 25 teams.

All newscasts and highlight shows emphasize the action
from Top 25 games. Participants need only watch a single
hour of television on Saturday evening or review one column of scores on their favorite sports Web site to apprise
themselves of the day's activity. The ability to find research
materials and track results serves to make the Top 25 the
standard configuration.

Be sure to find time to watch a Saturday wrap-up
show. The network analysts will provide information
on the strengths or weaknesses for virtually every team in a major
conference. This information will be invaluable in future weeks.

Another benefit of using the Top 25 is that this format does not require the participant to be particularly knowledgeable about the entire college football landscape. Most fans focus their attention on one particular conference and occasionally cast an eye toward the leader board or latest poll to see which team their particular favorite is chasing.

The number of games required for selection varies weekly. In 2005, participants had to make choices for between 12 and 22 games over the course of the season. The average week required 17 games last year.

CONFIGURATION OPTIONS

As previously mentioned, the basic configuration of the game forces participants to keep tabs on the Top 25 as it changes during the season. Participants who wish to confine their contest to the particular conference that house their favorite team will set up a contest on their own message board or Web site. At present, none of the major fantasy gaming sites allows for a straight conference contest.

The selection of a single conference aids in opening up the game to even the most time-strapped members of your office or family. In this system, you're looking at a maximum of 14 games per week (if you choose the Mid-American Conference), with most weeks rounding out between five and 10. Since all participants are at least somewhat invested in the chosen conference, there's no excuse for missed picks.

Scoring Styles

College football Pick'Em games are scored according to one of three systems. The straight-up scoring style requires participants to simply pick a winner. The use of confidence points or point spread adds another level of complexity to the competition. A small percentage of participants mix the confidence point and point spread styles to create a convoluted scoring system and truly difficult selection process.

Good: Straight Up

Most College Pick'Em games use the straight-up selection of winning teams. The process of completing selections under this format is quick, easy, and for the most part, boring.

A review over the past two seasons revealed that the team favored to win the game won almost 87 percent of the time. The final standings for a sample straight-up selection contest are shown in Figure 35.2. To some degree, the game fails to remain compelling over the course of the season.

Figure 35.2. College Pick'Em analysts' picks

Participants looking for the excitement that accompanies an upset prediction receive limited opportunities to do so in this format.

Choose the higher-ranked team for the majority of your selections. Over the course of the season, you will witness an average of two to three upsets per week.

Better: Confidence Points

A better use of the straight selection format forces participants to make their picks using a system called "confidence points." This configuration option requires the assignment of a point value to each game on the schedule based on how "confident" the participant feels about the outcome of the game.

The point modifiers available for assignment equal the number of games being selected in a given week. For instance, in a week where 15 games are being played, participants assign a point value of 15 to their top pick, 14 to their second-best pick, and so on.

Separate the games into three groups: automatic wins, toss-ups, and shoulder shrugs. Assign confidence points to the automatics and shoulder shrugs, and save the tossups for the end.

While the number of correct picks would remain unchanged when compared with the straight-up selection game without confidence points, the strategy of assigning points complicates the selection process and makes the game more compelling. In 2005, the consensus of participants in the Yahoo! Sports College Pick'Em game finished the season by correctly predicting 79 percent of games. Confidence points serve to create separation among the participants and to reward the timely selection of a big upset pick.

Best: Point Spread

The most compelling contest emphasizes knowledge of the sport and team trends. Groups among friends and co-workers generally utilize the point spread. In most sporting competitions, one team is decidedly better than the other. Therefore, in order to entice bettors to consider the alternative, the "point spread" was created to equalize the teams.

To make a correct pick with the favored team in this system, that team must win by more than the determined spread number. If you choose the underdog, the underdog must lose by less than the spread number in order for you to get credit for a correct pick.

By way of example, if you pick Northwestern and it is favored to beat Indiana by five points, then Northwestern must win the game by six or more points in order for your selection to be correct to get credit for a correct pick. If Northwestern wins by less than five, you would not get credit for the pick. If Northwestern wins by exactly five points, the game is a push, and no participants receive credit for a correct pick.

The selection of games against the spread truly changes the complexion of the contest. As I mentioned earlier, par-

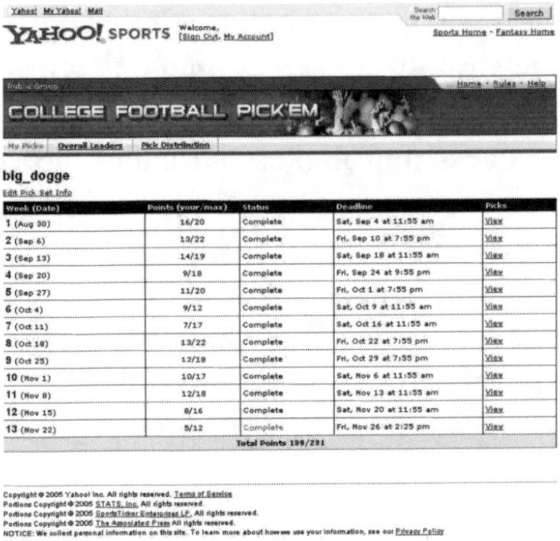

Figure 35.3. College Football Pick'Em season record

ticipants chose 79 percent of games correctly in straight-up selections. While I can't draw a direct comparison of digits to the general populace, as information of private groups cannot be reviewed, my own selection percentage dropped to 49 percent against the spread.

To further illustrate the complexity of using the spread to make selections, I present the records of two NCAA teams on both ends of the spectrum from last season. The University of Louisville Cardinals finished the season with a record of 9-2. On the other extreme sit the University at Buffalo Bulls, who finished the season with a woeful record of 1-10.

Against the spread, however, these teams were identical with 6-5 records. Despite a large disparity in final scores and certainly the actual game results of wins and losses, in the eyes of bettors and Pick'Em participants, they were equals. The inclusion of the spread takes away the sure selection and keeps all participants working hard to find an angle to make the next selection.

Don't dismiss the competitiveness of teams that languish at the end of the standings table. In this contest, they are just as formidable as a Top 25 team.

STRATEGY FOR MAKING SELECTIONS

The following section offers strategy points for the three scoring styles most common to college football Pick'Em games. Remember, as you veer away from the straight-up selection style, the number of variables to consider increases.

Straight Up

From the data provided earlier, it's clear that swinging wildly for the fences is not the appropriate strategy for picking games straight up. This past season, I spent considerable time and effort watching games and analyzing stats, trends, and injuries. Fortunately, my wife understands that this constitutes a normal workday for me. And believe you me, I turned in a number of 10-14-hour days on fall Saturdays in 2005. All my efforts and analysis yielded a success rate of 78 percent, a full six picks behind the general populace.

Don't overthink. In a straight-up contest, it's easy to look for reasons and scenarios that lead to an upset. Odds are that the upset won't materialize.

Confidence Points

In the average week using this system, participants make 17 selections. With a quick glance of the week's slate, there are a handful of games that jump off the page. For those selected games, either you know in an instant which team is going to win the game, or you throw up your hands in utter bewilderment. Take those games and assign your highest and lowest values immediately.

Use the highest point values on the top-ranked teams in the nonconference part of that week's schedule. Save the occasional top-tier matchup; these games are generally as close to a "sure thing" as you'll see.

Then take the remainder of the point modifiers that you need to assign and begin to rerank the games. Consider a number of decision points as you rank these games:

- Which team returns a larger number of starters from the previous season?
- Which teams are facing difficult challenges on the road?

- Is it a rivalry game against an in-state or key conference opponent?

- Whose offense has been playing well of late?

- Which team dropped the most slots in the prior week's poll?

- Is a team facing an opponent coming off a particularly bad defeat or huge win?

- Did the team win or lose its prior game in dramatic fashion?

- Has the coach struggled against a team throughout his career (such as Mack Brown versus Oklahoma prior to 2005)?

Use history as a base for your analysis, but be mindful that "past performances are not indicative of future results."

Point Spread

As I demonstrated earlier, the use of the point spread complicates the selection process and equalizes the mightiest of squads with the cellar dwellers.

Large spreads are a trap. With the number of available scholarships reduced, coaches cannot risk injury to top players late in a blowout. As such, the point differential generally dwindles late in the game.

Use of the spread offers drama early in the year, as participants start to see how a squad has changed from the previous year. Factoring in past performance, injuries, weather, and some weight to home-field advantage, the oddsmakers seek to equalize the number of participants/bettors choosing each team. Therefore, unlike the 85 percent victory rate achieved by the higher ranked team in the straight-up configuration, the spread pushes correct choices toward a 50/50 proposition.

With only 32 professional teams, college ball is the only game in town for many communities. Fans in Nebraska, Iowa, and Utah flock to home games and wear the school colors with pride. Naturally, these fans also want to show their knowledge of the game and support their favorite teams. As such, college fantasy football options continue to thrive and evolve.

Appendix

Appendicies for *The SAVVY Guide to Fantasy Football* can be found at **www.savvyfantasysports.com**. These charts and player lists are subject to change based on player information and will be periodically updated as the author finds this to be beneficial.

Index

C

D

E

F

G

M

manager 12, 26, 27, 28, 29, 36, 37, 38, 42, 49, 59, 61, 70, 86, 87, 95, 96, 97, 98, 99, 100, 101, 103, 106, 107, 108, 110, 111, 112, 115, 116, 117, 118, 119, 120, 122, 123, 126, 127, 128, 130, 131, 132, 136, 154, 157, 158, 214, 216, 219, 260, 296, 339, 363

message board 11, 15, 27, 34, 46, 57, 59, 127, 144, 442

mini-camp 176, 182, 185, 226, 258, 263, 365

mock draft 6, 98, 139, 261, 263, 265, 267

N

NFC 14, 37, 169, 174, 185, 195, 198, 206, 285, 323, 337, 341, 368, 374, 426

O

offensive coordinator 176, 207, 291, 317, 390

off-season 6, 14, 35, 51, 61, 106, 114, 134, 171, 173, 183, 186, 193, 196, 198, 209, 216, 241, 242, 245, 250, 281, 282, 283, 285, 286, 287, 288, 289, 291, 292, 293, 309, 313, 314, 318, 325, 326, 330, 332, 337, 343, 344, 347, 348, 349, 354, 359, 360, 364, 376, 383, 384, 386, 388, 389, 392, 394, 402, 407, 409, 413, 423, 424, 435

online draft 95, 98

P

pass rush 177, 178, 183, 184, 187, 190, 201, 202, 205, 207, 209, 409, 410, 413, 414, 421, 422, 424, 425

Pick'Em 6, 9, 13, 19, 20, 83, 84, 85, 86, 426, 427, 428, 429, 430, 431, 432, 433, 434, 435, 436, 437, 438, 439, 440, 441, 443, 445, 446, 447, 449

playbook 54, 171, 175, 179, 186, 240, 384

playoff(s) 12, 53, 54, 69, 70, 91, 120, 128, 161, 198, 213, 215, 216, 217, 218, 261, 270, 281, 292, 293, 301, 322, 331, 337, 340, 341, 357, 364, 369, 383, 385, 398, 409, 425

point spread 13, 20, 84, 85, 432, 433, 437, 443, 445, 449